Shinto (The Way of the Gods)

By

W. G. Aston

Published by Forgotten Books 2012

Originally Published 1905

PIBN 1000154255

# SHINTO

## (*THE WAY OF THE GODS*)

BY

## W. G. ASTON, C.M.G., D.Lit.

AUTHOR OF

'A GRAMMAR OF THE JAPANESE SPOKEN LANGUAGE,' 'A GRAMMAR OF THE
'APANESE WRITTEN LANGUAGE,' 'THE NIHONGI' (TRANSLATION),
'A HISTORY OF JAPANESE LITERATURE,' &C.

## LONGMANS, GREEN, AND CO.

39, PATERNOSTER ROW, LONDON

NEW YORK AND BOMBAY

1905

# TABLE OF CONTENTS.

# LIST OF ILLUSTRATIONS.

# ABBREVIATIONS.

Ch. K.—Mr. B. H. Chamberlain's translation of the *Kojiki*.

*Nihongi.*—Translation of the *Nihongi* by W. G. Aston.

*T.A.S.J.*—Transactions of the Asiatic Society of Japan.

---

# ERRATA.

For "Welhausen," note to p. 113, read *Wellhausen*.

For "of," p. 12, l. 18, read *on*.

P. 335, l. 24, read *to do her behests*.

---

# ADDENDA.

Add, bottom of p. 60, "St. Augustine says, in his 'Civitas Dei,' that funeral observances are rather solace to the living than help to the dead."

P. 41, line 25, after "deities" insert "a phrase which closely resembles the 'Zembla Bogh' used of the Czar by Russians."

P. 31, add to first note, "The Romans had an evil counterpart of Jupiter, viz., Vediovis or Vejovis."

# PREFACE.

As compared with the great religions of the world, Shinto, the old *Kami* cult of Japan, is decidedly rudimentary in its character. Its polytheism, the want of a Supreme Deity, the comparative absence of images and of a moral code, its feeble personifications and hesitating grasp of the conception of spirit, the practical non-recognition of a future state, and the general absence of a deep, earnest faith—all stamp it as perhaps the least developed of religions which have an adequate literary record. Still, it is not a primitive cult. It had an organized priesthood and an elaborate ritual. The general civilization of the Japanese when Shinto assumed the form in which we know it had left the primitive stage far behind. They were already an agricultural nation, a circumstance by which Shinto has been deeply influenced. They had a settled government, and possessed the arts of brewing, making pottery, building ships and bridges, and working in metals. It is not among such surroundings that we can expect to find a primitive form of religion.

The present treatise has two objects. It is intended, primarily and chiefly, as a repertory of the more significant facts of Shinto for the use of scientific students of religion. It also comprises an outline theory of the origin and earlier stages of the development of religion, prepared with special reference to the Shinto evidence. The subject is treated from a positive, not from a negative or agnostic standpoint, Religion being regarded as a normal function, not a disease, of humanity.   This element of the work owes much to the continental scholars Reville, Goblet D'Alviella, and Pfleiderer.

In anthropological matters, I have been much indebted to Dr. Tylor's ' Primitive Culture' and Mr. J. G. Frazer's ' Golden Bough.'   I should not omit to express my obligations to my friend Mr. J. Troup for assistance with the proofs and for a number of useful corrections and suggestions.

# CHAPTER I.

## MATERIALS FOR THE STUDY OF SHINTO.

**Prehistoric Shinto.**—Ethnologists are agreed that the predominant element of the Japanese race came to Japan by way of Korea from that part of Asia which lies north of China, probably by a succession of immigrations which extended over many centuries. It is useless to speculate as to what rudiments of religious belief the ancestors of the Japanese race may have brought with them from their continental home. Sun-worship has long been a central feature of Tartar religions, as it is of Shinto; but such a coincidence proves nothing, as this cult is universal among nations in the barbaric stage of civilization. It is impossible to say whether or not an acquaintance with the old State religion of China—essentially a nature-worship—had an influence on the prehistoric development of Shinto. The circumstance that the Sun was the chief deity of the latter and Heaven of the former is adverse to this supposition. Nor is there anything in Japan which corresponds with the Shangti of the ancient Chinese.

There are definite traces of a Korean element in Shinto. A Kara no Kami (God of Kara in Korea) was worshipped in the Imperial Palace. There were numerous shrines in honour of Kara-Kuni Idate no Kami. Susa no wo and Futsunushi have Korean associations.

Until the beginning of the fifth century of our era, writing was practically unknown in Japan. It is certain, however, that a considerable body of myth, together with formal rituals, was already in existence, having been transmitted from generation to generation by the *Nakatomi* and *Imbe*, two hereditary priestly corporations attached to the Mikado's Court.     We hear also of *Kataribe*, or corporations of reciters, who were established in various provinces, especially in Idzumo, a primæval centre of Shinto worship.     They are mentioned in the *Nihongi* under the date A.D. 465, and were still in existence in the fifteenth century.     Unfortunately we know little about them beyond the circumstance that they attended at the capital, and delivered their recitals of "ancient words" on the occasion of the Mikado's coronation.     These must have helped to furnish material for the written mythical and quasi-historical narratives which have come down to us.

**Kojiki.** — The oldest of these is a work entitled the *Kojiki*, or 'Records of Ancient Matters.'     It was compiled by Imperial order, and completed in A.D. 712.     The preface states that it was taken down from the lips of one Hiyeda no Are, who had so wonderful a memory that he could "repeat with his mouth whatever was placed before his eyes and record in his heart whatever struck his ears."     English readers may study this work in an accurate translation contributed by Mr. B. H. Chamberlain to the *Transactions* of the Asiatic Society of Japan in 1882.     It is preceded by a valuable introduction.

**Nihongi.** — The mythical narrative of the *Nihongi*, or 'Chronicles of Japan,' also an official compilation (A.D. 720), is not quite so full as that of the *Kojiki*, and it has the disadvantage of being composed in the Chinese language.     But it has one feature of great interest.     The author, or some nearly contemporary writer, has added to the original text a number of variants of the current myths, thus enabling us to correct any impression of uniformity or consistency which might be left by the perusal of the *Kojiki* or *Nihongi* alone.     These addenda show that there was then in existence a large body of frequently irreconcilable mythical material, which these works are attempts to harmonize.     A translation of the *Nihongi* by the present writer forms Supplement I. of the *Transactions* of the

Japan Society (1896). Dr. Florenz's excellent German version of the mythical part of this work may also be consulted with advantage. It has copious notes.

**Kiujiki.**—A third source of information respecting the mythical lore of Japan is the *Kiujiki*. A work with this name was compiled A.D. 620, *i.e.*, one hundred years before the *Nihongi*, but the book now known by that title has been condemned as a forgery by native critics. Their argu ments, however, are not quite convincing. The *Kiujiki* is in any case a very old book, and we may accept it provision ally as of equal authority with the *Kojiki* and *Nihongi*. It contains little which is not also to be found in these two works. Unlike them, the *Kiujiki* makes no attempt to be consistent. It is a mere jumble of mythical material, distinct and conflicting versions of the same narrative being often dovetailed into one another in the most clumsy fashion. It has not been translated.

**Idzumo Fudoki.**—This work, a topography of the pro vince of Idzumo, was compiled about A.D. 733. It contains a few mythical passages.

**The Kogoshiui** was written in 807. It adds a very little to the information contained in the *Kojiki* and *Nihongi.*

**Shôjiroku.**—In this work, which is a sort of peerage of Japan (815), the descent of many of the noble families is traced from the deities of the Shinto Pantheon.

**Yengishiki.**—Our principal source of information for the ceremonial of Shinto is the *Yengishiki*, or 'Institutes of the Period Yengi' (901-923). It gives a minute description of the official Shinto ritual as then practised, together with twenty-seven of the principal prayers used in worship. These prayers, called *norito*, were now, so far as we know, for the first time reduced to writing, but many of them must be in substance several hundreds of years older. Some have been translated by Sir Ernest Satow for the Asiatic Society of Japan (1879-81), and the series is now being continued by Dr. Karl Florenz, whose translation of the

*Ohoharahi* (1899) is a notable addition to the English reader's means of studying Shinto.

**Motoori and Hirata.** — The writings of the native scholars Motoori, Hirata, and others during the second half of the eighteenth century and the first half of the nineteenth are an indispensable source of information. No part of this voluminous literature has been, or is likely to be, translated. The English reader will find a good account of it in Sir Ernest Satow's 'Revival of Pure Shinto,' contributed to the *Transactions* of the Asiatic Society of Japan in 1875. By " Pure Shinto " is meant the Shinto of the *Kojiki, Nihongi*, and *Yengishiki*, as opposed to the corrupt forms of this religion which sprang up under Buddhist influence in later times.

The above-named works contain fairly ample materials for the study of the older Shinto. They have the advantage of showing us this religion as seen by the Japanese themselves, thus leaving no room for the introduction of those errors which so often arise from the unconscious importation of modern European and Christian ideas into the accounts of other rudimentary cults. It should be observed that it is the State religion to which these records chiefly relate. Of the popular beliefs and practices at this time we are told but little.

The *Nihongi*, and, to a lesser extent, the *Kojiki*, are somewhat influenced by Chinese ideas ; but this element is generally recognizable. Buddhism was introduced into Japan towards the middle of the sixth century, and was widely propagated under the regency of Shôtoku Daishi, who died A.D. 621 ; but there is little or no trace of it in the older Shinto. For a long time there was a marked antagonism between the two religions which served to protect the latter from such adulteration.

**The Fusoku Gwaho,** a modern illustrated magazine, is a rich store of information respecting modern Shinto and the folk-lore and superstitions which are associated with it.

# CHAPTER II.

**Religion.**—Religion, a general term which includes all our relations to the Divine, is a cord of three strands, namely, Emotion, Thought, and Conduct. Emotion com prises gratitude, hope, and fear. Thought yields conceptions and beliefs. Religious conduct consists in doing that which is pleasing to the superior powers, and in refraining from acts which are thought to be offensive to them. It includes worship, purity, and morality.

These elements of religion are inseparable. Emotion stimulates and sharpens the intellectual faculties, which in turn provide fresh food for emotion. Each without the other is evanescent and barren. Nothing worthy of the name of religion is possible without a long succession of alternate moods of thought and feeling.

Emotion and thought lead in all healthy minds to action of some sort. Man is impelled by his very nature to testify his gratitude to the powers on which he feels him self dependent, to express his hopes of future blessings from them, and to avoid acts which might offend them. Moreover, as a social animal, he is prompted to com municate his religious thoughts and feelings to his fellow men. Without such intercommunication, no religion is possible. No individual man ever evolved a religion out of his own inner consciousness alone.

**Emotional Source of Religion.**—The emotional basis of religion is gratitude, love, and hope, rather than fear. If life is worth living—and what sane man doubts it?—there are necessarily far more frequent occasions for the former than for the latter. The statement of the old Roman poet that "Primus in orbe Deus fecit timor" is untrue even of the Greek and Roman mythology to which he more particularly referred. Zeus, the Shining One, the Father of Gods and Men, though he may occasionally destroy a wicked man with his thunder, is loved rather than feared. "Alma Venus, hominum divomque voluptas," is not the offspring of our terrors. Nor is Ceres, Bacchus, Here Eileithuia, or Kora. In Mars, by an exception the malignant quality predominates.

Shinto is essentially a religion of gratitude and love. The great Gods, such as the Sun-Goddess and the Deity of Food, are beneficent beings. They are addressed as parents, or dear divine ancestors, and their festivals have a joyous character.* An eighth-century poet says, " Every living man may feast his eyes with tokens of their love." The *Kogoshiui* tells us that when the Sun-Goddess emerged from her cave, " Heaven above at length became clear, and all people could see each other's faces distinctly. They stretched forth their hands and danced and sang together, exclaiming, ' Oh! how delightful! how pleasant! how clear!'" The *Nihongi* says that on the same occasion all the Gods rejoiced greatly. Have we not here a rudiment of the beatific vision which in its higher developments embraces not only the sunlight but all things in Heaven and earth, and hell itself, founded, as Dante says, by the *primo Amore?* Even the boisterous Rain-Storm God, who of the *Dii Majores* most nearly approaches the type of an evil deity, has his good points. The demons of disease and calamity are for the most part obscure and nameless personages.

**Intellectual Basis of Religion. The Idea of God.**—A

---

* At the festival of Nifu Miōjin in Kii, when the procession bearing offerings arrives before the shrine, the village chief calls out in a loud voice, " According to our annual custom, let us all laugh." To which a hearty response is given. This is because this God does not go to Idzumo for an annual visit like the others.

God may be defined as a sentient being possessed of super
human power. The phrase "supernatural being," which is
sometimes used as equivalent to God, is open to objection
The word "supernatural" belongs to the vocabulary of a
comparatively scientific age. To the savage, phenomena
are ordinary or strange, not natural or supernatural. More
over, there are many objects of worship which are not at all
supernatural, as, for instance, the sun. "Spiritual being"
is insufficiently comprehensive as an equivalent for God.
The Lama of Tibet is a God ; but he is not a spiritual
being. Neither is the Wind nor the Moon. The assumption
that Gods are always spirits has been the source of much
confusion.

**Kami.**—The most common and comprehensive word for
deity in the Japanese language is *Kami*. It is probably
connected with *kaburu*, to cover, and has the general
meaning of "above," "superior." *Kami* is the part of
Japan which lies near the capital, as opposed to *Shimo*,
the lower country or provinces. *Kaha-kami* means the
upper waters of a river. *Kami no ke*, or simply *kami*, is
the hair of the head. *Kami* is applied not only to
Gods, but to Mikados and nobles. The heads of
State Departments were at one time called *Kami*, and
in later times this word became equivalent to our
"Lord" in territorial titles. *O Kami* is frequently said
vaguely of "the authorities," while *O Kami San* is the
domestic authority, namely, "the mistress." Whether
*Kami* is used of Gods or men, it is in both cases a
secondary application of the general meaning "upper."
The Gods are *Kami* because they reside in Heaven (*superi*,
*caelicoli*, 'Ουρανίωνες, Most High, Father in Heaven) ; men
are *Kami* on account of their higher rank. No doubt both
gain prestige by their association under the same title—the
Gods by a reflection from the pomp and ceremony which
attend on mortal *Kami ;* and men by assimilation with the
transcendent power and glory of the great nature-deities.

Why should height come to be everywhere associated with excellence and rank ? Herbert Spencer's characteristic con tribution* to the solution of this problem is as follows : " In battle it is important to get the force of gravity to fight on your side, and hence the anxiety to seize a position above that of the foe. Conversely the combatant who is thrown down cannot further resist without struggling against his own weight as well as against his antagonist's strength. Hence being below is so habitually associated with defeat as to have made maintainance of this relation (literally expressed by the words superior and inferior) a leading element in ceremony at large." To this it may be added that the upper part of the human body—namely, the head—is also the most important and honourable. "Chief" is derived from *caput :* "capital," as an adjective, means excellent. "Headman," "head-centre," "head and front of my offending," are familiar phrases which involve the assumption of the superior importance of the head. A Japanese raises to his head a present or other object to which he wishes to show respect. A further and decisive consideration is the circumstance that the most incom parably glorious, excellent, and majestic thing with which we are acquainted is also immeasurably the highest. Even pre-religious man cannot have been wholly insensible to the glory of the sky—" hoc sublime candens "—with its sun and moon, its dawns and sunsets, its clouds, thunders, and storms. No wonder that the words heavenly and celestial have come to convey the idea of supreme excellence.

The following quotations will help us to realize more fully what the Japanese mean by the word *Kami*. Mo-toori says :—

" The term *Kami* is applied in the first place to the various deities of Heaven and Earth who are mentioned in the ancient records as well as to their spirits *(mi-tama)* which reside in the shrines where they are worshipped.

* 'Sociology,' p. 153.

Moreover, not only human beings, but birds, beasts, plants and trees, seas and mountains, and all other things what soever which deserve to be dreaded and revered for the extraordinary and pre-eminent powers which they possess, are called *Kami*. They need not be eminent for surpassing nobleness, goodness, or serviceableness alone. Malignant and uncanny beings are also called *Kami* if only they are the objects of general dread.* Among *Kami* who are human beings I need hardly mention first of all the successive Mikados—with reverence be it spoken......Then there have been numerous examples of divine human beings, both in ancient and modern times, who, although not accepted by the nation generally, are treated as gods, each of his several dignity, in a single province, village, or family...... Amongst *Kami* who are not human beings I need hardly mention Thunder [in Japanese *Naru kami* or the Sounding God]. There are also the Dragon, the Echo [called in Japanese *Ko-dama* or the Tree Spirit], and the Fox, who are *Kami* by reason of their uncanny and fearful natures. The term *Kami* is applied in the *Nihongi* and *Manyoshiu* to the tiger and wolf. Izanagi gave to the fruit of the peach and to the jewels round his neck names which implied that they were *Kami* There are many cases of seas and mountains being called *Kami*. It is not their spirits which are meant. The word was applied directly to the seas† or mountains themselves as being very awful things."

Hirata defines *kami* as a term which comprises all things strange, wondrous, and possessing *isao* or virtue. A recent

---

* Compare with this the following description of the *huacas* of the ancient Peruvians. "All those things which from their beauty and excellence are superior to other things of a like kind ; things that are ugly and monstrous or that cause horror and fright ; things out of the usual course of nature."

† In the spirit of Wordsworth's

      " Listen, the mighty being is awake
      And doth with his eternal motion make
      A noise like thunder everlastingly."

dictionary gives the following essentially modern definitions of this word :—

*Kami.* 1. Something which has no form but is only spirit, has unlimited supernatural power, dispenses calamity and good fortune, punishes crime and rewards virtue. 2. Sovereigns of all times, wise and virtuous men, valorous and heroic persons whose spirits are prayed to after their death. 3. Divine things which transcend human intellect. 4. The Christian God, Creator, Supreme Lord.

**Double Current of Religious Thought.**—If we accept the definition of a God as a sentient being possessed of superhuman power, it follows that the idea of God may be arrived at in two ways. We may ascribe sense to those superhuman elemental powers of whose action we are daily witnesses, or we may reverse this process and endow sentient beings, especially men, with powers which they do not actually possess. In other words, the idea of God may be arrived at either by personification or by deification.

Strictly speaking, the first of these processes is the only legitimate one. The second involves the assumption that man may be or may become God. But without questioning the reality of an intimate union of the human with the divine, both in this world and the next, it is better to maintain a clear distinction between these two terms. Ultimately, after the errors of anthropomorphism, poly theism, and spiritism have been eliminated, the two methods of arriving at the idea of God yield the substantially identical formulas :—

A. God = infinite power + absolute humanity.

B. God = absolute humanity + infinite power.

But in the stage of religious progress represented by Shinto, we are far indeed from such a result.

The priority of the second of these two processes has been assumed or contended for by many writers, notably by Herbert Spencer. Others argue that there can be no deification until the idea of deity has somehow been arrived at previously, as for example, by the personification of natural powers. It appears to me impossible to say which of the two comes first in order of time. The germs of both may be observed at a stage of intellectual development prior to all religion. Children, as we have all observed, sometimes personify inanimate objects. I have known a boy of three years of age complain that, " Bad mustard did bite my tongue." The baby who cries for the moon credits his nurse—ignorantly of course—with powers far transcend ing those of humanity. The argument that there can be no deification without a previous acquaintance with the idea of deity loses sight of the circumstance that deity is a compound conception, which combines the ideas of great power and sense. Of these two a man has sense already. To make him a God all that is necessary is to ascribe to him transcendent power. Deification, therefore, does not necessarily imply a previous knowledge of the conception of deity. In practice, however, men are usually deified by being raised to the level of already known deities.*

Each of these two processes rests on a basis of truth. The personification of natural objects and powers springs from some glimmering notion that the so-called inanimate world is really alive. Everything physical has its meta physical counterpart. There is no motion without some thing akin to sensation, and no sensation without motion. As all our sensations, emotions, and thoughts are accom panied by corresponding disturbances of the molecules of our brain and nervous system, so all natural phenomena have associated with them something varying in quality

* M. Goblet d'Alviella says : " I maintain that neither of these two forms of worship necessarily presupposes the other ; but that man having been led by different roads to personify the souls of the dead on the one hand and natural objects and phenomena on the other, subsequently attributed to both alike the character of mysterious superhuman beings. Let us add that this must have taken place everywhere, for there is not a people on earth in which we do not come upon these forms of belief side by side and intermingled." Dr. Pfleiderer's view is substantially identical.

and intensity, for which our human language has no better word than sensation, while along with the sum of the infinitely interwoven physical energies of the universe there goes what we, in our imperfect speech, must call emotion, purpose, thought.

Ordinarily the lower animal, the child, the savage, and the primitive man do not realize this truth. Under the pressure of imperious practical necessities they recognize with sufficient accuracy the difference between the animate and the inanimate. They do not take the further step of seeing that there is animation in the so-called inanimate. Sense and volition are not habitually attributed by them to inanimate objects. Much less do they assume, as we are sometimes told, the presence in them of a conscious agent not visible to the senses. There are, however, exceptions to this rule. Some of these are simple mistakes. I have known a dog take a doll for a living person, and only discover his error after close examination and long consideration. A large stone-ware image of the Buddhist Saint Daruma, of stern aspect, which stood in my garden in Tokio, caused unmistakable alarm to stray dogs who unexpectedly found themselves face to face with it. Children sometimes beat inanimate objects by which they have been hurt, and savages have been known to regard a watch as a living being.

A second exception is the case of conscious make-believe, of which we may observe instances in the play of children, and even of the lower animals. Errors and fancies of this kind do not constitute religion, though they may prepare the way for it. A time comes, however, when some savage or primitive man, gifted beyond his fellows, arrives at a partial and hesitating recognition of the truth that with the energies of nature there really goes something of the same kind that he is conscious of in himself, and has learned to recognize in his fellow beings—namely, sense and will. He sees the sun move across the heavens, diffusing light

and warmth, and says to himself, " He is alive." With the
intellectual perception there is associated emotion. He
feels that the sun is kind to him, and bows his head as he
would to his chief, partly to express his thanks and partly
in order that others may share his thoughts and feelings.
This is religion. It comprises the three elements of
thought, emotion, and action. Religion is at first excep
tional. Every primitive man is not a seer or maker of
religious myth. His ordinary attitude towards the powers
of nature is that of the Chinaman, who thought that the
moon was " all the same lamp pigeon." He is an unconscious
Agnostic, and knows nothing of volition in the inanimate
world.

The deification of men, although involving a contradiction in terms, has yet a substantial and most important
truth associated with it. Great captains, wise rulers, in
spired poets, sages and seers, whether alive or dead, deserve
honour to which it is not easy to place a limit. Napoleon
said that one of his generals was worth an army division.
Who shall estimate the value to their respective races, and,
indeed, to humanity, of such men as Shakespeare, Con
fucius, Mahomet, or Buddha ? Nor are they dead. They
live in their works, and subjectively in the hearts and
minds of their countrymen. And may we not go a step
further ? Our actions, even the most insignificant, do not
remain locked up in ourselves. As by sensation the whole
universe affects us, so does every impulse of our ego react
upon the universe, leaving an impression which is indelible.
The physical world is different for the most trifling act of
the meanest human being that ever lived. All our emotions
and thoughts have a counterpart in our physical constitu
tion, which is resolvable into motion, and is therefore
indestructible. The doctrine of the conservation of energy
is the physical counterpart of the doctrine of the immor
tality of the soul. Each involves the other. Assuming,
therefore, that all motion is accompanied by something

akin to sensation, it will be seen that dead men may con
tinue to have perhaps even a sentient existence equal to
the sum of the reactions of their ego upon its environment,
animate or inanimate, during life. It is the remembered
total energies of the man which, I take it, form the object
of honour and worship after he is dead, and not his corpse
or ghost. The latter is a mere accident, of secondary
origin, and is by no means universally recognized.

In justification of man-worship, it may also be pleaded
that if the nature-deity is truer, the man-deity is nearer to
us and more capable of vivid realization. And as it is from
the sympathetic recognition of life in our fellow men that
we proceed to the recognition of life in the so-called inani
mate universe, so it is by the contemplation of the highest
types of humanity that we are able to refine and exalt our
conception of divinity.

The two great sources of religious thought, personification
and deification, are constantly intermingling their streams
and reacting upon each other. A deity who begins his
career as a Nature-God often in course of time loses this
quality, and becomes hardly distinguishable from a magnified
man. The Zeus of Homer is an example. He is much
more the Father of Gods and men than a Sky or Weather-
God. In Japan it is only the scholar who recognizes in
Susa no wo the deity of the Rain-storm. To the people
even Tenshodaijin (the Sun Goddess) is nothing more than
the great providential deity who resides at Ise. Her solar
quality is practically forgotten. Men, on the other hand,
may be exalted to such a height by the ascription to them
of nature-powers that their original humanity is much
obscured.

It is sometimes difficult to determine to which of the two
currents of religious thought a particular deity belongs.
For example, we find a sword worshipped as a deity. Is
it on account of its wonderful cutting property, or because
it was once an offering to a nature or a man-deity, and

had therefore at length absorbed to itself a portion of his divinity? Or is it the Excalibur of some forgotten deified chieftain? There is no general answer to such questions. They must be decided, if at all, by the evidence in each case. To call objects of this kind "fetishes" helps us nothing. In the *Yengishiki* we find mention of a shrine to Iha no hime (the lady of the rock). At first sight this looks like a Nature-God. But when we find that an Iha no hime was the mother of the Mikado Richiu (end of fourth century) it seems more probable that the Iha no hime of this shrine was a deified mortal.

In Shinto it is the first of the two great currents of religious thought with which we are chiefly concerned. It is based much more on the conception —fragmentary, shallow, and imperfect as it is—of the universe as sentient than on the recognition of pre-eminent qualities in human beings, alive or dead. It springs primarily from gratitude to—and, though in a less degree, fear of—the great natural powers on which our existence depends. The desire to commemorate the virtues and services of great men and to perpetuate a loving remembrance of departed parents and forefathers takes a secondary place.

**Classification of Deities.**—Both Nature-Gods and Man-Gods may be deities of individuals, of classes, or of abstract qualities. We have, therefore, six classes of Gods, as follows :—

*Nature-Gods.*

Individuals, as the Sun.
Classes, as the God of Trees.
Properties, as the God of Growth.

*Man-Gods.*

Individuals, as Temmangu.
Classes, as Koyane.
Properties, as Ta-jikara no wo (Hand-strength-male).

This is the logical sequence ; but it by no means follows that all Gods of individuals precede all Gods of classes, or that there were no deities of abstractions before some of the later individual or class deities were evolved.

The distinction between individual objects deified and deities of classes is not always well maintained in Shinto. It is doubtful, for example, whether Kamado no Kami is the God of all cooking furnaces, or whether there is a separate God for each. Different worshippers might give different answers. The habitual neglect by the Japanese nation of the grammatical distinction between singular and plural is a potent obstacle to clearness in such matters.

**Phases of Conception.**—The conception of individual parts of the universe as deities passes through the phases represented in the following formulas :—

I. The Sun (Moon, Wind, Sea, &c.) is alive.

II. The Sun is a man, a father, a chief or a king—first rhetorically, and then literally.

III. The Sun is a material object, ruled by an unseen but not incorporeal being with human form and passions.

IV. The Sun is (*a*) a material object ruled by an anthropomorphic being which has a spiritual double, or (*b*) is animated by a spiritual being.

These formulas exhibit the logical sequence of develop ment. In practice the various phases are found to overlap one another considerably. Even in the latest Shinto the direct conception of the natural object as alive is not forgotten.

The first stage,* in which we have the religious concep tion before it is clothed in myth or metaphor, is abundantly exemplified in Shinto. A well, for example, is, like Horace's " Fons Bandusiæ," worshipped without name or myth attached to it, or anything to show whether it is regarded as male or female. The same is the case with

---

* Max Müller speaks of " that ancient stratum of thought which postulated an agent in the sky, the sun, &c." This is really a secondary conception.

sites, buildings, provinces, trees, all of which are deified and have religious rites in their honour without any very definite personality being attributed to them.    They are simply thought of as in some sort of way living things. Mud and sand are dubbed *Kami*, and there the personifica tion ends.    There are a good many colourless deities of this kind in Shinto.    Motoori declares explicitly that when a sea or a mountain is called *Kami*, it is not the spirit of the sea or mountain which is meant, but the sea or mountain itself.    A poet of the Manyoshiu says of Fujiyama :—

> Of Yamato, the Land of Sunrise,
> It is the peace-giver, it is the God,
> It is the treasure.

When a kitchen wench at the present day speaks of the *Hettsui-sama* —*sama* is a honorific and personifying word— she means the cooking-furnace itself regarded as a God, not a spirit inhabiting it.    She will even speak of the plasterer making a *Hettsui-sama*.

The second or anthropomorphic stage of the develop ment of the idea of God arises out of the rhetorical necessity of rendering more vivid, even at the expense of exact truth, the presentation of the conception of the powers of nature as living things.    Finding that the bare assertion that they are alive produces little impression, the poet or seer goes a step further, and boldly ascribes to them human form, passions, actions, and character.    Myth and metaphor are his instruments.    The God has bodily parts, parents, sex, and children.    He eats, drinks, is angry or alarmed, loves, fights, weaves, cultivates the ground, fishes, hunts, and dies.    With the advance of social organization he is a chief or a king.    Sometimes in these metaphors we can trace a special application to the deity's natural functions.    Sometimes they are introduced merely for general effect.    The results of this process for good and for evil are written large in the pages

of human history.    It is, on the one hand, the indis
pensable means by which the high intuitions of the seer
are brought home, more or less imperfectly, to the multi
tude. On the other hand, the true original nature divinity
is often lost sight of in a profusion of anthropomorphic
fancies, and nothing is left but a magnified man, whose
ultimate fate it is to be disavowed by advancing knowledge
and enlightenment.

It has been said that the primitive man knows no distinc
tion between fancy and reality.    In truth, life would be
impossible for such a simpleton.    However primitive he
may be, he cannot hold a fire in his hand by thinking of
the frosty Caucasus.    The difference between a real dinner
and an imaginary one is palpable even to his limited intelli
gence.    The hunter who could not distinguish between
the game of his imagination and the reality could never
earn a living. He would be fit only for an imbecile asylum.
The child is well aware that his mud pies are not fit to eat.
The savage woman who pretends to herself that a stone is
her lost baby, knows in her heart that this is nothing more
than make-believe.    Even a dog appreciates the distinction
between a real rat and the object which it pleases him to
fancy one, and worries accordingly.    The seer is conscious
that his anthropomorphic language is only metaphorical.
Dante felt this when he said :—

> Per questo la Scrittura condescende
> A nostra facultate e piedi e mano
> Attribuisce a Dio ed altro intende.

Metaphor is of the very essence of myth.    But the literal-
minded vulgar are at all times prone to confound the *altro*
which is clothed in myth and metaphor with its outward
husk, and the literal-minded scholar or scientific man is often
little better.    Hirata says that "what we call *kami* are all
men.    Even among men those who are excellent are called
*kami*.    The natural difference between men and Gods is

that the Gods are high and men are low, owing to the greater care taken by the creator deities in producing the former." He thinks that the Shinto deities are about ten feet high.

The humanization of the nature deities is reflected in the vocabulary of Shinto. The term *mioya*, or "august parent," is frequently used of them. *Tsuchi* or *tsutsu*, old forms of *chichi*, father, occurs in the names of several. It is primarily by no means physical fatherhood which is meant in such cases, although there are no doubt vulgar minds who are unable to rise above this conception and have thereby done much to corrupt religion.

In Western religions a God must be either male or female. The grammatical structure of their languages compels Europeans to say either he or she in speaking of deities. In Japan this necessity does not exist. The forms of Japanese speech take little account of sex. Many Shinto deities have no sex at all. In others sex is indicated by the incidents of the myth or by the additions of such termina tions as *wo* male, *me* female. There are several pairs of married deities. In art, sex is comparatively little distin guished in Japan.

The reason for attributing one sex to a deity rather than the other is not always evident. Provinces and mountains are sometimes male and sometimes female. The Food Goddess is naturally feminine, as representing the productive principle of nature, and perhaps also because cooking is the business of women. The male sex is more suitable to Susa no wo's violent character as the Rain-storm. Warlike gods like Hachiman are naturally masculine.

The "chieftain" conception of divinity is represented by the use of the word *wo*, male, *i.e.*, virile or valiant one, in many of the names of deities, and by the ascription to some of warlike qualities. There is nothing to show that these are deified chieftains. On the contrary, the term *wo* is applied, like *tsuchi*, father, to what are unmistakably nature deities, such as the Sea-Gods Soko-tsutsu-wo (bottom-father-male) Naka-tsutsu-wo (middle-father-male), and Uwa-tsutsu-wo (upper-father-male), produced by the lustrations of Izanagi in the sea after his return from Yomi.

*Tohe*, another word for chieftain, occurs in the name of the Wind-God, Shina tsu tone.

*Nushi*, master, is found in the names of several deities.

The application to the Shinto deities of words implying sovereignty is illustrated by *sube* or *sume*, which enters into a number of compounds relating to the Gods or Mikados. This word means "to collect together into one," and hence "to hold general rule over." *Sumera* or *sumeragi no mikoto* is the Mikado. Several deities enjoy the honorary epithet of *Sume-gami*, or *Subera-gami*.

*Mi-koto*, august thing, is also applied equally to Gods and Mikados, and in ancient times even to parents. It is nearly equivalent to our "majesty."

*Wake*, a branch, that is to say, a branch of the imperial family, a prince, is applied to deities.

*Hiko* and *hime* occur frequently in the names of gods. These words mean literally sun-child and sun-female, but in practice they are equivalent to prince and princess, or lord and lady. In the history of these words one may observe the operation of both of the great currents of deity-forming thought. *Hi*, sun, is used as an epithet for the glorification of human personages, and the compounds *hiko* and *hime* are in turn applied to nature powers as a personifying term. The Wind-God is a *hiko*.

The rhetorical impulse to realize in its various phases the human character of the nature deities of Shinto has produced a number of subsidiary personages, who are attached to them as wives, children, ministers, or attendants. Some of these are also nature deities. In others we find a union of the two deity-making tendencies. Thus Koyane, by the circumstance of his descent from Musubi, the God of Growth, and by his position of high-priest to the Sun-Goddess, belongs to the category of nature deities, while as an embodiment of the collective humanity of the Nakatomi sacerdotal corporation, whose ancestor he is feigned to be, he belongs to the class of deified human beings.

In Japan, the myth and metaphor-making faculty—in other words the imagination—though prolific enough, is comparatively feeble. The ancient Japanese especially were appreciably more neglectful than Western races of the distinction between the animate and the inanimate, and there was therefore less scope for the play of fancy in which religious personification consists. Like other Far-Eastern peoples, they realized the personal conception of deity with less intensity than the Aryan or Semitic nations. In this respect Homer and the Bible stand at the opposite pole from Confucius, whose *Tien* has as little about it of humanity as is possible for a being who is said to know, to command, to reward, and to punish. Shinto approaches Confucianism in this respect. There is, no doubt, a profuse creation of personified nature-deities, but we find on examination that they are shadowy personages with ill-defined functions and characters wanting in con sistency. Moreover, owing to the neglect by the Japanese of grammatical forms indicating number, it is frequently hard to tell whether a given name is that of one deity or of several. Musubi, the God of Growth, is sometimes one God, sometimes two, while at a later period he became split up into five or more deities. The Wind-God is at one time a single deity, at another a married couple. Susa no wo has in recent times been made into a trinity. Such fissiparous reproduction of deities is characteristic of a low degree of organization.* To meet the difficulties arising from this state of things Motoori, in the eighteenth cen tury, propounded his theory of *bun-shin*, or " fractional bodies," which may remind us of the " three persons and

---

* It was not unknown in ancient Greece and Rome. Zeus, Hercules, and other deities became divided up in this way.

one substance " of Christian theology.    Hirata, his
pupil, speaking of the three Sea-deities, Uha tsutsu no wo,
Naka tsutsu no wo, and Soko tsutsu no wo, says : " This
deity, although, strictly speaking, born as three deities, is
described as though one deity were present.    This is to
be understood of the God dividing his person and again
uniting it.    The descent of the *Adzumi no Muraji* (a noble
family) from him shows that in this respect he is to be
regarded as one."

The circumstance that many of the Gods, like the
Japanese themselves, have numerous aliases, adds to the
uncertainty.    The nomina and the numina do not invariably
go together.    There is sometimes reason to suspect that it
is the same God who appears under different names, while,
on the other hand, the same name may cover what are in
reality two or more different deities.

There were no arts of sculpture or painting in Japan
before their introduction from China in historical times,
and the consequent want of images and pictures for which
Shinto has been commended must have contributed
materially to prevent the Gods from acquiring distinct
personalities like those of ancient Greece.

The feeble grasp of personality indicated by the above
facts is profoundly characteristic of the Japanese genius.
It is illustrated by their unimaginative literature, which
makes but sparing use of personification, allegory, and
metaphor, by their drama, with its late and imperfect
development, and by their art, which has produced little
monumental sculpture or portrait painting of importance.
It may also be traced in the grammar, which has piac-
tically no gender, thus showing that the Japanese mind
is comparatively careless of marking the distinction
between animate and inanimate and male and female.  The
law takes far less cognizance of the individual and more
of the family than with us.    Another fact of the same
order is the neglect of distinctions of person shown by the

sparing use of personal and other pronouns.    In a passage
translated from Japanese into English, without any intention of illustrating this fact, there occur only six pronouns
in the former against nearly one hundred in the latter.  The
verb has no person.  *Yuku* for example, means equally I go,
thou goest, he goes, we go, you go, and they go.  It is
true that person may be indicated by the use of honorifics
to mark the second person and humble forms for the
first, but even when these are taken into account, the
absence from Japanese of indications of person is very
remarkable.

Herbert Spencer, in his 'Principles of Sociology,' suggests
that the comparative fewness of personal pronouns in the
languages of the Far East is owing to the circumstance
that they "establish with the individual addressed a relation
too immediate to be allowed where distance is to be main
tained."   Now, not only is it possible, and even common,
for pronouns to be used for the express purpose of magni
fying the distance between the speaker and the person
whom he addresses, as in the case of the German *er* when
used as a pronoun of the second person, but Spencer's
explanation does not meet the case of pronouns of the
third person, which are just as rare in these languages as
those of the first and second.   Nor is there anything in
the relations between men of high and low degree in these
countries which is so radically different from those which
have prevailed in Europe as to produce such a far-reaching
difference in the language of all classes of society.   The
truth is that these nations do not *avoid* pronouns.  Their
minds are still in a stage of development in which they
have not yet realized the advantages in clearness of
expression which are to be gained by a more systematic
distribution of their ideas into the three categories of first,
second, and third person.   It is with them not a matter
of etiquette, but of poverty of imagination, that power
which, as Mr. P. Lowell has remarked, is to the mental

development what spontaneous variation is to organic development.*

In Stages I. and II. of the evolution of nature-deities, it is the nature power or object itself which is the deity. Stage II. (Anthropomorphism), so long as it is not meant literally, is not inconsistent with a direct worship of natural objects and phenomena. But the vulgar are always prone to mistake metaphor for reality. When they are told that the Sun is a goddess, who walks, weaves, wears armour, sows rice, and so on, they take these statements literally, combining an implicit belief in them with the worship of the Sun itself. Even Motoori says that it is the actual Sun in Heaven which we worship as Amaterasu no Oho-Kami (the Heaven-shining-great Deity), while he believes at the same time that the Sun-myth of the *Kojiki* is real history. A time comes when it is objected that the Sun has no arms or legs necessary for the performance of the actions attributed to her. It is pointed out that the wind has no bodily form at all. Instead of going back to the true explanation—that these things are only metaphorical, the literal-minded man prefers to accept the suggestion (which brings us to Stage III.) that the deity is not the actual sun, or wind, or sea, or mountain, but a powerful being who rules it. Such beings, however, are not at first conceived of as in any way incorporeal.

* " Mr. Tylor has justly observed that the true lesson of the new science of Comparative Mythology is the barrenness in primitive times of the faculty which we most associate with mental fertility, the imagination......Among these multitudes (the millions of men who fill what we vaguely call the East) Literature, Religion, and Art—or what correspond to them—move always within a distinctly drawn circle of unchanging notions......This condition of thought is rather the infancy of the human mind prolonged than a different maturity from that most familiar to us.'—Maine, ' Early History of Institutions,' pp. 225-6. This characteristic of the mental development of the races of the Far East is discussed in ' A Comparative Study of the Japanese and Korean Languages,' by W. G. Aston, in the *Transactions* of the Royal Asiatic Society, August, 1879, and more fully by Mr. Percival Lowell, in his ' Soul of the Far East,' 1888. See also Mr. B. H. Chamberlain's ' Kojiki,' Introd., lxvi.

There is considerable confusion observable in Shinto between Stages I. and II. and Stage III. We have seen that Motoori identified Ama-terasu with the Sun. His pupil Hirata, on the other hand, says that the Sun-Goddess was born on earth, and was sent up to Heaven as " Ruler of the Sun." And while it is true that a sea may be directly called *Kami*, we have also a Sea-God, Toyotama-hiko, who is as clearly distinguished from the physical ocean as Neptune is. This fluctuation is common to all mytho logies. Greek literature is full of examples of reverence paid at one time to natural objects and phenomena, and at another to deities which rule them. They adored Apollo as well as Helios. Muir, in the introduction to vol. v. of his ' Sanskrit Texts,' says :—" The same visible object was at different times regarded diversely as being either a portion of the inanimate universe, or an animated being and a cosmical power. Thus in the Vedic hymns, the sun, the sky, and the earth are severally considered, sometimes as natural objects governed by particular gods, and some times as themselves gods who generate and control other beings." Our own poets are not a whit disturbed by such inconsistencies. In ' Paradise Lost ' the Sun is apos trophized in one place as the " God of this new world," while in another passage of the same poem we have a " Uriel, Regent of the Sun." Shakespeare, in the ' Tempest,' puts into the mouth of an anthropomorphic Iris the words :—

> The Queen of the Sky,
> Whose watery arch and messenger am I.

**Spiritism.**—We now come to Stage IV., or spiritism. The great and obvious difficulties connected with the anthropomorphic conception of deity, even in the modified form of a belief in corporeal beings detached from natural phenomena, led to spiritism, which may be defined as a partial or complete negation of the material properties of the Gods. Spiritism is therefore far from being a

"primitive" religious development, as is so often sup
posed. "Primitive man," it has been said, "thinks that the
world is pervaded by spiritual forces." I would rather
describe his mental attitude as a piecemeal conception of
the universe as alive, just as he looks on his fellow man as
alive without analyzing him into the two distinct entities
of body and soul. A dog knows quite well the difference
between alive and dead ; but the distinction between body
and soul is far beyond his intellectual capacity.

In Japan the process of spiritualizing the Gods has not
gone very far. Like the Gods of the Homeric Olympus,*
the Shinto deities are, on the whole, unspiritual beings.

The doctrine of spiritism is associated in Shinto with the
word *Mitama*, for which "spirit" is the nearest English
equivalent. Strictly speaking, the *Mitama* is not the God,
but an emanation or effluence from him, which inhabits his
temple, and is the vehicle of his action at a distance from
the place where he himself resides. It therefore corre
sponds to the Shekinah (that which dwells) of the Jews,
and, though in a less marked degree, to the Roman *numen*.
The Shekinah, like the *Mitama*, is a later development.
Where Habakkuk, ii. 20, says, "The Lord is in his holy
temple," the Targums have, "Jehovah was pleased to
cause his Shekinah to dwell in his holy temple." I cannot
see that the Shekinah and *Mitama* owe anything to the
analogous doctrine of the separability of the human soul
and body. The ghost is not the parent of either.†

The unavoidable assumption that an anthropomorphic
God can act at a distance from his own abode in Heaven
or elsewhere really involves the doctrine of spiritism,
though time and thought are required for its development.

---

* Homer implicitly denies the spirituality of his Gods when he says that the
Hercules which was summoned up by Ulysses was only his *eidolon*, or phantom,
the real man being in Olympus among the happy Gods.

† See an instructive article on ' Shekinah ' in Dr. Hastings's ' Dictionary of
the Bible,'

It is clearly not the Sun-Goddess herself who lives in Ise. •
Her true place is in Heaven ; but she is present in some
way on earth, as is proved by her answering the prayers
which are addressed to her at her shrine.   The explanation
which is ultimately forthcoming is that it is the *Mitama*, or
spirit, of the Goddess which resides there.   We have here
a foreshadowing of the doctrine of the omnipresence of
deity.

The etymology of the word *Mitama* will repay examina
tion.   *Mi* is simply a honorific prefix.   *Tama* contains the
root of the verb *tabu*, to give, more often met with in its
lengthened form *tamafu*.   *Tama* retains its original signifi
cation in *tama-mono*, a gift thing, and *toshi-dama*, a new
year's present.   *Tama* next means something valuable, as
a jewel.   Then, as jewels are mostly globular in shape, it
has come to mean anything round.   At· the same time,
owing to its precious quality, it is used symbolically for the
sacred emanation from the God which dwells in his shrine,
and also for that most precious thing, the human life or
soul.•

The meaning of *tama* is illustrated by the following story,
which is related in the *Nihongi* of Ohonamochi, the Creator
or Kosmos-deity of Idzumo myth :—

" *Coming at last to the province of Idzumo, he spake and
said : ' This Central Land of Reed-plains had been always
waste and wild.   The very rocks, trees, and herbs were all
given to violence.   But I have now reduced them to submis
sion, and there is none that is not compliant.'   Therefore he
said finally : ' It is I, and I alone, who now govern this
land.   Is there perchance any one who could join with me in
governing the world ?'   Upon this a divine radiance† illumi
nated the sea, and of a sudden there was something which*

---

• "And mine eternal jewel given to the common enemy of man."—
' Macbeth,' Act III. scene i.

† The Shekinah was also associated with a divine radiance, or glory.

*floated towards him and said : ' Were I not here, how couldst thou subdue this land ? It is because of my presence that thou hast been able to accomplish this mighty task.' ' Who art thou ?' asked Ohonamochi. It replied and said : ' I am thy spirit (tama) of good luck, the wondrous spirit.' Then said Ohonamochi : ' True ; I know, therefore, that thou art my spirit (tama) of good luck, the wondrous spirit. Where dost thou now wish to dwell ?' The spirit answered and said: ' I wish to dwell on Mount Mimoro, in the province of Yamato.' Accordingly he built a shrine in that place and made the spirit to go and dwell there. This is the God of Oho-miwa."*

The distinction between the God and his spiritual double so clearly indicated in this extract is often neglected and the deity of Miwa spoken of simply as Ohonamochi. The same uncertainty as to the spiritual character of the God is reflected in his names Oho-kuni-nushi (great-country-master) and Oho-kuni-dama (great-country-spirit), and in a legend told of him in the *Kojiki*, where he is corporeal enough to have a child by a mortal woman and yet sufficiently spiritual to pass through a keyhole.

In the *Idzumo Fudoki*, Susa no wo speaks of the village of Susa as the place where his *mitama* was settled, that is to say, where a shrine was dedicated to him. The *Nihongi* states that Izanami's *mitama* was worshipped at Kumano with music and offerings of flowers. In a modern book the Hi no mitama (spirit of the Sun) is not the Sun-Goddess, but a separate deity of a lower class.

The element *tama* enters into the names of several deities. The Food-Goddess is called either Ukemochi no Kami or Uka no mitama.* But the meaning " spirit " is not applic able in every case in which a God's name contains this ele ment. Futo-dama, for example, the name of the supposed ancestor of the Imbe priestly corporation, probably means

---

* *Mi mi* (august body) in the names of others involves a more material conception of deity.

"great gift or offering." Yorodzu-dama no Kami is not the God of ten thousand spirits, but the God of ten thousand offerings.

It is a curious circumstance that in later times the *mitama* par excellence were the phallic Sahe no Kami. Their festival was formerly called the *mitama matsuri*. It is now known by the Chinese equivalent *Gorioye*.

In a few cases the *mitama* is in duplicate, a *nigi-mitama*, or gentle spirit, and an *ara-mitama*, or rough spirit.* In the *Idzumo Fudoki* a man who is praying for revenge calls upon the *nigi-tama* of the *Oho-kami* (great deity) to remain quiet, and asks the *ara-tama* to attend to his petition. The legendary Empress Jingo was attended on her expedition to Korea by two such sea-god *mitama*, one to guard her person, the other to lead the van of her army. But we hear little of this distinction in the older records. The *aragami-matsuri* (rough-God-festival) of later days was a sort of saturnalia when license was permitted to servants.

The *Kojiki* and *Nihongi* do not theorize about the *mitama*. Hirata's statement that they do not distinguish between the *utsushi-mi-mi* (real-august-body)† and the *mitama* of the Gods is, as the case of Ohonamochi shows, not quite correct. But there is much foundation for it. In one myth, for example, the Sun-Goddess in handing over the divine mirror to Ninigi, enjoins on him to regard it as her *mitama*, and in another version of the story to look upon it as herself.

Another indication of an advance towards spirituality in the older Shinto literature is the distinction which is made between *araha-goto* (public things) and *kakure-goto* (hidden things), the former term being applied to temporal and the latter to spiritual matters, namely, the service of the unseen Gods. Mystery is not the vital element of religion. It depends on what we know, not on what we

---

* Corresponding to the *mo acha*, uncle of peace, and *shi acha*, rough uncle, of the Ainus.

† Homer's αὐτός.

do not know. Still, there perhaps never was a religion which did not betray some feeling that what we know is only an infinitesimal portion of that infinite sum of knowledge for which mankind is possessed with an eternal yearning. Religion, though not based in mystery, must always proceed, like other knowledge, from the known towards the unknown. A good deal, however, that is mysterious in religion is of our own making. Hirata, when he can find no way out of the difficulties arising from his crude, literal-minded anthropomorphism, constantly resorts to the time-honoured expedient of declaring his problems mysteries which transcend human intelligence, exclaiming, "Oh! how wonderful! Oh! how strange! Oh! how strange! Oh! how wonderful!"

Motoori and Hirata account for the invisibility of such Gods as Musubi, the God of Growth, by the theory that since the Age of the Gods they have removed further from the earth, so that they are now beyond the scope of human vision. In other respects, however, they have, under unacknowledged Chinese influence, greatly developed the hints of the spiritual nature of the Gods which are found in the *Kojiki* and *Nihongi*. Of the *mitama*, Motoori says* :—

" *In general, when such or such a God is mentioned in the old scriptures, we must distinguish between the real God and his mitama. The real God is his actual body ; the mitama is his divine spirit : the mitama-shiro (spirit-token) is the thing, be it a mirror or aught else, to which the divine spirit attaches itself. It is commonly called the Shintai (God-body). Now both the real body and the spirit are spoken of simply as the God. Thus when we are told that Amaterasu no Ohokami was entrusted to Toyo-suki-iri-bime and Yamato no Oho-kuni-dama to Nunaki-iri-bime, it is not to be supposed that the real bodies of these two deities were in the*

* *Sakitake no Ben,* 21,

*Imperial Palace. It is unquestionably their mitama-shiro
which are spoken of as if they were the real bodies......Again,
when we are told in the history of the same reign that the
Mikado assembled the eighty myriads of Gods on the plain
of Kami-asachi and inquired of them by divination, this is
not like the assembly in the divine age of the real Gods in
the Plain of High Heaven. The invitation is to their
mitama."*

The same writer says that of the attendant deities who
came down from Heaven with Ninigi, some came in their
real bodies, some as *mitama*. Among the former he
naturally classes all those who are represented as having
human descendants. Hirata regards this as a discovery
which will endure to all ages.

The following quotation from Hirata's *Koshiden* (vi. 9)
illustrates further the ideas of this school of theology
regarding the spiritual nature of the Gods :—

*" Both this God (Chigaheshi) and Kunado\* were produced
by the great mitama of the great God Izanagi applying itself
earnestly to preventing the entrance into this world of the
things coming furiously from the Land of Yomi, and which
accordingly became separated from him and adhered to a
staff and a stone. Remaining there, it (the mitama) did
good service in both cases. These Gods, moreover, sometimes
reveal their real bodies and dispense blessings. This may
not be doubted. We find below that Kunado no Kami acted
as a guide to Futsunushi; and that Chigaheshi no Oho-Kami
was two deities distinguished as hiko and hime (prince and
princess)."*

Hirata thinks that Gods (and men too) have two
doubles, the *nigi-tama* and an *aratama* mentioned above.
These he distinguishes from the *Zentai no mitama*, or
" spirit of the entire body." But he admits that these
distinctions are not recognized in the old Shinto. There is

\* See Index.

no limit to the subdivision of the *mitama*. Hirata explains that the deity is like a fire, which may be communicated to a lamp or to firewood while the original fire remains the same. " But the world knows not this." In other words, this is a philosophic refinement too subtle for the popular taste.

While the old records rarely distinguish between the God's real body and his *mitama*, in later times the *mitama* is often confounded with the *mitama-shiro* (spirit-token), or *shintai* (god-body) as the concrete representative of the God is called. Even in the *Nihongi* there is a case in which a sword is called Futsu no mitama. The *Kiujiki* calls the mirror of the Sun-Goddess her *mitama*. The *Shinto Miomoku* (1699) says that Futsu no mitama is the sword of the great deity of Kashima, and speaks of the Toyo-uka no mitama (the Food-spirit) as being, or residing in, a stone. Hirata himself calls a stone idol the *mitama* of the God, and speaks of the Sun-Goddess's *mitama* as going backward and forward between Ise and the sky. The unspiritual vulgar naturally find it hard to distinguish between the spirit of the God and its concrete representative.

The doctrine of the separability of the human body and soul, and of the continued existence of the latter after death, whether in a material or semi-material form, or as a pure spirit, may have been a factor in the spiritualizing of the cruder anthropomorphic conceptions of deity. But there is little or no evidence to this effect in the old Shinto scriptures, and the above pages show that other important influences were at work in producing this result. Whether the idea of God had its origin in the doctrine of separable human souls is a question which may be left to the discerning reader's judgment.

**Gods of Classes and Qualities.**—No language is possible without some exercise of the powers of generalization and abstraction. In Japanese, however, we miss many of the

more general, and especially of .the more abstract, con
ceptions embodied in European languages, a circumstance
which limits the scope of the personifying faculty, none
too vigorous in itself.  Supposing that we take the series
of conceptions beginning with the concrete individual tree,
and passing through evergreen oak, oak, tree, and vegetable,
to the definitive generalization of the universe.  The
Japanese language has no word for vegetable except
*somoku*, a recent compound of Chinese origin.  The word
for universe is *Ame-tsuchi* (Heaven + earth) which is almost
certainly a translation of the Chinese *ten-chi*.  The con
sequence is that neither the class of vegetables nor the
universe is recognized in the Japanese scheme of nature-
deities.  Individual trees are deified, and there is a God of
trees, but that is all.  The neglect of grammatical number
in the Japanese language often obscures the distinction
between the Gods of individual objects and of classes.
*Ki no Kami* means equally the God of the tree and the
God of trees.*

There is a marked poverty of abstract terms in the
Japanese language, and the personification of abstract
qualities is correspondingly restricted.  There is scarcely
anything in Shinto to compare with the numerous
personified abstractions of Greek and Roman mythology.
Izanagi and Izanami, embodiments of the creative or
generative powers of nature, are probably not originally
Japanese, but an echo of the *Yin* and *Yang* of Chinese
philosophy.  I have a suspicion that Musubi, the God of
Growth, may yet be traced to a Chinese source.

* For deities of classes consult Dr. Tylor's ' Primitive Culture,' ii. 242.

# CHAPTER III.

## DEIFICATION OF MEN.

THE importance of the deification of human beings in Shinto has been grossly exaggerated both by European scholars and by modern Japanese writers. Grant Allen, for example, says, in his 'Evolution of the Idea of God': "We know that some whole great national creeds, like the Shinto of Japan, recognize no deities at all, save living kings and dead ancestral spirits." He was probably misled by the old writer Kaempfer, whose ignorance of the subject is stupendous. The truth is that Shinto is derived in a much less degree from the second of the two great currents of religious thought than from the first. It has comparatively little worship of human beings. In the *Kojiki*, *Nihongi*, and *Yengishiki* we meet with hardly anything of this element. None of their great Gods are individual human beings, though at a later period a few deities of this class attained to considerable eminence and popularity. An analysis of a list of "Greater Shrines," prepared in the tenth century, yields the following results: Of the Gods comprised in it, seventeen are nature deities, one is a sword, which probably represented a nature deity, two are more or less legendary deceased Mikados, one is the deified type and supposed ancestor of a priestly corporation, one is the ancestor of an empress, and one a deceased statesman.

**Deified Individual Men.**—Like Nature-Gods, Man-Gods may be divided into three classes—namely, deified individual men, deified classes of men, and deified human qualities. The first of these classes comprises the Mikados, living or dead, and numerous heroes, of whom Yamato-dake, the legendary conqueror of the eastern part of Japan, and Sugahara (Tenjin), the god of learning, may be quoted as examples.

**Phases of Conception.**—They are variously conceived of, as follows :—

I. X, alive or dead, is a great man, worthy of our love, reverence, gratitude, or fear.

II. X, sometimes when alive, more frequently when dead. is possessed of superhuman powers, usually borrowed from those of nature, such as the control of the weather and the seasons, and of diseases.

III. X's powers reside not in his body but in a more. or less spiritual emanation from it.

In the first of these three phases, man-worship is not religion. So long as a man is honoured for those qualities only which he really possesses or possessed, he cannot be called a God. But although rational man-worship is not in itself religion, it is a necessary factor in its development. Our sentiments of gratitude and awe towards the great nature-powers spring up in hearts already prepared by the feelings which we entertain towards our parents, superiors, and other fellow-men. Whether individually or collec-tively, a man loves his parents before he loves God. The outward signs of divine worship are almost exclusively in the first place acts of reverence towards men. A man bows his head or makes presents to his superiors before he worships or sacrifices to a deity.

There is a tendency to restrict the word worship to the adoration of deity. Thus, when we speak of ancestor-worship, we are apt to think of it as implying deification. But there is much worship of living and dead men which is perfectly rational, and implies no ascription to them of superhuman powers.

The second, or religious, phase of man-worship involves the assumption that some men are possessed of powers of a kind different from those of ordinary mortals. The mere exaggeration of the human faculties may produce an inferior

sort of deity, but no really great man-God can be pro
duced without borrowing some of the transcendent powers
of Nature, or in some way identifying him with that
increasing cosmic purpose, which from one point of view
is te⁻dency and evolution, and from another is a loving
Providence.   Until this is done a deified king, ancestor, or
ghost (if there be such a thing) is a poor specimen of a
God.   To become a deity of any consequence, the man-
God must make rain, avert floods, control the seasons, send
and stay plagues, wield thunderbolts, ride upon the storm,
or even act as Creator of the world.*   When the practice
of deifying men was once established it was enough to
entitle them Gods, the term itself implying the possession
of those powers which we call supernatural, but which are
only so when predicated of men.

    **Deification of Mikados.** — The misunderstanding of
metaphorical language is a fertile source of apotheosis.
The deification of the Mikados is a case in point.   The
Mikado is called " the Heavenly Grandchild," his courtiers
are " men above the clouds," rural districts are spoken of
as "distant from Heaven," that is, from the Imperial Palace.
The heir to the throne was styled *hi no miko*, or " august
child of the Sun," and his residence *hi no miya*, " the august
house of the Sun."   The native names of many of the
Mikados contain the element *hiko*, or " Sun-child."   The
appearance in Court of the Empress Suiko (A.D. 612) is
compared to the sun issuing from the clouds.   *Tenshi*, or
" Son of Heaven," a Chinese term freely applied to the
Mikado in later times, is a variant of the same idea, which,
it need hardly be said, is known in other countries besides
Japan   The Chinese Emperor is said to call the sun his
elder brother, and the moon his sister.   Images of the sun

* " Laotze finit par n'etre plus que le principe vital universel existant avant
le ciel et la terre et qui s'est plu à chaque epoque a se montrer sous les traits
d'un personnage quelconque souvent des plus obscurs."—' Religion de la Chine,'
De Harlez.

and moon were depicted on the banners which were borne
before him on State occasions.  The same practice had
been adopted in Japan as early as A.D. 700, and there is a
relic of it at the present day in the Japanese national flag,
which is a red sun on a white ground.*  The ancient kings
of Egypt called themselves earthly suns.  Our own poet
Waller, addressing James II., says :—

> To your great merrit given,
> A title to be called the sonne of Heaven.

Let us not pass by these metaphors with a disdainful
smile, as mere unsubstantial poetic fancies.  They are
more or less rude attempts to give expression to the
very important truth that the benefits which a nation
derives from the rule of a wise and good sovereign are
comparable to the blessings of the sun's warmth and light.
As Browning, in ' Saul,' has well said :—

> Each deed thou hast done
> Dies, revives, goes to work in the world, and is as the sun
> Looking down on the earth, though clouds spoil him, though tempests
>     efface,
> Can find nothing his own deed produced not, must everywhere trace
> The results of his past summer prime—so each ray of thy will,
> Every flash of thy passion and prowess long over, shall thrill
> Thy whole people, the countless, with ardour till they too give forth
> A like cheer to their sons, who in turn fill the south and the north
> With the radiance thy deed was the germ of  .

It may be objected that it is contrary to the general law
of human development to make the higher metaphorical
conception precede the lower physical one.  It is no doubt
true that the physical idea of fatherhood must come before
the metaphorical use of this relationship.  But it does not
follow that when once the metaphor is arrived at, it may
not relapse into its original physical acceptation.  The
forces which produce religious progress act by waves, with

* See a paper on the *Hi no maru* (sun-circle) in the *T. A. S. J.*, Nov. 8th,
1893.

intervals of stagnation or retrogression. Even when the general religious condition of a country :s advancing it will be found that the lower popular stratum of thought consists less of undeveloped germs of future progress than of a breccia of the debased or imperfectly assimilated ideas of the wise men of preceding generations. In this retrograde movement a large part is played by the in vincible tendency of the vulgar to give metaphors their literal signification. This, I take it, is the source of the numerous actual children or descendants of the Sun and other deities who are found all over the world, in Greece, Peru, Japan, and elsewhere. The sequence of ideas may be thus represented :—

I. The King or sage is like the Sun.

II. He is (rhetorically) a Sun, or the Sun's brother or offspring.

III. He is actually descended from the Sun in the $n$th generation, the intermediate links of the genealogy being $a$, $b$, $c$, $d$, &c., and he is therefore himself a divinity.

Herbert Spencer, in his 'Sociology,' says :—

" There are proofs that like confusion of metaphor with fact leads to Sun-worship. Complimentary naming after the sun occurs everywhere, and where it is associated with power, becomes inherited. The chiefs of the Hurons bore the name of the Sun ; and Humboldt remarks that ' the " Sun-Kings " among the Natches recall to mind the Heliades of the first eastern colony of Rhodes.' Out of numerous illustrations from Egypt may be quoted an inscription from Silsilis—' Hail to thee ! King of Egypt ! Sun of the foreign peoples.. Life, salvation, health to him ! he is a shining Sun.' In such cases, then, worship of the ancestor readily becomes worship of the Sun .... Personalization of the wind had an origin of this kind."

" Nature-worship, then, is but an aberrant form of ghost-worship."

Surely this is an inversion of the true order of things.

Why do kings bear the name of Sun, or child of the Sun? Is it not because the Sun is already looked upon as a glorious being (a God?) with whom it is an honour to be associated? Herbert Spencer himself speaks of "*complimentary* naming after the Sun." The Chinese call deification *hai-ten*, or "matching with Heaven," showing that with them at least it is the man who acquires his divinity by being placed on a level with Heaven, not *vice versâ*. Worship of the Sun must be anterior to the very existence of Mikados, and there are certainly more substantial reasons for it than the transfer to him, suggested by metaphorical language, of the reverence paid to human sovereigns or ancestors.

The deification of living Mikados was titular rather than real. I am not aware that any specific so-called miraculous powers* were authoritatively claimed for them. In 645 a Japanese minister, addressing some envoys from Korea, described his sovereign as "the Emperor of Japan, who rules the world as a manifest deity." The same official recognized the Korean princes as "Sons of the Gods." The Mikado Keiko, admiring the strength and courage of his son Yamatodake, says to him: "Whereas in outward form thou art our child, in reality thou art a God." The Mikados called themselves, in notifications and elsewhere, *Akitsu Kami*, that is, manifest or incarnate deities, and claimed a general authority over the Gods of Japan. Yuriaku conversed on equal terms with the God Hito-koto-nushi. He expected obedience from the Thunder-God, but speedily had cause to repent his audacity.†

The honours paid to deceased Mikados stand on a somewhat different footing. There is little, however, in the earlier period of Shinto to distinguish the respect shown to

---

* Such as touching for scrofula or the assurance of fine weather.

† The statements of Kaempfer, in his 'History of Japan,' regarding the sacred character of the Mikado's person cannot be depended on. His account of Shinto generally is grossly erroneous, or rather imaginary.

deceased Mikados from the customary observances towards
the undeified dead.  The *Kojiki* and *Nihongi* have hardly
a trace of any practical recognition of their divinity.  We
are told in the *Nihongi* (A.D. 679) that the Mikado Temmu
did reverence to the tomb of his mother who had died
eighteen years before.  In 681 worship was paid (no doubt
by the Mikado) to the august spirit of the Mikado's grand
father (or ancestor).  There is nothing in these notices to
show that divine worship is intended.  An oath made by
Yemishi or Ainus, when tendering their submission in 581,
is more to the point.  They pray that " if we break this
oath, may all the Gods of Heaven and Earth, and also the
spirits of the Mikados destroy our race."  Still it must be
remembered that the author of the *Nihongi* was a profound
Chinese scholar, and that his work is deeply tinctured with
Chinese ideas.  I should not be surprised to find that the
above oath was simply copied from some Chinese book.

In the time of the *Yengishiki* (tenth century) the honours
paid to deceased Mikados had become regularized, and
offerings similar to those made to nature-deities were ten
dered to them periodically.  It is, however, a significant
circumstance that of the twenty-seven *norito* contained in
that work not one relates to their worship, and that the
care of their tombs did not belong to the Department of
Shinto.  Hirata protests vigorously against a modern
practice of using a Chinese word meaning Imperial Mauso-
leum for the shrines of Ise and Kamo.

As early as the ninth century there are several cases of
prayers addressed to deceased Mikados for rain, to stay a
curse sent by them for disrespect to their tombs, for the
restoration of the Mikado's health, for preservation from
calamity, &c.  In more recent times shrines were erected
to them, and prayers put up for blessings which it is far
beyond the power of man to grant.  Under the name of
Hachiman, the Mikado Ojin, visibly owing to Chinese and
Buddhist influences, became an important deity in later

Shinto. The same may be said of the Empress Jingo. The *Kojiki* and *Nihongi* treat both as mere mortals.

The honours paid to deceased Mikados were much neg lected before the Restoration of 1868. At present th*e*y consist in four solemn mourning services held in the Palace, one on the anniversary of the death of the late Emperor, the second on that of the death of Jimmu Tennō, the third and fourth in spring and autumn, in memory of all the Imperial ancestors.* Embassies are also despatched to the Imperial tombs (*misasagi*), which now have *toriwi* (the distinctive Shinto honorary gateway) erected in front of them. Two of the Mikados, namely, Ojin and Kwammu, have special State shrines dedicated to them. Concurrent with the enhancement of the political prestige of the Crown there has been a strong tendency in the present reign to increase the respect paid to the Imperial House, so that it now amounts to something like religious worship. The ceremony of the *naishi dokoro*,† which in ancient times was in honour of the sacred sun-mirror, now includes the tablets of the deceased Mikados.

**Other Deifications.**—Even in the case of the deification of living and dead Mikados there is much room for suspicion of foreign influence. Of the deification of other men I find no clear evidence in the older records. It is probable, however, that some of the numerous obscure deities mentioned in the *Kojiki* and *Nihongi* are deified men. A number of the legendary and historical personages named in these works were deified at a subsequent period. Others have been added from time to time. The case of the God of Suha has a special interest. Here the God's living descendant, real or supposed, is regarded as a God, and a cave (probably a tomb) occupies the place of the shrine. A fuller account of this cult is given below.‡

* ' Japan,' edited by Capt. Brinkley.
† See Index, *sub voce.*
‡ See Index—' Suha.'

The high-priest of the Great Shrine of Idzumo is called an *iki-gami*, or living deity. Not only good but bad men might be deified or canonized, as in the case of the arch-rebel Masakado, the robber Kumasaka Chohan, and in our own day, Nishitaro Buntarō, the murderer of Mori, the Minister for Education.

Lafcadio Hearn, in his 'Gleanings in Buddha Fields,' tells a typical story of the deification of a living man. A certain Hamaguchi Gohei, head man of his village, saved the lives of his fellow villagers from destruction by a tidal wave, at the sacrifice of his crop of rice, which he set fire to in order to attract them away from the sea-shore to the higher ground. "So they declared him a God, and there after called him Hamaguchi Daimyojin, and when they rebuilt their village, they built a temple to the spirit of him, and fixed above the front of it a tablet bearing his name in Chinese text of gold ; and they worshipped him there, with prayer and with offerings......He continued to live in his old thatched home upon the hill, while his soul was being worshipped in the shrine below. A hundred years and more he has been dead ; but his temple, they tell me, still stands, and the people still pray to the ghost of the good old farmer to help them in time of fear or trouble."

**Ancestor-Worship.**—If we restrict this term to the religious cult of one's own ancestors, as in China, this form of religion has hardly any place in Shinto. The only case of it, except in modern times and under foreign influences, is that of the Mikados, and even then there is no evidence of its existence before the sixth century. The term ancestor-worship is often used more generally of the worship of dead men of former generations. There is no good reason, however, for distinguishing between the cult of dead and that of living men. If the former is the more common, it is because absence and lapse of time are usually necessary to allow their obviously human character to be forgotten and to raise the popular imagination to the height of attributing to them superhuman powers. Deifica tion is the result of an exaggerated appreciation of what the man was during life, though there is often associated with this primary reason the ascription of imaginary powers to his corpse or ghost.

It is often assumed by English writers that Shinto is substantially, or at least is based on, ancestor-worship. The modern Japanese, imbued with Chinese ideas, throw them back into the old Shinto, and have persuaded themselves that it contains a far more important element of this kind than is actually the case. A recent Japanese writer says : " Ancestor-worship was the basis of Shinto. The divinities, whether celestial or terrestrial, were the progenitors of the nation, from the sovereign and the princes surrounding the throne to the nobles who dis charged the services of the State and the soldiers who fought its battles." Hirata, notwithstanding his anti-Chinese prejudices, was unable to resist the influence of Chinese ideas as regards ancestor-worship. He devotes vol. x. of his 'Tamadasuki' to the inculcation of an ancestor-worship which is plainly nothing but the well-known Chinese cult. His *tama-ya* (spirit-house, or domestic ancestral shrine) is a Chinese institution under a Japanese name, and the *tama-shiro*, or spirit-token, is the Chinese *ihai* (ancestral tablet). He would have his followers address their prayers, as in China, to their ancestors of every generation, from the parents of the worshipper up to the " Great Ancestor," the founder of the family. Their spirits (*mitama*) are to be adjured to avert evil from their descendants, to keep watch over them by night and day, and to grant them prosperity and long life. This is genuine ancestor-worship, but it is not Shinto. It was to meet the case of a failure of direct heirs to continue such ancestor-worship that the practice of adoption, unknown in ancient Japan, was introduced from China. The truth is that only a very small part of the Japanese nation knew, or pretended to know, anything about their ancestors. Even of those who had genealogies, many traced their descent from mere undeified mortals, some being Koreans or Chinese. There remain in the *Shōjiroku* and elsewhere a good number of genealogies in which the descent of noble families from Shinto deities is recorded. To what class do these deities belong? It is impossible to assert that some may not be genuine deified ancestors, though I cannot point to any undoubted case of this kind. Many are nature-deities. The descent of the imperial family from the Sun-Goddess is a typical example. The God of Growth, Kuni-toko-tachi, the Yatagarasu or Sun-Crow, the sword Futsunushi, and many other nature-deities appear among the ancestors of the *Shōjiroku*. In the ' Ideals of the East,' a work recently published in English by Mr. Takakura Okasu, the author speaks of the "immaculate ancestrism of Ise and Idzumo." The so-called ancestral Gods worshipped at these places are the Sun-Goddess, the Food-Goddess, Ohonamochi (an Earth-God) and Susa no wo (the Rainstorm). Dr. E. Caird's observation that " in the majority of cases it is not that the being worshipped is conceived of by his worshipper as a God because he is an ancestor, but rather that he is conceived as an ancestor because he is believed to be their God,"* obviously applies to this feature of Shinto.

Other nobles traced their lineage from, and paid a special worship to, personages who never existed as individual human beings. Such is Koyane, the reputed ancestor, but really only a personified type of the Nakatomi priestly corporation.

If we have any regard for correct terminology we must call this recognition of nature-deities and class-types as ancestors not ancestor-worship, but pseudo-ancestor-worship. When Britain's sons declare, as they do with

* ' Evolution of Religion,' p. 239.

sufficient emphasis, that "Britannia rules the waves," is this ancestor-worship? Or supposing that Macaulay's New Zealander found a remnant of the English people wor shipping John Bull as their reputed ancestor, would he be right to conclude that ancestor-worship was an English institution?

**Uji-Gami.**—These pseudo-ancestors are called in Japanese *uji gami*, or surname gods. The *uji* were originally official designations, whether of Court officials or of local officials or chieftains, which, as these offices became hereditary, took the character of hereditary titles, and eventually became mere surnames. They may be compared with such titles as Duke of Wellington or with surnames like Chamberlain, Constable, or Baillie. In ancient times the common people had no surnames, and therefore no ancestor-worship, pseudo or real.

The word *uji* is also used collectively of the noble house of persons bearing the same surname. It does not seem a very ancient institution, and must date from a time when an organized Government had already been established. Of the cult of the *Uji-gami* as such we know very little. The *Kojiki* mentions the fact of various deities being worshipped by certain noble families. A modern authority says: "All descendants of deities had *uji*. Every *uji* consisted of members called *ukara*. The chief of the *uji* was termed the *uji no kami* (the superior of the *uji*). It was his duty, on festival occasions, to convene the *ukara* for the worship of the ancestral God." In later times the *Uji-gami* became simply the tutelary deity of one's birth place, and was also called *ubusuna* (birth-sand). Infants born in his jurisdiction are presented to him soon after birth, and parturient women pray to him for relief. They also procure earth from the site of his shrine, in the belief that it has a magical power to assist their delivery. The same earth is credited with the property of relaxing the rigidity of a corpse

The modern *Uji-gami* are taken indiscriminately from all classes of deities, perhaps including even a few genuine ancestors. One or two Indian deities have been made *Uji-gami*. The Nakatomi had three *Uji-gami*— namely, Take-mika-dzuchi, Futsunushi, and Koyane. Noble families have been known to change their *Uji-gami*.

The *Uji-gami* correspond in some respects to the Greek ἀρχηγός.

**Biso.** —Analogous to the *Uji-gami* are the trades-deities of modern times. They are called *biso* (author or inventor), and may be either nature-deities, deceased men, or merely the deified type of the particular trade or profession. Wrestlers worship Nomi no Sukune, who was probably a real person, and Chinese doctors the legendary Chinese Emperor Shinnung. Confucian pundits worship Confucius, poets honour Hitomaro, and Haikwai poets Bashô. Professors of the art of tea-drinking show reverence to the founder of that particular branch of it which they practise. Soothsayers, *miko*, football players, flower-arrangers, and actors worship the so-called ancestral gods of their several professions. There is a *Kaji-so-sha*, or blacksmith-ancestor-shrine. Carpenters, for some reason, have adopted Shotoku Daishi, an Imperial Prince who lived in the seventh century, as their patron. Merchants worship Yebisu. They also pay some sort of respect to Fukusuke,* a dwarfish figure with a large head, attired in the ceremonial *kami-shimo*, and seated in a squatting position, which may often be seen in the larger shops. A figure of a cat with uplifted paw, called the *maneki-neko*, or "beckoning cat," and a recumbent cow covered with rugs are also objects of respect with them. It is in many cases a question whether the honour shown amounts really to divine worship.

**Spirits.**—The older Shinto scriptures afford but scanty evidence of the spiritualization of deified human beings. In the *Nihongi* there is one reference to the worship

* Fuku means good fortune.

of a Mikado's *mitama* (spirit). In another case the *mitama* of the Mikados are called upon to punish oath-breakers. Yamato-dake's *mitama* is in one place said to have been changed into a white bird. Of the *mitama* of ordinary undeified human beings there is no mention in the *Kojiki* or *Nihongi;* but, of course, this may be owing to the imperfection of the record. *Tamashiï*, a derivative of *tama*, is the ordinary word for soul at the present day, and is undoubtedly of considerable antiquity. Still there are cases where we should expect to find *mitama* spoken of, but where a more material conception—namely, that of metamorphosis—takes its place. Among several instances of this kind may be quoted that of Yamato-dake. He died, and was buried, upon which he took the form of a white bird, which flew away leaving the tomb empty. The modern name for ghost testifies to the prevalence of this conception in Japan. It is *bake-mono*, or "transformation," and is applied to foxes which change into human form as well as to the ghosts of the dead and to hobgoblins of uncertain origin. *Bake-mono* are not worshipped in Japan, any more than ghosts are with ourselves, but there is a beginning of reverence to them in the honorific particle *o* which is frequently prefixed to the word, especially by women. There are no proper ghosts in the *Kojiki* or *Nihongi*, although the writers of these works were fond of recording strange and miraculous occurrences. The metamorphosed appearances mentioned in them are never phantoms with a resemblance to the human form, and possess no spiritual qualities. Even now the *bakemono*, though differing little from our ghost, is quite distinct from the human *mitama* or *tamashiï* (soul).

*Tama*, as we have seen above,* may mean either a jewel, a round object, or the effluence of a deity or a spirit. Here literal-minded Dullness, with whom the Gods themselves contend in vain, leaps to the conclusion that the

* See p. 27.

physical globular *tama* is not merely a symbol of the soul, but the soul itself. By the ignorant in modern times it is conceived of as a small round black object, which has the power of leaving the body during sleep. The popular name for the will-of-the-wisp, namely, *hito-dama* (man-ball-soul) enshrines a like superstition.* It is asserted that the souls of the newly dead have been seen to float away over the eaves and roof as a transparent globe of impalpable essence.

We may compare with these Japanese notions the follow ing cases, which I quote from Herbert Spencer's 'Socio logy': " According to Ximenes, when a lord died in Vera Cruz, the first thing they did after his death was to put a precious stone in his mouth. The object of it was that the stone should receive his soul. The Mexicans along with a man's remains put a gem of more or less value, which they said would serve him in place of a heart in the other world." Such material conceptions of the soul are to be found every where. Mr. Hartland, in his ' Legend of Perseus,' observes : " To the savage, as to our own forefathers, and to the folk of all civilized countries still, the idea of an incorporeal soul is incomprehensible. It is everywhere in the lower culture conceived of as material, though capable of changing its form and appearance without losing its identity."† Hirata, after pointing out correctly that the *mitama* (jewel or spirit) is so called because there is nothing in the body so precious as the soul, immediately relapses into a more material con ception when he proceeds to explain that, although we can not discern its shape, seen from the Gods it must have the shape of a jewel (that is, spherical).‡

The history of the *mitama* suggests that the material,

---

* In Teutonic mythology the will-of-the-wisps are souls which have not attained heavenly peace.

† See also Mr. Frazer's ' Golden Bough,' ii. 297.

‡ The Stoics held that the world was not only animated and immortal, but likewise happy and round, because Plato says that that is the most perfect form.

or partially material, conceptions of the soul are a com
paratively recent development. Though religion is on
the whole progressive, it by no means follows that all
movements of religious thought are in a forward direc
tion. The spiritual edifice which poets and seers build
up is being constantly reduced to ruin by the inept
handling of the material-minded vulgar, to be reared
anew by others more splendid than before. But let us
not mistake the ruin for the first courses of a new build
ing, the dead husk for the living germ. Ghosts and ball-
souls are aberrant conceptions which belong to the former
category. The dullards to whom such notions are due are
quite incapable of originating the pregnant, though artificial,
conception of body and soul as two distinct entities.

Let me add a few more etymological facts which bear on
the question of spirituality.

*Mi-kage*, or "august shadow," is an ancient synonym for
*mi-tama*. It is unnecessary to suppose that anything but
a metaphorical meaning was originally intended. There
is, however, a modern superstition that when a man is near
his death his shadow becomes thinner.

The ordinary Japanese word for "to die" is *shinuru*, that
is to say, "breath-depart." Death is also called conceal
ment, long concealment, body-concealment, rock-conceal
ment (in allusion to the practice of burial in dolmens),
change, and ending. In the case of the Gods, death is
called divine departure or divine ascent.

*Iki*, "breath," one of the vital functions, is put by
metonymy for their sum, that is, life. It has not, like our
word "spirit" and the Greek "psyche," taken the further
step of coming to mean the human soul, except we identify
it with the *ke* of *hotoke*, which has been plausibly derived
from *hito*, "man," and *ke*, "spirit." It is now the common
Buddhist term for Buddha and his saints, and also for the
spirits of the sainted dead. The material-minded man, as
usual, drags it down to his own level. To him the corpse

\

at a funeral is the *hotoke*.   It is not certain, however, that
the element *ke* of this word is not of Chinese origin.
China, always far in advance of Japan in spirituality, has
exercised a profound influence on the development of
Japanese ideas regarding spiritual matters.

Another material conception of the life or soul is con
tained in a poem of the *Manyōshiu*, in which a fisherman
named Urashima is related to have found his way to the
*Toko yo no kuni*, or "Eternal Land."   When about to
return to earth he received from his wife a casket, with the
injunction that he must not open it.   He does open it,
upon which his life or soul comes out and flies away like
a white cloud to the "Eternal Land."   He dies soon after.
But this is a poetic fancy, open to strong suspicions of
Chinese inspiration.

There is a ceremony called *iki-mitama* (living soul),
which consists in paying respect to an absent parent, &c.,
as if he were present.   Another similar practice is that of
*kage-zen* (shadow-food), in which a meal is set out for an
absent member of the family, especially when it is not
known whether he is dead or alive.   The term *iki-su-
dama* (living spirit) is applied to the angry spirit (double?)
of a living person, which is supposed to work a curse,
sometimes unknown even to himself.   *Su-dama* are
defined as the essences of woods or mountains, which
assume a metamorphosed form—elves, as we should say.
All these are comparatively modern ideas.

The *Shinto Do-itsu*, a modern Shinto manual. frankly
adopts the Chinese views of the soul.   A manual of this
sect has the following : "The *kom-paku* are in China the
animal and rational souls.   When a man dies, his *kon* goes
up to Heaven and his *haku* returns to Earth.   Man at birth
derives his breath (or life) from Heaven and Earth.   There
fore when he dies it returns to Heaven and Earth.   The
*kon* is the *yang* or male, positive spirit ; the *haku* is the *yin*
or female, negative spirit (*tama*).   In everything there is

the *yin* and the *yang* heart. All men have *ki* (breath), *kei* (form), and *sei* (life). The *kon* rules the *ki* and the *sei*. The *haku* rules the form and the body. *Ki* means literally breath, on which man's life depends. From the Buddhist point of view there are two functions of the material body, namely, life and death, each of which has its soul. The *saki-dama* (spirit of luck) is the *kon;* the *kushi-dama* (won drous spirit) is the *haku* * Again the five viscera have each a God in shape like a man."

**State of the Dead.**—Like the Old Testament, the ancient Japanese records afford but few and uncertain glimpses of the condition of the dead. The doctrine of the immortality of the soul is nowhere taught explicitly. There are no prayers for the dead or for happiness in a future life. There is a land of *yomi* (darkness) which corresponds to the Greek Hades and the Hebrew Sheol. It is also termed *Ne no kuni* (root-land), *Soko no kuni* (bottom-land), *Shita-tsu-kuni* (lower-land), or the *Yaso-kumade*, that is to say, the eighty road-windings, a euphemistic phrase resembling our "going on a long journey." Yomi, however, does not seem to be peopled by human beings or ghosts. Nor do we find any actual cases of their descending thither at death, although the conception was no doubt originally a metaphor for the grave. In the *Nihongi* myth we find that where one version speaks of Izanami in Yomi, another uses the expression "temporary burying - place." The same work mentions an opinion that the " Even Pass of Yomi " is not any place in particular, but means only the space of time when the breath fails on the approach of death. The *Kojiki*, after relating the death and burial of Izanami on Mount Hiba, at the boundary of the Land of Idzumo, goes on to speak of her descent to Yomi as if it were the same thing. From this it would appear that to many persons, even in these early times, Yomi was a tolerably transparent metaphor for the state of the dead.

* Hirata denies this.

How difficult it is for even learned and intelligent men to rise above the literal interpretation of metaphor is illus trated by the fact that Motoori treats this suggestion with great scorn, pointing out that there is an actual entrance to Yomi in the province of Idzumo.

Izanami went to Yomi when she died.  She is called the Great Deity of Yomi.  It is also spoken of as the abode of Susa no wo, who, according to one myth, 'vas appointed to rule this region.  We also hear of the deities of Yomi, the armies of Yomi, the ugly females of Yomi, and the Road-Wardens of Yomi.  Thunder-Gods are said to have been generated there from the dead body of Izanami.  All these are probably various personifications of death and disease.

In modern times Yomi has been identified with *Jigoku*, the inferno of the Buddhists, which is a place of torture for the wicked.  Our own word hell has undergone a similar change of application.

In the *Manyoshiu* heaven is mentioned as the destina tion of a deceased Mikado, while in the very same poem a prince is spoken of as dwelling in his tomb in silence and solitude.  The *Toko-yo no kuni*, or Eternal Land, is another home of the dead.  The God Sukunabikona went thither when he died.  So did a brother of the first Mikado, Jimmu.  The *Toko-yo no kuni* is identified by some with Horai-san, the Chinese island paradise of the Eastern Sea, and by others with China itself.  The orange is said to have been introduced from the *Toko-yo no kuni*.  In the Manyoshiu poem of Urashima, the *Toko-yo no kuni* is the same as the submarine palace of the Sea-Gods, where death and old age are unknown.  *Toko-yo tachi* (ye immortal ones!) is a complimentary exclamation in a poem of the *Nihongi*.

The most definite statement regarding the continued existence of men after death occurs in the *Nihongi* under the legendary date A.D. 367 :—

" *The Yemishi rebelled. Tamichi was sent to attack them.
He was worsted by the Yemishi, and slain at the harbour of
Ishimi. Now one of his followers obtained Tamichi's armlet
and gave it to his wife, who embraced the armlet and strangled
herself. When the men of that time heard of this they shed
tears. After this the Yemishi again made an incursion and
dug up Tamichi's tomb, upon which a great serpent started up
with glaring eyes and came out of the tomb. It bit the
Yemishi, who were every one affected by the serpent's poison,
so that many of them died, and only one or two escaped.
Therefore the men of that time said : 'Although dead Tamichi
at last had his revenge. How can it be said that the dead
have no knowledge ?'* "

Evidently at this time there were two opinions on the
subject. Motoori says that this is a subject which tran
scends human comprehension. He leans to the view of
the old books, that men when they die go to the Land of
Yomi, in preference to the sceptical ratiocinations of the
Chinese sophists. Hirata takes a more decided attitude.
He points to the story just quoted as an example of dead
men executing vengeance upon those who were their
enemies during life.

**Funeral Customs.**—Let us now inquire whether any
thing is to be learned regarding the views of the ancient
Japanese as to the condition of the dead from their funeral
customs. The bodies of nobles, princes, and sovereigns
were deposited in megalithic vaults which were covered
by huge mounds of earth.* Pending the construction of
these, the body was placed temporarily in a building called
a *moya*, or mourning house. It was enclosed in a wooden
coffin and in some cases in a sarcophagus of stone or
earthenware. These sarcophagi have been found to

---

* For full details of the construction of the Japanese dolmen, the reader
may consult two admirable papers by Mr. W. Gowland, in the Japan Society's
*Transactions*, 1897-8, and the *Journal* of the Society of Antiquaries, 1897.

contain traces of cinnabar.* In all the more modern megalithic tombs the entrance faces the south. This arrangement is connected with the idea, common to the Japanese with the Chinese and other far-eastern races, that the north is the most honourable quarter. The Mikado, on state occasions, stands on the north side of the Hall of Audience. His palace fronts the south. Immediately after death corpses are laid with the head to the north, a position scrupulously avoided by many Japanese for sleep. They say they are unworthy of so great honour.

With the more eminent dead there were buried food, weapons, ornaments, vessels of pottery, and other valuables. Eulogies were pronounced over them, and music was performed at the funeral. Posthumous honours—a Chinese institution—were conferred on those who had merited them by distinguished services. In the more ancient times human sacrifices were made at the tombs of deceased Mikados and princes. The *Nihongi*, under the legendary date B.C. 2, states :—

"*10th month, 5th day. Yamato-hiko, the Mikado's younger brother by the mother's side, died.*

"*11th month, 2nd day. Yamato-hiko was buried at Tsuki-zaka in Musa. Thereupon his personal attendants were assembled, and were all buried alive upright in the precinct of the tomb. For several days they died not, but wept and wailed day and night. At last they died and rotted. Dogs and crows gathered and ate them.*

"*The Emperor, hearing the sound of their weeping and wailing, was grieved at heart, and commanded his high officers, saying 'It is a very painful thing to force those*

---

* "Blood, which is the life, is the food frequently offered to the dead......
By a substitution of similars, it is considered sufficient to colour the corpse, or some part thereof, with some red substance taking the place thereof."—Jevons, 'Introduction to the History of Religion,' p. 52. But see Index—'Red.'

*whom one has loved in life to follow him in death. Though it be an ancient custom, why follow it if it is bad? From this time forward, take counsel so as to put a 'stop to the following of the dead.'*

"*A.D. 3, 7th month, 6th day. The Empress Hibasu-hime no Mikoto died. Some time before the burial, the Emperor commanded his Ministers, saying: 'We have already recog nized that the practice of following the dead is not good. What should now be done in performing this burial?' There upon Nomi no Sukune came forward and said: 'It is not good to bury living men upright at the tumulus of a prince. How can such a practice be handed down to posterity? I beg leave to propose an expedient which I will submit to Your Majesty.' So he sent messengers to summon up from the Land of Idzumo a hundred men of the clay-workers' Be. He himself directed the men of the clay-workers' Be to take clay and form therewith shapes of men, horses, and various objects, which he presented to the Emperor, saying: ' Henceforward let it be the law for future ages to substitute things of clay for living men, and to set them up at tumuli.' Then the Emperor was greatly rejoiced, and commanded Nomi no Su kune, saying: ' Thy expedient hath greatly pleased Our heart.' So the things of clay were first set up at the tomb of Hibasu-hime no Mikoto. And a name was given to these clay objects.* They were called haniwa, or clay rings.*

"*Then a decree was issued, saying: ' Henceforth these clay figures must be set up at tumuli: let not men be harmed.' The Emperor bountifully rewarded Nomi no Sukune for this service, and also bestowed on him a kneading-place, and appointed him to the official charge of the clay-workers' Be. His original title was therefore changed, and he was called*

---

* Some of these figures are still in existence, and one may be seen in the British Museum, where it constitutes the chief treasure of the Gowland Collec tion. The Uyeno Museum, in Tokio, also possesses specimens, both of men and horses.

*Hashi no Omi. This was how it came to pass that the Hashi no Muraji superintend the burials of the Emperors"*

This narrative is too much in accordance with what we know of other races in the barbaric stage of culture to allow us to doubt that we have here a genuine bit of history, though perhaps the details may be inaccurate, and the chronology is certainly wrong. In an ancient Chinese notice of Japan we read that "at this time (A.D. 247) Queen Himeko died. A great mound was raised over her, and more than a hundred of her male and female attendants followed her in death."

Funeral human sacrifice is well known to have existed among the Manchu Tartars and other races of North-Eastern Asia until modern times. The Jesuit missionary Du Halde relates that the Emperor Shunchi, of the T'sing dynasty (died 1662), inconsolable for the loss of his wife and infant child, "signified by his will that thirty men should kill themselves to appease her manes, which cere mony the Chinese look upon with horror, and was abolished by the care of his successor "—the famous Kanghi.

Another missionary, Alvarez Semedo, in his history of the Tartar invasion, says : " It is the custome of the Tar tars, when any man of quality dieth, to cast into that fire which consumes the dead corpse as many Servants, Women, and Horses with Bows and Arrows as may be fit to atend and serve them in the next life."

This custom was also practised in China in the most ancient times, though long condemned as barbarous. An ode in the ' Sheking' laments the death of three brothers who were sacrificed at the funeral of Duke Muh, B.C. 621. When the Emperor She Hwang-ti died, B.C. 209, his son Urh said, " My father's palace-ladies who have no children must not leave the tomb," and compelled them all to follow him in death. Their number was very great.

A King of Kokuryo in Corea died A.D. 248. He was beloved for his virtues, and many of his household wished

to die with him. His successor forbade them to do so, say
ing that it was not a proper custom. Many of them, how
ever, committed suicide at the tomb. ('Tongkam,' iii. 20.)

In A.D. 502, Silla prohibited the custom of burying peo
ple alive at the funerals of the sovereigns. Before this time
five men and five women were put to death at the King's
tomb. ('Tongkam,' v. 5.)

Cases of suicide at the tomb of a beloved lord or sove
reign have not been uncommon in Japan even in modern
times. There was one in 1868.

The Japanese, like the Chinese, make no distinction
between voluntary deaths and human sacrifices. Both are
called *jun-shi*, a term which means "following in death."
Indeed, as we may see by the Indian suttee, it is often hard
to draw the line between these two forms of what is really
the same custom.

In the case of common people, of course, no such costly
form of burial could have been practised. It was called
*no-okuri* (sending to a moor or waste place), by which
simple interment, or perhaps exposure at a distance from
human habitations, was probably meant. The offerings
consisted of a little rice and water.

It is often assumed as too obvious to require proof that
such funeral customs as these imply a belief in the con
tinued sentient existence of the dead. It is taken for
granted that it is for their personal comfort and gratifica
tion that wives and attendants are put to death and
offerings of food deposited at the tomb.* 'If we reflect,
however, on the reasons for our own funeral observances,
which are less different in principle from those of barbarous
nations than we are willing to admit, we shall see cause to
doubt whether this is really the ruling motive. Most of
us have laid flowers on the coffin of some dear one, or

* "Rites, performed at graves, becoming afterwards religious rites per
formed at altars in temples, were at first acts done for the benefit of the ghost."
—Herbert Spencer's 'Sociology,' ii. 8.

erected a tombstone to his memory, or subscribed for a monument to a statesman who in life has deserved well of his country. Were these things done for the physical gratification of the dead? We cannot divide them in principle from more barbarous rites. We do not suppose that the dead see or smell the wreaths laid upon the coffin. Why should it be thought that in a more barbarous state of society it is believed that they enjoy the society of the wife who is sacrificed at the tomb?

The ruling motives for such rites are to be sought else where. In addition to the practical considerations which, as Sir Alfred Lyall has shown, are potent in the case of the Indian suttee, it is to be remembered that the memory of the great dead is a national asset of the highest value (as the memory of our parents is in the domestic circle), and that it is worth while going to great expense in order to perpetuate it. In an age before writing or epic poems existed, cruel sacrifices, pyramids, great tumuli, and other rude monuments were more necessary for this purpose than they are in our day. And if barbarians sacrificed human beings, do not we spend the financial equivalent of many human lives in statues, memorials, and otherwise useless funeral pageantry? The difference between them and us lies not so much in the motive as in the lower value placed by them on human life.

The truth is that offerings to the dead, from a flower or a few grains of rice to a human victim, are partly a symbolical language addressed to the deceased, and partly constitute an appeal for sympathy by the mourners and a response by their friends. They symbolize the union of hearts among those who have suffered by a common bereavement. We must also allow something for the despair which counts nothing that is left of any value, and prompts the survivors to beating of breasts, tearing of garments, cutting the flesh, sitting in sackcloth and ashes, lavish expenditure, and even suicide.

Yet it must be admitted that there is a broad, though secondary and lower, current of opinion, which holds that the dead benefit in some more or less obscure physical sense by the offerings at their tombs. Hirata believed that food offered to the dead loses its savour more rapidly than other food. The ghosts summoned up by Ulysses from Erebus eagerly lapped up the blood offered them. This, although poetry, no doubt represents a real belief.

Mr. Andrew Lang mentions the case of an Irish peasant woman, who, when her husband died, killed his horse, and, to some one who reproached her for her folly, replied, "Would you have my man go about on foot in the next world?" But may we not suspect that the real motive of my countrywoman's action was to express dumbly to the world the love she bore her husband by sacrificing something which she valued highly, and that the answer quoted was nothing more than a consciously frivolous reason, invented for the benefit of an unsympathetic, dull-minded intruder?

Whether or not the dead, apart from any physical benefit from funeral offerings, are grateful for the affectionate remembrance which they symbolize, it may be doubted whether the recognition of such a feeling on their part enters very largely into our motives. Was it for the gratification of Nelson's spirit that the column was erected in Trafalgar Square? Or do those who annually deposit primroses before the statue of Lord Beaconsfield think that his spirit is sensible of this observance?

Funeral ceremonies were not recognized as having anything to do with the older Shinto. It avoided everything connected with death, which was regarded as a source of pollution. Not until the revolution of 1868 was there instituted an authorized form of Shinto burial.*

**Deified Classes of Men.**—In the older Shinto this category of deities had more importance than it has at

* See an article by Mr. W. H. Lay in *T. A. S. J.*, 1891.

present. Several of the pseudo-ancestors are in reality
deified types, analogous to such conceptions as Tommy
Atkins or Mrs. Grundy. As a general rule they have two
aspects, one as man-Gods, and another as satellites of the
Sun-Goddess, a nature deity. They are more particularly
described in a later chapter.

**Deities of Human Qualities.**—·As might be expected,
Shinto has comparatively few deities of this class. It is
represented by the Gods of Pestilence, of Good and Ill
Luck, the phallic deities, and the *oni*, or demons of disease.
Such deified abstractions as the Fates, the Furies, Old Age,
Time, Themis, Fear, Love, &c., are conspicuously absent.

It will be observed that both of the two great currents of
religion-making thought are concerned in the evolution of
the last two categories of man-deities. They involve not
only the exaltation of human types and qualities to the
rank of divinity, but the personification of these general
and abstract conceptions. This complication indicates
that they belong to a secondary stage of development.
Ta-jikara no wo (hand-strength-male), for example, is not a
primary deity of the Japanese Pantheon. He is little more
than an ornamental adjunct to the myth of the Sun-
Goddess. It may be gathered from the myths of the
*Kojiki* and *Nihongi* that the phallic deities—personifica
tions of lusty animal vigour--were at first mere magical
appliances, which were afterwards personified and raised to
divine rank. It was a personified human abstraction—
namely, Psyche, who was described by Keats as

> The latest born and loveliest by far
> Of all Olympus' faded hierarchy.

Mnemosyne, Styx, and all the numerous deified abstrac
tions of humanity in Greek mythology are obviously of
later origin than Gaia and Ouranos, or even Zeus and
Here.

It is on the narrow basis of these two secondary classes
of conceptions that Comte strove to establish his Religion

of Humanity. But it is difficult tó conceive how on
Positivist principles Humanity, whether we regard it as a
class or as a quality, could have a sentient existence or
transcendent power, without a combination of which there
can be no deity and no religion, properly so called. His
worship of deceased individual men is open to the same
objection. Comte's recognition of nature-deities is brief
and contemptuous. He allows a certain reverence to the
Sun and Earth as " fetishes."*

**Animals in Shinto.**—Animals may be worshipped for
their own sakes, as wonderful, terrible, or uncanny beings.
The tiger, the serpent, and the wolf are for this reason
called Kami. But there are no shrines in their honour, and
they have no regular cult. A more common reason for
honouring animals is their association with some deity as
his servants or messengers. Thus the deer is sacred to
Take-mika-tsuchi at Kasuga, the monkey is sacred at
Hiyoshi, the pigeon to the God Hachiman, the white egret
at the shrine of Kebi no Miya, the tortoise at Matsunoo, and
the crow at Kumano. The *wani*, or sea-monster, belongs
to the sea-God, and the dragon belongs to (or is) Taka
okami (the rain-God). There is also mention of a thunder-
beast. In later times the rat is sacred to Daikokusama.
The pheasant is the messenger of the Gods generally. The
best-known case of the worship of an associated animal is
that of Inari, the rice-God, whose attendant foxes are
mistaken by the ignorant for the God himself, and whose
effigies have offerings of food made to them. The mythical
*Yatagarasu*, or Sun-Crow, had formerly a shrine in its
honour. The stone *Koma-inu* (Korean dogs), seen in front
of many Shinto shrines, are meant not as Gods, but as

---

* " Comte ramenait toutes les religions a l'adoration de l'homme par
l'homme. Comte, il est vrai, ne faisait pas de l'homme individuel l'objet du
culte normal : il proposait a nos adorations l'homme en tant qu' espece en tant
qu' humanité et parvenait a deployer une veritable mysticité sur cette etroite
base."—Reville, ' Prolegomena,' p. 26.

guardians, like the Buddhist Nio. They are a later introduction.

The Gods are sometimes represented as assuming animal form. Kushiyatama no Kami changes into a cormorant, Koto-shiro-nushi into a *wani* (sea-monster or dragon) eight fathoms long. The God of Ohoyama takes the form of a white deer. The most usual form assumed by deities is that of a snake, serpent, or dragon. Ohonamochi, in his amours with a mortal princess, showed himself to her as a small snake. In the Yamato-dake legend, there is a mountain-deity who takes the shape of a great serpent. At the command of the Mikado Yuriaku, the God of Mimuro was brought to him by one of his courtiers. It was a serpent. Water-Gods are usually serpents or dragons.

**Totemism.**—I find no distinct traces of totemism in ancient Japan. Tattooing, which some have associated with this form of belief, existed as a means of distinguishing rank and occupation. The most probable derivation of the tribal name *Kumaso* is from *kuma*, bear, and *oso*, otter. A very few surnames are taken from names of animals. Dances, in which the performers represented various animals, were common.

The piecemeal immigration of the Japanese race from the continent of Asia must have done much to break up their original tribal system and to destroy any institutions associated with it.

The law of exogamy, with which totemism is connected, was very narrow in its operation in ancient Japan.*

* See Index—'Incest.'

# CHAPTER IV.

## GENERAL FEATURES.

**Functions of Gods.** — Nature deities seldom confine themselves to their proper nature functions. Shinto exhibits an increasing tendency to recognize in them a providence that influences human affairs. Even in the older Shinto there are examples of the Gods exercising a providential care for mankind outside of their proper spheres of action. The Sun-Goddess not only bestows light on the world, but preserves the seeds of grain for her beloved human beings. She watches specially over the welfare of her descendants the Mikados. Susa no wo, the Rain-storm personified, is the provider of all kinds of useful trees. Practically, all the deities are prayed to for a good harvest, or for rain. Even man-Gods, like Temmangu, may be appealed to for this purpose. Any God may send an earthquake or a pestilence. In 853 there was a great epidemic of small pox. An oracle from Tsukiyomi, the Moon-God, indicated the means of obtaining relief from this plague, and since then people of every class pray to him when it is prevalent. The *Ujigami* and *Chinju*, family and local protective Gods, might be chosen from any class of deities. A modern Japanese writer* says: "No one knows what spirit of heaven or earth is venerated at the Suitengu,† in Tokyo. But despite the anonymity of the God, people credit him with power to protect against all perils of sea and flood, against burglary, and, by a strange juxtaposition of spheres

---

\* In 'Japan,' edited by Capt. Brinkley.

† Dr. Florenz, in his 'Japanische Mythologie,' says that Sui-tengū is a fusion of the Sumiyoshi Sea-Gods with the Indian Sea-God Sui-ten, that is, Varuna, subsequently identified with the youthful Emperor Antoku (who lost his life by drowning in 1185),

**D**

of influence, against the pains of parturition. The deity of Inari secures efficacy for prayer and abundance of crops ; the Taisha [great shrine of Idzumo] presides over wed lock ; the Kompira shares with the Suitengu the privilege of guarding those that 'go down to the deep.' The rest confer prosperity, avert sickness, cure sterility, bestow literary talent, endow with warlike powers, and so on."

**Polytheistic Character of Shinto.**—A nature-worship, such as the older Shinto was in substance, is inevitably polytheistic. The worship of a single nature-God, as the Sun, is indeed conceivable. But in practice, the same impulse which leads to the personification of one nature object or phenomenon never rests there. The Living Universe is a possible monotheistic nature-deity. But this conception requires a greater amount of scientific know ledge than the ancient Japanese possessed. They had necessarily only imperfect and fragmentary glimpses of the vision splendid.

There is some evidence that Shinto took the place of a still grosser and more indiscriminate polytheism. We are told that Take-mika-tsuchi and Futsunushi prepared Japan for the advent of Ninigi by clearing it of savage deities who in the daytime buzzed like summer flies and at night shone like fire-pots, while even the rocks, trees, and foam of water had all power of speech.

The number of Shinto deities is very great. The Yengi- shiki enumerates 3,132 officially recognized shrines, and although the same Gods are reckoned more than once, as being worshipped in different places, still their name is legion. They are popularly spoken of as eighty myriads, eight hundred myriads, or fifteen hundred myriads. The number of effective deities fluctuates greatly. Oblivion dis poses of many. The identification of distinct deities is another cause of depletion in their ranks. This happens very readily in a country where, to parody Pope's line, "most deities have no characters at all." On the other hand their numbers are recruited from time to time by new Gods produced by various processes. The same deity, worshipped at different places, comes to be recognized as so many different deities. Horus in ancient Egypt, the Virgin Mary in Italy, and many of the Greek and Roman deities illustrate this principle. We may be sure that the Ephesians would have resented any attempt to identify their Diana with that of other cities. This process is facilitated in Japan by the practice of speaking of the God, not by his name, but by that of his place of residence—another illustration of the impersonal habit of the Japanese mind already noticed. Indeed the Japanese care little what God it is that is worshipped at any particular place. It is enough for the average pilgrim to know that some powerful deity resides there. A poem composed at the great shrine of Ise says : "What it is that dwelleth here I know not, yet my heart is filled with gratitude and the tears trickle down." Of one of the " Greater Shrines " of the Yengishiki Murray's 'Handbook' informs us that "considerable divergence exists among scholars as to the identity of the Gods to whom this temple is dedicated." During the present reign Kompira was converted by the Japanese Government from a Buddhist to a Shinto deity, without detriment to the popularity of his shrine as a resort of pilgrims. The same God may have greater credit for efficacy in one place than another. Thus the Inari of a certain village has a high reputation for the recovery of stolen property. Such specialties were recognized even by the Government, which awarded different ranks to the same deity at different places. Distinctions of this kind, of course, facilitate the disruption of one deity into several. Another cause of multiplication is the mistake of supposing the same deity with different epithets to be different Gods. In modern times the Shinto Pantheon has been recruited pretty largely from the ranks of human beings. Trees are still deified, and we have sometimes a new deity making his appearance from nobody knows where.

The polytheistic character of Shinto is intimately connected with the weakness of the Central Government of Japan during the period of its development. Or perhaps it may be more correct to say that it is another manifestation of the same want of national cohesion.* The ancient Mikados were anything but autocrats. Their authority was almost always overshadowed by the influence of ministers who struggled among themselves for the direction of the power nominally vested in the sovereign The Central Government had little effective jurisdiction beyond the capital and the five home provinces. No wonder that under these circumstances local deities retained their vitality and prestige.

Monotheism was an impossibility in ancient Japan. But we may trace certain tendencies in this direction which are not without interest. A nation may pass from polytheism to monotheism in three ways : Firstly, by singling out one deity and causing him to absorb the functions and the worship of the rest ; secondly, by a fresh deification of a wider conception of the universe ; and thirdly, by the dethroning of the native deities in favour of a single God of foreign origin. It is this last, the most usual fate of polytheisms, which threatens the old Gods of Japan. Weakened by the encroachments of Buddhism and the paralyzing influence of Chinese sceptical philosophy, they already begin to feel

The rays of Bethlehem blind their dusky eyne.

Our business, however, is with the past, not with the future. The first of the three paths which lead to monotheism is illustrated by the tendency to ascribe to several of the Shinto deities a certain superiority over the others. The Sun-Goddess, Kuni-toko-tachi, the first God in point of time

* "The different peoples conceived and developed this divine hierarchy *pari passu* with their own approximation to political unity" (Goblet d'Alviella, Hibbert Lectures). Aristotle recognized the same principle.

according to the *Nihongi*, Ame no mi naka nushi, and in Idzumo, Ohonamochi have been in turn exalted to a unique position by their adherents. But, for reasons which will appear when we come to examine these deities more closely, none of them really deserves the title of Supreme Being. Max Muller's opinion that "the belief in a Supreme Being is inevitable" is not borne out by the facts of Shinto.

The second path, which leads to monotheism through a more comprehensive conception of the universe, is exempli fied by the Creator deities, Izanagi and Izanami, personifi cations of the male and female principles of Nature, and still more so by Musubi, the God of Growth, which might conceivably have developed into a Pantheistic Supreme Being. But philosophic abstractions of this kind are unfitted for human nature's daily food. Musubi never acquired much hold on the people, though at one time his worship held a very prominent place at the Court of the Mikados. He eventually split up, first into two, then into a group of deities, and finally became almost wholly neglected.

The *Nihongi*, under the date A.D. 644, gives the following account of a blind and abortive movement towards a supreme monotheistic deity which claims from us a measure of sympathy :—

"*A man of the neighbourhood of the River Fuji, in the East Country, named Ohofube no Ohoshi, urged his fellow-villagers to worship an insect, saying : ' This is the God of the Everlasting World. Those who worship this God will have long life and riches' At length the wizards [kannagi] and witches [miko] pretending an inspiration of the Gods, said : ' Those who worship the God of the Everlasting World will, if poor, become rich, and, if old, will become young again.' So they more and more persuaded the people to cast out the valuables of their houses, and to set out by the roadside sake, vegetables, and the six domestic animals. They also madethem cry out :* ' *The new riches have come !'* Both *in the country and in the metropolis people took the insect of the Everlasting World and, placing it in a pure place, with song and dance iuvoked happiness.* They *threw away their treasures, but to no purpose whatever.* The *loss and waste was extreme.* Hereupon *Kahakatsu, Kadono no Hada no Miyakko, was wroth that the people should be so much deluded, and slew Ohofube no Ohoshi.* The *wizards and witches were intimidated, and ceased to persuade people to this worship.* The *men of that time made a song,* saying :

> *Udzumasa*
> *Has executed*
> *The God of the Everlasting World*
> *Who we were told*
> *Was the very God of Gods.*

" *This insect is usually bred on orange trees, and some times on the hosoki.* It *is over four inches in length, ind about as thick as a thumb.* It *is of a grass-green colour with black spots, and in appearance very much resembles the silkworm* "

We may note here the popular identification of the prophet with the God whom he served, and the worship of a caterpillar, which apparently played the part of the ear of corn in the Eleusinian mysteries.

**Shintai.** — Concurrent with the development of the spirituality of Shinto there arose a greater necessity for some visible concrete token of the presence of the God.[*] This is known as the *mitama-shiro* (spirit representative, spirit-token), or more commonly as the *shintai* (god-body). The *shintai* varies much in form. It is frequently a mirror

---

[*] " The symbol or permanent object, at and through which the worshipper came into direct contact with the God, was not lacking in any Semitic place of worship, but had not always the same form, and was sometimes a natural object, sometimes an artificial erection."—Robertson Smith, ' Religion of the Semites,' p. 160.

or a sword, but may also be a tablet with the God's name, a sprig of sakaki, a gohei, a bow and arrows, a pillow, a pot, a string of beads, a tree or river-bank, or even the shrine itself. A stone is a very common *shintai*, doubtless because it is inexpensive and imperishable. The *shintai* is usually enclosed in a box, which is opened so seldom that some times the priest himself does not know what it contains. It is not always the same for the same God worshipped in different places.

The *shintai* in some respects resembles the Greek ἄγαλμα. Both were originally offerings which became tokens of the God's presence, and by virtue of immemorial association with the deities to whom they were presented came at length to be regarded as sharing their divinity. The ἄγαλμα, however, developed into the statue, while the *shintai*, with a very few exceptions of later origin, did not take this form. Broadly speaking, Shinto has no idols. There is usually no attempt to give the *shintai* any resemblance to the supposed form of the God whom it represents. A few exceptions may be noted. The mirror of the Sun-Goddess, which was in reality originally an offering, is stated in one of the myths to have been made in imitation of the form of the sun. The phallic Gods, Yachimata-hiko and Yachi-mata-hime, were represented by human figures. The scarecrow God, Kuhe-biko, may be regarded as a rude idol. In the province of Noto there are stone idols said to be the images of the Gods Sukuna-bikona and Ohona-mochi. The pictures of the Gods sold at Shinto shrines in the present day are owing to Chinese or Buddhist influence.

In the old language the word *hashira*, pillar, is added to the numerals for deities and Mikados. For instance, " three Gods " is *Kami mi-hashira*, that is to say, " three pillars of Gods." Now in Korea, a country inhabited by a race closely allied to the Japanese, there are seen by the roadsides posts carved at the top into a rude semblance of the human form.* Some serve as milestones, and some are erected at the outskirts of villages to keep away the demon small-pox. These figures are called the Opang Chang-gun, or Generals of the Five Quarters. The name is Chinese, but the deities themselves may nevertheless be of Korean origin. If the ancient Japanese had rude figures of this kind it would explain the use of *hashira*, pillar, as a numeral for Gods. I am rather disposed, however, to surmise that the use of this term was really owing to the fact that the symbols of divinity most familiar to the ancient Japanese were the phallic emblems set up every where by the roadsides. The term *wo-bashira*, applied to the phallic end-post of the parapet of a bridge, contains the same element.†

There is a tendency in Japan, as in other countries, for the token of the God to become regarded, firstly, as the seat of his real presence, and, secondly, as the God himself. Many persons do not distinguish between the mitama and the shintai, and some go so far as to confound the latter with the God's *utsushi-mi*, or real body. This is a form of idolatry. The shintai may even be erected into an inde pendent deity. The mirror, which is the shintai of the Sun-Goddess, is the object of a separate worship, under the name of Ame kakasu no kami. Even at the present day religious honours are paid to this mirror or its repre-sentative.‡ The sword Futsu no mitama has shrines dedi cated to it. Another sword, called Kusanagi, has been worshipped for centuries at Atsuta, near Nagoya. It was this sword which Susa no wo found in the tail of the great serpent slain by him to rescue the Japanese Andromeda, and sent as an offering to his sister the Sun-Goddess.

---

* simulacra que maesta deorum
Arte carent, cæsis extant informia truncis.

Lucan, ' Pharsalia.'

† See Index—*Sahe no kami.*

‡ See Index—*Naishidokoro.*

Fetish worship of this kind is a later and degenerate form of religion; and must not be confounded with the worship of the great nature-deities.

Some artificial inanimate objects of worship are not shintai, but are worshipped for their own sakes as helpers of humanity. The fire-place is honoured as a deity. Potters at the present day pay respect to their bellows, which are allowed one day of rest annually, and have offerings made them. The superstitious Japanese housewife still, on the 12th day of the 2nd month, gives her needles a holiday, laying them down on their side and making them little offerings of cakes, &c.*

The absence of idols from Shinto is not owing, as in Judaism and Islam, to a reaction against the evils caused by the use of anthropomorphic pictures and images, but to the low artistic development of the Japanese nation before the awakening impulse was received from China. It indicated weakness rather than strength. Much of the vagueness which characterizes the Japanese conceptions of their Gods would have been avoided by a freer use of images. In principle the image and the metaphor are the same. There is no more harm in representing a God, pictorially or in sculpture, as an old man than there is in addressing him as Father, though practically a wide experience shows that the common people do not stop here in either case. There is a strong tendency to debase religion by attributing special virtue to the particular physical object of devotion, or even to forget that there is a God of which it is only a very imperfect symbol.

**The Infinite.**—Max Müller says that without the faculty of apprehending the Infinite there can be no religion. In that case Shinto is not a religion. The Gods are not

---

* In an official report by Mr. H. Risley he says that at the time of the spring equinox there is a festival (in India) called Sri Panchami, when it is incumbent on every religious-minded person to worship the implements or insignia of the vocation by which he lives.

conceived of as infinite. They are superior, swift, brave, bright, rich, &c., but not immortal, omnipresent, omniscient, or possessed of infinite power. Where the word infinite is used it is said of infinite time. We hear of the infinite succession of the Mikados, and of infinite or perpetual night (*tokoyami*). Perhaps what Max Muller really meant was "transcendent," that is, beyond man's power to rival, or even fully to comprehend.

# CHAPTER V.

## MYTH.

**Nature of Myth.**—Myth and religion have distinct sources. We have seen above* that there is a phase of religion antecedent to myth. On the other hand, the earliest form of myth has no religious significance. It is the result of an idle play of fancy without any definite purpose. I have known a child of two or three years of age, who, when he saw a light cloud pass over the rising moon, exclaimed " She is putting on her clothes." Not that he believed the moon to be an animated being, or that he thought that clouds were really her clothes. His childish imagination was stirred by an instinctive impulse, to be compared with that which prompts the gambolling of a kitten who rushes from one place to another without any definite object, or to the butting of a young ruminant before his horns have grown. Closely related to such spontaneous efforts is the myth invented solely for the amusement of the hearer. May we not place in this category some of the nature myths of savages which to all appearance have no worship or belief associated with them, and belong to a pre-religious stage of development. Then we have the myths which are explana tory of some custom, rite, natural phenomenon, political institution, names of places or persons, &c. With these we may associate the genealogical myth. There is also the blunder myth, arising frequently from a misunderstanding of language, and the lie — a myth framed with intent to deceive. All these classes of fiction are abundantly exemplified in the old Japanese books.

* P. 16.

More important for our present purpose is the religious
myth, that
>    Mysterious veil, of brightness made,
>    At once the lustre and the shade

of religious conceptions.  Like the metaphor, of which it
may be regarded as an expansion, it suggests the True by
means of the Untrue.  It is an acknowledged necessity of
religious teaching.  In the infancy of language there is no
other means of expressing spiritual verities than by physical
symbols—in other words by myth and metaphor.  And
even when a language has acquired some capacity for the
direct expression of spiritual facts, it is found that the old
methods must still be resorted to in order to excite the
interest and impress the imagination of the ignorant multi
tude.  It is not to be supposed that the makers of such
myths believed that they were true in their natural physical
acceptation.  Take for example the parable of the prodigal
son.  There is no reason to believe that the " far country,"
" the husks that the swine did eat," " the fatted calf," and
the prodigal himself were not figments of Our Lord's imagi
nation.  Nor if the story had been true in all its details
would this circumstance have added one whit to the value
of the lesson taught by it.  I believe that the author of the
Mosaic story of the Fall of Man would be much surprised
to know that his drama, which deals so forcibly in concrete
form with temptation, sin, and its punishment, had been
taken by the world for many centuries as a narrative of
actual fact.

Some high authorities apply a different measure to pagan
and savage myth.  Dr. Pfleiderer, in his ' Philosophy of
Religion,' says that " it must be carefully borne in mind
that the religious phantasy, in producing such poetic sym
bolical legends, is not in the habit of distinguishing, nor
can distinguish between the ideal truth and its sensible
investment."  The late Mr. Fiske held substantially the
same view.  He goes so far as to apply it to Dante, whose

"Charon beating the lagging shades with his oar," "Satan crushing in his monstrous jaws the arch-traitors Judas, Brutus, and Cassius," "Bertrand de Born looking at his own dissevered head," he regards as "in the minds of Dante and his readers living, terrible realities." True it is that a stern reality underlies these grotesque fancies. But it is not of the physical order. No one knew better than Dante the virtue of the *altro intende* in such matters. We may be quite sure that he did not believe in a real inscription over the gate of Hell, in Italian *terza rima*, and composed by himself. It is a mistake, I sub mit, to imagine him, "like Katerfelto, with his hair on end at his own wonders." When Dickens tells us that he decidedly looked on his heroes as living per sons we must take this statement *cum grano salis*. We know what would have happened if some one had offered him, by way of payment, a cheque bearing the signature of Mr. Boffin, Dombey & Son, or the Brothers Cheeryble.

Mere inferences are often taken for facts, but, under normal conditions, the imaginative man is not the dupe of his own inventive faculty. It may be said that, however true this may be of more modern religious myth. the attitude of the "primitive man" towards the naïve creations of his fancy is different. Strictly speaking, there is no such thing as a primitive man. However far we may go back, we shall find men with parents. and preceded by an infinite line of ancestors. Still there can be no harm in using this term to designate mankind at some ill-defined stage of progress above the highest lower animal and below the savage of our own days. Strange things are told us of the primitive man. He is said to be unable to distinguish between his imaginations and facts, and that he is in the habit of taking his dreams* for real occurrences. Fiske says: "Our primitive ancestors knew

* See above, p. 12, and Index—'Dreams.'

nothing about laws of nature, nothing about physical forces,
nothing about the relations of cause and effect, nothing about
the necessary regularity of things......The only force they
knew was the force of which they were directly conscious—
the force of will.    Accordingly, they imagined all the
outward world to be endowed with volition and to be
directed by it."    Of course our primitive ancestors
expressed themselves differently from ourselves.    They did
not talk about laws of nature and the necessary regularity
of things.    But can we conceive them ignorant of the law
of the regular alternation of night and day, of summer and
winter, of the phases of the moon ?    Did not the " primitive
man " know just as well as Newton that when an apple
is detached from a tree it falls to the ground ?    He knew
that from a blow as cause we may expect pain, wounds, or
even death as the effect.    He had sufficient acquaintance
with dynamics to be aware that he could not raise himself
from the ground more than a few feet, and with chemistry
to have learnt that the savour of food is improved or spoilt,
according to circumstances, by the application of fire.    Nor
is it true that he ascribed all forces to volition.    It is only
by exception that the child, the savage, and the primitive
man attribute life to inanimate things.    This requires
imagination, a faculty which is notoriously feebler with
them than with the adult civilized man.    The progress of
humanity is from a sporadic towards a general recognition
of will in or behind the material universe, from fitful and
sportive fancies involving this idea to an earnest and steady
conviction of its truth, and from the fragmentary personifica
tion of the part as animated to the conception of a living,
universal whole.    Agnosticism, which ignores volition in
matter, belongs, therefore, to the lower end of the scale of
progress.    Where it appears in civilized man, it is a case
of arrested development.    The average savage is a mate
rialist, who associates volition with the energies of nature
in a much less thorough and systematic way than the

Christian, who believes that a sparrow cannot fall to the ground without the Father.

We must not confound the primitive maker of religious myth with the primitive man. It would lead to error if we modelled our idea of the average modern European on Bunyan, Milton, or Dante.

It is sometimes asserted that the impossible and mira culous occurrences which we so often meet with in the narratives of the primæval myth-maker are to him true. Why should he be limited to fact in this way? No doubt his standard of truth is different from our own. He would regard as possible many things which we know to be impossible. But is it necessary to suppose that his know ledge that a thing was impossible should prevent him, any more than our modern storytellers, from utilizing it in his imaginative work? Jules Verne well knew that a voyage round the moon is an impossibility. The unknown author or authors of 'Cinderella' surely need not be credited with a belief that pumpkins can be converted into coaches by the stroke of a fairy wand ; the inventor of the story of the birth of Minerva from the brain of Jupiter knew quite well that such obstetrical operations were not feasible ; and it is unnecessary to believe that the myth-makers of the *Kojiki* and *Nihongi* thought that children could be pro duced by crunching jewels in the mouth and spitting them out.

There is, however, an exception to the rule that a story teller does not believe in the truth of his own inventions. It is notoriously possible for the author of a fictitious narrative to become, after a time, unable to distinguish it from a statement of actual facts. There is a case on record in which a learned judge communicated to the Psychical Society in perfect good faith a ghost story, all the prin cipal features of which were proved to be imaginary. They had their origin in his own talent as a distinguished raconteur. But this is a morbid phenomenon which must

not be confounded with the normal action of the imagi
nation in the child, the savage, or the primitive (or, indeed,
any other) myth-maker.

The inability to distinguish between imagination and
fact is really not a special characteristic of the primitive
man or savage, but of the literal-minded of all ages, in
presence of the creations of imaginative genius. Some few
primitive men may distinguish between the spiritual kernel
and its imaginative envelopment. But for the multitude
this is impossible. Unable to discriminate between these.
two elements, and dimly conscious that the whole is a
valuable possession, they wisely accept it indiscriminately
as actual fact.

De Gubernatis, in his 'Zoological Mythology,' relates a
story which illustrates the respective attitudes of the myth-
maker and his hearers. He tells us that "when he was four
years old, as he was walking one day with a brother, the
latter pointed to a fantastical cloud on the horizon, and
cried, 'Look down there : that is a hungry wolf running
after the sheep.' He convinced me so entirely of that
cloud being really a hungry wolf that I instantly took to
my heels and escaped precipitately into the house." Take,
again, the following sun-myth, fresh coined from the mint
of Mr. George Meredith :—

"The sun is coming down to earth, and the fields and
the waters shout to him golden shouts. He comes, and
his heralds run before him, and touch the leaves of oaks
and planes and beeches lucid green and the pine stems
redder gold : leaving brightest footprints upon thickly
weeded banks, where the foxglove's last upper bells incline
and bramble shoots wander amid moist herbage," &c.

This myth, like the old Greek tales of Prometheus and
Tantalus, which Wordsworth calls

Fictions in form, but in their substance truths,

has a spiritual significance of which Mr. Meredith cannot

have been unconscious. Though nobody at the present day supposes that the author or his readers take it for a narrative of actual events, cannot we fancy Macaulay's New Zealander, being told as a fact some traditional, time-worn, corrupt, and ill-interpreted version of it, and, especially if he is a literal-minded philosopher, wondering how it was possible for the English to believe in such a concatenation of anthropomorphic fancies?

The literal acceptation of myth or metaphor is not confined to the lower class of intellect. It was a " teacher of Israel " who could not see how " a man could enter into his mother's womb and be born again." Motoori and Hirata, highly educated scholars, well versed in Chinese and Indian religious literature, received the stories of the *Kojiki* and *Nihongi* as genuine history.

Even Dante and Milton, men of profound spiritual insight, probably accepted in their most literal sense some, of the imaginative figments of their predecessors.

There have always been literal-minded unbelievers, who reject the myth and its religious contents without dis crimination, and simply value it, if at all, for its æsthetic merits. Of them, as of the literal-minded believer, " Si exempla requiris, circumspice."

The history of the religious myth may be summarized as follows : A, a man of genius, creates it, clearly distin guishing in his own mind between the kernel of religious truth and its imaginative embodiment. His disciples B and C understand him thoroughly. In this stage a myth is called a parable or allegory. Many myths proceed no further. D, F, H, * * * T and V, unable to discriminate the true element from the false, accept the whole confusedly as actual fact. E, G, * * S and U are dense to its religious significance, and think it idle nonsense, or at best, simply a good story. W and X have a glimmering notion that the imaginative part cannot be literally true, but do not dare to question it, lest they should sacrifice at the same time the valuable religious kernel. Z is a philosophic inquirer who, not without difficulty, regains the standpoint of B and C. But by this time the myth has been super seded as a vehicle of religious truth by fuller and more exact forms of expression.

The chief ideas underlying Japanese myth are, firstly, the conception—piecemeal it is true, and inadequate—of the so-called inanimate universe as being really instinct with sentient life, and exercising a loving providential care over mankind ;* and secondly, the doctrine that honour and obedience are due to the sovereign whose beneficent rule secures to the people blessings comparable to that of the sun's light and warmth. For such, I take it, is the real meaning of the story by which the Mikados are feigned to be descendants of the Sun-Goddess. It is the Japanese version of the doctrine of the divine right of kings. With out these and similar vital elements Japanese myth would be nothing more than what some writers have supposed it, a farrago of absurdities, and its examination would belong not to the physiology, but to the pathology of the human mind.

It can hardly be maintained, however, that the poets and seers of ancient Japan achieved much success in clothing their spiritual conceptions in mythical form. There is little force or beauty in their stories, and there is a plentiful admixture of matter which, to us at least, is frivolous, revolting, or devoid of religious significance.

There is no summer and winter myth in the old Japanese books, no deluge myth, and no eclipse myth. There is, strange to say, no earthquake myth, and but one solitary mention of a God of Earthquakes. There are no astral myths, no " Returning Saviour " myth, and no " Journey of the Dead " beyond the bare mention of an " Even Pass of Yomi," or Hades. The creation of mankind is not accounted for.

* See Dr. Tylor's ' Primitive Culture,' second edition, i. 285.

**Myth and Ritual.**—When a myth and a ceremony relate to the same subject-matter, which comes first in order of time? Is the ceremony a dramatic commemoration of the events related in the myth, or, *vice versa*, is the myth an attempt to explain the origin of the ceremony? Some go so far as to say that ritual is the source of all religious myth. The late Mr. D. G. Brinton, on the other hand, held that " every rite is originally based on a myth." Robertson Smith's view was that "in almost every case the myth was derived from the ritual, and not the ritual from the myth." No general rule can be laid down in these cases. Every such question must be decided according to the available evidence. A myth is a narrative, and a ceremony a kind of dramatic peformance. It will not be disputed that dramas have been founded on narratives, and that narratives are sometimes taken from dramas, as in the case of Lamb's 'Tales from Shakespeare.' Novels are every day dramatized, and the reverse process, though not common with ourselves, is familiar in Japan. Several of the Shinto deities are worshipped for no other reason than because they are mentioned in the myths of the *Kojiki* and *Nihongi*. It was probably the mythical account of the friendship of Ajisuki and Ame-waka-hiko which led to shrines being erected to these deities side by side at Idzumo. A literal interpretation of the obviously allegorical story of Iha-naga-hime and Kono-saku-hime led, in later times, to an actual cult of these personages. On the other hand, the ceremony of religious ablution is certainly older than the myth which represents Izanagi as washing in the sea in order to remove the pollutions of the land of Yomi. The worship of the Sun is assuredly not the outcome, but the source, of the Japanese solar myths, though it may owe to them some of its more modern features.

Many myths have no ceremonial associated with them, and there is much ceremony for which the myth-makers have not attempted to account.

# CHAPTER VI.

## THE MYTHICAL NARRATIVE.

No really adequate idea of the old Japanese myths can be gained without a direct study of the *Kojiki*, *Nihongi*, and *Kiujiki*, with all their repetitions, inconsistencies, and obscurities. In the following outline, taken mainly from the two first-named works, a selection has been made of such incidents as have an interest and significance for European students of mythology.

Both the *Nihongi* and the *Kiujiki* begin with a passage which is justly repudiated by the modern school of Shinto theologians as in reality belonging to the materialistic philosophy of China.* It runs as follows :—

"*Of old, Heaven and Earth were not yet separated, and the In and Yo†  not yet divided. They formed a chaotic mass like an egg, which was of obscurely defined limits, and con tained germs. The purer and clearer part was thinly diffused and formed Heaven, while the heavier and grosser element settled down and became Earth. The finer element easily became a united body, but the consolidation of the heavy and gross element was accomplished with difficulty. Heaven was therefore formed first, and Earth established subsequently. Thereafter divine beings were produced between them*"

Pfleiderer says :‡ "There is not unfrequently found in

---

* See ' Rig-veda,' x. 129, for a similar rationalistic dissertation on the origin of the universe. Here and below the italics indicate translations.

† In Chinese, *Yin* and *Yang*. The *Yin* is the dark, negative, passive, feminine, and terrene principle ; the *Yang* is light, positive, active, male, and celestial.

‡ ' Philosophy of Religion,' i. 269.

the mythology of the nature-religions a combination of Theogony and a Divine formation of matter in such a way that the Gods—whether one or all of them—are the first products of chaos, but then they form the rest of the world out of it. In the Indian mythology Prajapati proceeded out of the golden world-egg and then became the creative former of the world. Likewise in the Chaldæan mythology the great Gods arose at first out of chaos, and they then created the other Gods and the living beings of heaven and earth."

But are not such speculations later accretions on the original myth? In Japan, at any rate, formation out of chaos is undoubtedly an afterthought.

**First Gods.**—We have next what is called "the seven generations of Gods," ending with the creator - deities, Izanagi and Izanami. Of the first six of these generations the most confused and contradictory accounts are given in the various authorities. There is no agreement as to the name of the first God on the list. The *Nihongi* tells us that the first deity produced between Heaven and Earth while still in a state of chaos sprang up like a reed-shoot, which then changed into a God,* and was called Kuni-toko-tachi no Mikoto,† or "Earth-eternal-stand augustness." The *Kojiki* calls the first God Ame no mi-naka nushi no Kami, that is to say, "Heaven-august-centre-master-deity," identified by some with the Polar Star, a hypothesis for which there is no other ground than the name itself. The same authority gives Kuni-toko-tachi a place lower down in the genealogical table. The *Kiujiki* has a first God called Ame yudzuru hi ame no sagiri kuni yudzuru tsuki kuni no sagiri, and describes him (or her, for there is no indication of sex) as the "Heavenly Parent." It is impossible to translate this rigmarole; but as it contains the words

---

* "Into human shape" is another version.

† I shall usually omit this purely honorific addition to the names of Japanese Gods and sovereigns.

"earth," "sun," "moon," and "mist," a nature-deity is evidently intended. Both the *Kojiki* and *Kiujiki* first Gods disappear at once from the mythical record. There is little trace of their worship in later times, and they must be pro nounced mere abortive attempts at deity-making. Two other first deities are mentioned in the various myths quoted in the *Nihongi*, namely, Umashi-ashi-kabi-hiko-ji (sweet-reed-shoot-prince-father) and Ama-toko-tachi (Heaven-eternal-stand). The latter forms, along with Kuni-toko-tachi, one of those pairs of deities, not necessarily male and female, which are common in Japanese mythology. An enumeration of the Gods of the five generations which follow would be tedious and unprofitable. Some of them had probably no existence outside of the imagination of individual writers. They were doubtless invented or collected in order to provide a genealogy for Izanagi and Izanami. With one exception, they have left no trace in myth or in ceremonial. There are no shrines in their honour. Little is to be learnt from their names, the derivation of which is often doubtful. Several of them, however, show that the divinely mysterious process of growth, so all-important to an agricultural nation, had attracted attention.*

Musubi no Kami (the God of Growth), who forms the sixth generation of deities, is a genuine divinity, of whom more remains to be said hereafter.

**Izanagi and Izanami.**—The seventh generation consisted of two deities, Izanagi and Izanami. It is with them that Japanese myth really begins, all that precedes being merely introductory and for the most part of comparatively recent origin.

---

* Hirata says that "the five generations of deities which in the *Kojiki* precede Izanagi and Izanami are only names descriptive of the successive stages of formation of these deities. Their functions are obscure, and they have no shrines or worship. They are unnecessary, as all that are required are two Gods for the creation of Heaven, two of Yomi and two of Earth."

The *Nihongi* tells us that—

"*Izanagi and Izanami stood on the floating bridge of Heaven, and held counsel together, saying 'Is there not a country beneath?' Thereupon they thrust down the 'Jewel-Spear of Heaven' (Ame no tama-boko) and groping about with it, found the ocean. The brine which dripped from the point of the spear coagulated and formed an island which received the name of Onogoro-jima or the 'Self-Coagulating Island.' The two deities thereupon descended and dwelt there. Accordingly they wished to be united as husband and wife, and to produce countries. So they made Onogoro-jima the pillar of the centre of the land.*"

The *Kojiki* says that Izanagi and Izanami were com manded by all the heavenly deities "to regulate and fully consolidate" the floating land beneath. But all the accounts, the *Kojiki* included, proceed to represent the islands of Japan as having been generated by them in the ordinary manner. We have therefore three distinct conceptions of creation in Japanese myth—first as generation in the most literal sense, second, as reducing to order, and third, as growth (*Musubi*) *

The " floating bridge of Heaven " is no doubt the rainbow. It is represented on earth by the *Sori-bashi* or *Taiko-bashi* (drum-bridge) a semi-circular bridge over a pond before some Shinto shrines. It has too steep a slope for ordinary use, and is reserved for the Deity and for the priest on solemn occasions, the custom having been in this instance probably suggested by the myth.

The *Ame no tama-boko* or Jewel-Spear of Heaven has been the subject of much dissertation. Hirata, whose view is endorsed by several eminent scholars, native and foreign, thinks that it is a phallus. Its use in creating, which in Japanese myth is the same thing as begetting, the first

---

* There is a close association in Hebrew between the ideas of creation and begetting. *Bara*, create, and *jalad*, beget, are often interchanged.

island, countenances this idea. The derivation of *tama-boko* also lends itself to it. *Tama* may be rendered ball or knob as well as jewel, and the *tama-boko* might therefore be a shaft surmounted by a knob representing the glans, reminding us of the spears tipped with pine cones which were carried by the Bacchantes in the Dionysia. We have another Japanese case of a conventionalized phallus in the *wo-bashira*.* Moreover, on the theory that the *tama-boko* is a phallus, we have a satisfactory explanation of the cir cumstance that *tama-boko no* is used as a standing epithet of *michi*, road, which has puzzled Japanese scholars. The *tama-boko no michi* would then mean "the road where phallic symbols are set up." There is abundant evidence that objects of this kind were a familiar sight by the road sides near the capital in ancient times. The poet Tsura-yuki (tenth century) has left a short poem in which he expresses his intention of praying to the Tamaboko no chi-buri no kami when starting on a journey. The Chiburi no kami were the phallic road deities, protectors of travellers. Notwithstanding the Japanese poets' habit of using stock epithets without much regard to their proper meaning, this juxtaposition is highly suggestive. Another name for the phallic Sahe no kami† was Chimata no kami, or road-fork-gods, because they had no temples and were worshipped by the road-sides and at cross-ways. The road between Utsu-nomiya and Nikkô, when I travelled along it in 1870, was still a *tama-boko no michi*—in the phallic sense.‡ Another link between the *hoko* and the phallus is suggested by a state ment in the *Shiki Monogatari* that the weapon which formed, and still forms, the central object in the great *Gorïoye* festival procession at Kioto is known as the *Sai no*

---

* See Index.

† See Index.

‡ It was deprived of this character soon after by order of the Mikado's Government, the only monument of the old cult left standing being Nantai (male form), a mountain which towers above Nikko to the height of 8,500 feet.

*hoko.* Now the *Gorioye* is a survival of the old festival in honour of the phallic Sahe no kami.

But in mythology one explanation does not necessarily exclude another and apparently contradictory one. Whether the myth-makers had in their minds the phallus conception of the *tama-boko*—and I am persuaded that they had—it is impossible in this connexion to ignore the function of the *hoko*, or spear, as a symbol of authority. Herbert Spencer* has shown how universally the spear has this meaning. Britannia's trident is a familiar example. Theseus, in the 'Hippolytus' of Euripides, speaks of " the land ruled by my spear." Lances or arrows are emblems of authority in Korea. In Japan itself there is an abundance of similar evidence. In the *Nihongi* we hear of local governors being granted shields and spears in token of authority. When Ohonamochi abdicates in favour of Ninigi he delivers over the Kuni-muke no hiro-boko, or land-subduing-broad-spear. The epithet Ya-chi-boko no kami, or God of eight thousand spears, applied to the same deity, has a similar symbolical meaning. The Empress Jingo set up her spear at the palace gate of the King of Silla, in Korea, as a token of conquest. A holly spear, eight fathoms long, was given to Prince Yamatodake when he was despatched on his expedition to subdue Eastern Japan.

It will be observed that the *tama-boko* as a phallus belongs to the generative conception of creation, and as a spear to the idea of it as a cosmic or regulating process :—

" *The two deities having descended on Onogoro-jima erected there an eight fathom house with an august central pillar. Then Izanagi addressed Izanami, saying : ' How is thy body formed ? ' Izanami replied, ' My body is completely formed except one part which is incomplete.' Then Izanagi said, ' My body is completely formed and there is one part which is superfluous. Suppose that we supplement that which is*

---

* ' Sociology,' ii. 177.

*incomplete in thee with that which is superfluous in me, and thereby procreate lands.' Izanami replied, ' It is well.' Then Izanagi said, ' Let me and thee go round the heavenly august pillar, and having met at the other side, let us become united in wedlock.' This being agreed to, he said, ' Do thou go round from the left, and I will go round from the right.' When they had gone round, Izanami spoke first and exclaimed, ' How delightful ! I have met a lovely youth.' Izanagi then said, ' How delightful ! I have met a lovely maiden.' After wards he said, ' It was unlucky for the woman to speak first.' The child which was the first offspring of their union was the Hiruko (leech-child), which at the age of three was still unable to stand upright, and was therefore placed in a reed-boat and sent adrift"*

The "eight fathom house" built by Izanagi and Izanami as a preliminary to their marriage is the *fuseya*, or nuptial hut, several times referred to in the old records. It was erected less for practical purposes than to avoid the cere monial contamination of the ordinary dwelling-house by the consummation of a marriage within it.

The number eight is often met with in Japanese myth. It would be a mistake, however, to regard it as in any way sacred. The primary meaning of *yatsu* is " many," and it might be better to translate it so in this passage.

The central pillar of a house (corresponding to our king post) is at the present day an object of honour in Japan as in many other countries. In the case of Shinto shrines, it is called the *Nakago no mibashira* (central august pillar), and in ordinary houses the *Daikoku-bashira*. The circum-ambulation of the central post by Izanagi and Izanami reminds us of the Hindu *pradakchina.*[*] Hirata's conjecture that we have here an ancient marriage rite is very plausible.

---

[*] See Index, ' Circumambulation.' Also Simpson's ' Praying Wheel,' p. 285, and Jevons's ' Introduction to Religion,' p. 210. The corresponding Highland ceremony, called Deasil, is described in Sir Walter Scott's ' Fair Maid of Perth.' See also Brand's ' British Antiquities.'

The circumambulation of the dwelling, the fire, a tree, or an altar by the bride and bridegroom is a familiar feature of marriage ritual. It does not follow that the Japanese rite had a religious character. Nothing in the mythical record suggests that this is the case, and at no time in Japanese history has the marriage ceremony had the sanction of religion. Shinto neither consecrates wedlock nor condemns adultery.

It must not be inferred from this narrative that unions between brothers and sisters of the full blood were per mitted by ancient Japanese custom. Cain and Abel must have married their own sisters, but this proves nothing against the morality of the Jews. The necessity of the story is the compelling motive in both cases. It is true that marriages were allowed between a man and his sister by the father's side only, but we learn from the *Nihongi**\** that in the case of full brothers and sisters such connexions were considered criminal. The fact that *imo*, younger sister, is also used in addressing a wife proves no more than the "How fair is thy love, my sister, my bride!" of the Song of Solomon. The author of the myth of the Sun-Goddess endeavours to smooth over the difficulty of her conjugal relations with her brother Susa no wo by giving them a miraculous character.

The story of the abandonment of Hiruko by his parents, like the similar legends of Sargon and Moses, is evidence that the custom of casting away weakly or deformed infants was known to the authors. The real significance of the Hiruko myth will be shown hereafter.

The two deities next gave birth to the islands of Japan. Of the birth of Tsukushi, now called Kiushiu, the *Kojiki* says :—

"*Next they gave birth to the island of Tsukushi. This island likewise has four faces, and each face has a name.*

* I 324.

*So the land of Tsukushi is called Shira-bi-wake (white-sun-youth) ; the land of Toyo is called Toyo-bi-wake (rich-sun-youth) ; the land of Hi is called Take-hi-mukahi-toyo-kuji-hine-wake (brave-sun-confronting-rich-wondrous-lord-youth) ; the land of Kumaso is called Take-bi-wake (brave-sun-youth)."*

At this point the *Nihongi* inserts the rationalistic observation that the islands of Tsushima and Iki with the small islands in various parts were produced by the coagulation of the salt water.

Izanagi and Izanami then procreated a number of deities, among whom were Iha-tsuchi-biko (rock-earth-prince), Oho-ya-biko (great-house-prince), the Wind-Gods, a variety of marine deities, Ame no Mikumari (the heavenly water distributor), the God of Moors (who is also the God of Herbs and Grasses), the God of Trees, the Gods of Mountains and Valleys, and the Goddess of Food. The last deity to be produced was the God of Fire, Kagu-tsuchi, also called Ho-musubi (fire-growth). In giving birth to him Izanami was burnt so that she sickened and lay down. From her vomit, fæces, and urine were born deities which personify the elements* of metal, water, and clay, while from the tears which Izanagi shed when she died there was produced a deity called Naki-saha-me, or the Weeping Female. In his rage and grief, Izanagi drew his sword and cut Kagu-tsuchi to pieces, generating thereby a number of deities. Of these two were widely worshipped in later times. One, named Take-mika-tsuchi (brave-awful-father), is the God of the famous shrine of Kashima in the east of Japan. The other, named Futsunushi, is worshipped under the form of a sword at Kadori in the same neighbourhood. Izanami, by one account, was buried at the village of Arima at Kumano, in the province of Kii.

*"In the time of flowers the inhabitants worship her*

* A strong suspicion of Chinese origin attaches to these elemental gods.

*mitama by offerings of flowers. They also worship her with
drums, flutes, flags, singing and dancing."*

When she died Izanami went to the land of Yomi, or
darkness.

" *Thereafter Izanagi went after Izanami, and entered the
land of Yomi. When he rejoined her, they conversed together.
Izanami said: ' My lord and husband, why is thy coming so
late? I have already eaten of the cooking-furnace of Yomi.
But I am about to lie down to rest. Do not thou look on me.'
Izanagi did not give ear to her, but secretly took his many-
toothed comb, and breaking off its end-tooth\* made of it a
torch and looked at her. Her body was already putrid,
maggots swarmed over it, and the eight thunder-gods had
been generated in her various members. Izanagi, greatly
shocked, exclaimed, ' What a hideous and polluted land I
have come to unawares!' So he speedily ran away. Izanami
was angry, and said, ' Why didst thou not observe that which
I charged thee? Now am I put to shame' So she sent the
Ugly Females of Yomi to pursue and slay him. Izanagi,
in his flight, threw down his many-toothed comb, which forth
with became changed into bamboo-shoots. The Ugly Females
pulled them up and ate them. When they had done eating
them they again gave chase. He then threw down his head
dress, which became changed into grapes, and so once more
delayed his pursuers. On reaching the foot of the ' Even
Pass of Yomi' he gathered three peaches† that were growing
there, and smote his pursuers with them, so that they all fled
back. Moreover, he said to the peaches, ' As ye have helped
me, so must ye help all living people in the Central Land of
Reed-plains when they are in trouble' And he gave them
the title Oho-kamu-dzu-mi no mikoto (their augustness great-
divine fruit). This was the origin of the custom of
exorcising evil spirits by means of peaches.*

---

\* The significance of the *wo-bashira*, or end-tooth, is explained elsewhere.
See Index.

† See Index—' Peach.'

"*At the Even Pass of Yomi, Izanagi was overtaken by
Izanami herself.   He took a great rock\* and blocked up the
pass with it, pronouncing at the same time the formula of
divorce—namely, 'Our relationship is severed.'   He also
said, ' Come no further,' and threw down his staff, which was
called Funado no Kami ( pass-not-place-deity), or Kunado no
Kami (come-not-place-deity).   Moreover, he threw down his
girdle, which was called Nagachiha no Kami.   Moreover,
he threw down his upper garment, which was called
Wadzurahi no Kami (God of disease).   Moreover, he
threw down his trowsers, which were called Aki-guhi no
Kami.   Moreover. he threw down his shoes, which were
called Chi-shiki no Kami*"

The *Kojiki* represents Izanami as assuming the position
of the "Great Deity of Yomi," a personification of death.
In this character she says to Izanagi, "If thou dost so
(divorce me), I will in one day strangle to death a thousand
of the people of thy land."   To which he replied " If thou
dost so, I will in one day build a thousand and five hun
dred parturition houses."

The fatal consequences of tasting the food of the lower
regions are well known to mythologists.  Proserpine's return
to the upper world became impossible when once

> Puniceum curvâ decerpserat arbore pomum
> Sumpta que pallenti septem de cortice grana
> Presserat ore suo.

The same principle is recognized in Indian myth :

> Three nights within his (Yama's) mansion stay,
> But taste not, though a guest, his food.†

The natural aversion of human beings from touching or
even looking on the dead is made a characteristic of the
Gods in Greek mythology as well as in Japanese myth.
Artemis, in the ' Hippolytus' of Euripides, says, " It is not
*themis* for me to look upon the dead."

---

\* Deified as *Chi-gaheshi no Oho-kami* (road-send-back-great-deity).

† Muir's ' Sanskrit Texts,' v. 320.

The "Even Pass of Yómi" takes the place of the water to be crossed of other mythologies. Grimm, in his 'Teutonic Mythology,' says that "to Death is ascribed a highway levelled, smooth, and kept in repair, on which the dead travel."

On returning from Yomi, Izanagi's first care was to bathe in the sea in order to purify himself from the pollutions which he had contracted by his visit to the Land of Yomi. A number of deities were generated by this process, among whom were the Gods of Good and Ill Luck, and certain ocean deities held to be the ancestors of some families of local chieftains and worshipped by them. The Sun-Goddess was born from the washing of his left eye, and the Moon-God from that of his right, while a third deity, named Susa no wo, was generated from the washing of his nose. To the Sun-Goddess Izanagi gave charge of the " Plain of High Heaven," and to the Moon-God was allotted the realm of night. Susa no wo was at first appointed to rule the sea, but he cried and wept till his beard grew down to the pit of his stomach. He wept the green mountains bare and the seas and rivers dry. Izanagi inquired of him, " Why dost thou continually weep ?" He answered, " I wish to follow my mother to the Nether Land." Izanagi said, " Go, as thy heart bids thee," and drove him away.

Another account of the birth of these three deities says that they were born to Izanagi and Izanami on earth before the descent to Yomi. The Sun-Goddess was sent up to Heaven by the " Pillar of Heaven," which then served as a means of communication. Heaven and earth were still "not far separated." *Ame no mi-hashira* (Heaven-august-pillar) is one of the names of the Wind-God. An island is described as " Heaven's single pillar." Other myths speak of the *Ama no iha-bune*, or Rock-boat of Heaven, as used for com munication by the deities. There is also mention of an *Ama no hashidate* (Heaven-bridge-erection) which is distin guished by Hirata from the " Pillar of Heaven." He thinks the former was a sort of pier used by the Rock-boat of Heaven. A spit of land two miles long and 190 feet broad near Miyadzu in Tango is now called by this name.*

*Ame*, or the firmament, where the Gods live, is to be distinguished from *Oho-sora*, the Great Void, which is the space between heaven and earth.

Izanagi's ablutions (*harahi*)† represent a wide-spread rite. They remind us of Juno's lustration by Iris after a visit to Hades, and of Dante's immersion in Lethe when he had completed his ascent through Purgatory and was preparing for admission to the circles of Paradise. Alcestis, after her rescue by Herakles from Thanatos, had to be purified, and was not allowed to speak for three days. We have in the Japanese myth the counterpart of a custom described by Chinese travellers to Japan centuries before the *Kojiki* and *Nihongi* were written. It was then, we are informed, the practice, when the funeral was over, for the whole family of the deceased to go into the water and wash. Lustration is a wide-world practice,‡ and the myth was clearly suggested by it, not *vice versâ*.

Izanagi's career having come to an end, he built himself an abode of gloom in the island of Ahaji, where he dwelt in silence and concealment. Another account says that he ascended to Heaven, where he dwelt in the smaller Palace of the Sun.

It will be observed that Izanagi was not immortal, and that he did not go to Yomi when he died.

**Susa no wo.**—The mythical narrative now turns to the doings of the Sun-Goddess and her brother Susa no wo (the rainstorm personified).

Susa no wo, before proceeding to take up his charge as Ruler of the Nether Region, ascended to Heaven to take leave of his elder sister, the Sun-Goddess. By reason of

---

* See Murray's ' Japan,' fifth edition, p. 408.
† See Index.
‡ See Dr. Tylor's ' Primitive Culture,' ii. 435.

the fierceness of his divine nature there was a commotion in the sea, and the hills and mountains groaned aloud as he passed upwards. The Sun-Goddess, in alarm, arrayed herself in manly garb, and confronted her brother* wearing her royal necklace of jewels, and armed with sword and bow and arrows. The pair stood face to face on opposite sides of the River of Heaven.† Susa no wo then assured his sister of the purity of his intentions, and proposed to her that they should each produce children by biting off and crunching parts of the jewels and swords which they wore and blowing away the fragments.‡ Eight children born in this way were worshipped in after times as the *Hachôji*, or eight princely children. They figure largely in the Shôjiroku genealogies of Japanese noble families. Through one of them, named Masa-ya-a-katsu-kachi-haya-hi-ama-no-oshi-ho-mi-mi, the Mikados trace their descent from the Sun-Goddess. *A-Katsu* means I conquer. The allusion is to Susa no wo's having triumphantly proved the purity of his intentions by producing male children.§

Susa no wo's subsequent proceedings were very rude and unseemly. He broke down the divisions between the rice-fields belonging to his sister, sowed them over again, let loose in them the piebald colt of Heaven, and committed nuisances in the hall where she was celebrating the solemn festival of first-fruits. The climax to his misdeeds was to flay a piebald colt of Heaven with a backward flaying and to fling it into the sacred weaving-hall where the Sun-Goddess was engaged in weaving the garments of the deities. She was so deeply indignant at this last insult

---

* As Horus, in Egyptian myth, confronts the powers of darkness.

† The Milky Way : a Chinese expression.

‡ This is one of several miraculous births and pregnancies in Japanese myth. Mankind have a rooted propensity for imagining that it is possible to improve on the means ordained for this purpose by Divine Providence. See Mr. Hartland's ' Legend of Perseus ' for numerous examples.

§ The *Kiujiki* makes Masa-ya, &c., the son of the Sun-Goddess by Taka-

石窟幽居

that she entered the Rock-cave of Heaven and left the world to darkness.

The piebald colt of Heaven may be compared to Prisni, the speckled cow of Indian myth, which is explained as a personification of the variegated appearance of the starry heavens.

The retirement of the Sun-Goddess to the Rock-cave of Heaven produced great consternation among the heavenly deities. They met on the dry bed of the River of Heaven and took counsel how they should entice her from her seclusion. By the advice of Omohi-kane no Mikoto (the Thought-combiner or Counsellor deity) the long-singing birds of the Eternal Land (cocks)* were made to utter their prolonged cry before the door of the cave. Ame no Koyane no Mikoto, ancestor of the Nakatomi and Futo-dama no Mikoto, ancestor of the Imbe, dug up by the roots a five-hundred branched true *Sakaki* tree of Heaven and hung on its higher branches strings of jewels, on its middle branches a mirror, and on its lower branches pieces of cloth. Then they recited their liturgy in her honour. Moreover, Ame no Uzume (the Dread Female of Heaven) arrayed herself in a fantastic manner, kindled a fire and standing on a tub which resounded when she stamped upon it, performed a (not very decent) mimic dance and gave forth an inspired utterance. The Plain of High Heaven shook, and the eight hundred myriad deities laughed together. The Sun-Goddess wondered how Ame no Uzume and the other gods could be so jolly while the world was wrapped in complete darkness, and peeped out from the half-opened door of the cave. She was at once seized by Ta-jikara no wo (Hand-strength-male) and prevented by main force from re-entering, to the great joy of all the deities.

Susa no wo was then tried by a council of Gods, who mulcted him in a fine of a thousand tables of purification

* Represented at Ise by dancers called *tonako* (bird-cry).

offerings. They also pulled out the nails of his fingers and toes, and banished him to the land of Yomi. Finally Ame no Koyane, the ancestor of the Nakatomi, recited his Oho-harahi or " Great purification " liturgy.

The above episode is the kernel of the mythical lore of Japan. Belonging to the class of light and darkness myths, it professes to give the origin of some of the principal ceremonies of the Shinto religion as they were practised at the Mikado's Court at the time when they became current. In addition to the Nakatomi and Imbe, some versions of the story show the Sun-Goddess surrounded by other officials, such as jewel-makers, mirror-makers, &c., obviously borrowed from the actual functionaries of the Court, and introduced with an eye to genealogical requirements. By a curious coincidence, the Smith-God attached to her train, like the Cyclops of Greek myth, has but one eye.

Ame no Uzume, the Dread Female of Heaven, who danced and gave forth an inspired utterance before the Rock-cave where the Sun Goddess was hidden, is the supposed ancestor of the Sarume (monkey-women) or female mimes attached to the Mikado's Court, whose performances were the origin of the pantomimic religious dances still kept up in Japan and known as *Kagura*, while her divinely inspired utterance is the prototype of the revelations of the Miko, or Shinto priestesses. One version of the story gives us the actual words used by Uzume on this occasion—namely, *Hi, fu, mi, yo, itsu, mu, nana, ya, kokono, towo.* A Japanese baby knows that these are simply the numerals from one to ten. But they have given much trouble to later Shintoists, who have endeavoured to read into them a deep mythical signification.

The fire kindled by her is the prototype of the *nihabi*, or " courtyard fire," of Shinto ceremonial. It is plainly one of those numerous imitative magic devices for making sunshine, of which Mr. Frazer has given several examples.[*]

* 'The Golden Bough,' second edition, i. 115.

Modern Shinto explains the darkness produced by the Sun-Goddess's retirement as emblematic of the darkness of sin. The renewal of light typifies repentance. Of course, this was far from the thoughts of the original myth-makers.

Susa no wo did not at once proceed to the land of Yomi. He went and begged food of the Food-Goddess, who produced dainty things of all kinds from various parts of her body, and offered them to him. But Susa no wo took offence at her proceedings, which he considered filthy, and at once slew her. Whereupon there were produced in her head silkworms, in her eyes rice, in her ears millet, in her nose small beans, in her genitals barley, and in her funda ment large beans. These Musubi, the God of Growth, took and caused to be used as seeds.

The above is the *Kojiki* version of the story. The *Nihongi* makes the Moon-God the culprit, and gives it as the reason of his alienation from the Sun-Goddess, who had sent him to visit the Food-Goddess. This is not the only attempt of myth-makers to account for the aloofness maintained by these two deities. The same variant of this episode makes the Sun-Goddess the recipient of the various seeds produced in the body of the Food-Goddess :—

"*She was rejoiced, and said, 'These are the things which the race of visible men will eat and live.' So she made the millet, the panic, the wheat and the beans the seed for the dry fields, and the rice she made the seed for the water-fields. Therefore she appointed a Mura-gimi (village-lord) of Heaven, and forthwith sowed for the first time the rice-seed in the narrow fields and in the long fields of Heaven*"

Probably in the slaying of the Food-Goddess we have an echo of some of those practices so fully examined by Mr. Frazer, in which the Corn-maiden, or other representative of the corn, is slain—a tragedy of perennial interest to mankind. Witness the rape of Persephone and the death of John Barleycorn. Susa no wo then visited Corea, but not finding that country to his liking, returned to Japan, and went to the province of Idzumo.

"*Here he observed a chopstick floating down the river Hi, so thinking that there must be people living further up the stream, he went in quest of them, and found an old man and an old woman weeping, with a young maiden set between them. He asked of them, ' Who are ye ? ' The old man replied, ' Thy servant is a deity of earth, and his name is Ashinadzuchi, son of the great God of the Mountain. My wife's name is Tenadzuchi, and my daughter is called Kushinada hime.' He further inquired, ' Why weep ye ? ' He answered, saying, ' I have had eight children, girls ; but the eight-forked serpent of Koshi came year after year and devoured them. It is now the time of its coming, and therefore do we weep.' ' Describe to me this serpent,' said Susa no wo. ' Its eyes are as red as the winter cherry. It has one body with eight heads and eight tails. Moreover, its body is overgrown with moss, pines and cedars. Its length extends over eight valleys and eight hills. Its belly is always all bloody and inflamed to look upon' Then Susa no wo said to the old man, ' If this be thy daughter, wilt thou give her unto me ? ' ' With reverence be it said,' replied the old man, ' I know not thy honourable name.' ' I am the elder brother of the Sun-Goddess, and have now come down from heaven,' replied Susa no wo. Then the deities Ashinadzuchi and Tenadzuchi said, In that case, with reverence we offer her to thee.' Susa no wo straightway took that young maiden and changed her into a many-toothed comb, which he stuck into his hair, and said to the deities Ashinadzuchi and Tenadzuchi, ' Do ye brew some saké of eight-fold strength. Also make a fence round about, and in that fence let there be eight doors, at each door let there be eight stands, on each stand let there be a saké-tub, and let each saké-tub be filled with the saké of eight-fold strength. Then wait' So having prepared everything in accordance with his august bidding, they waited.   Then the eight-forked serpent came, indeed, as had been said, and bena ing down one head into each of the tubs, lapped up the saké. Hereupon it became drunken, and all the heads lay down to sleep, when straightway Susa no wo drew his ten-span sword from his girdle and slew the serpent, so that the river had its current changed to blood.   Now, when he cut the middle part of the tail the edge of his august sword was broken. Wondering at this, he pierced it and split it open, when he found that within there was a great sharp sword.   He took this sword, and thinking it a wonderful thing, reported his discovery to the Sun Goddess.   This is the great sword Kusanagi (Herb-queller)."*

On the occasion of his marriage to Kushinada hime, Susa no wo composed the following verses :—

> *Many clouds arise,*
> *On all sides a manifold fence :*
> *To receive within it the spouses,*
> *They form a manifold fence,*
> *Ah! that manifold fence!*

Eventually he entered the Nether Land.

Few of my readers will require to have pointed out to them the striking resemblance of this story to that of Perseus and Andromeda, or will need to be referred to Mr. Sidney Hartland's ' Legend of Perseus,' in which everything relating to its numerous variants has been so thoroughly examined. I would direct special attention to chapter xviii. of this work, where the hypothesis is offered, " that we have in this incident a reminiscence of the abolition of human sacrifices to deities in the shape of the lower animals......In certain stages of civilization, sacrifices of the kind are practised, and are frequently offered to water-spirits conceived in animal form.,.....It may, of course, be that the monster sent to devour Andromeda is to be regarded simply as the personifi cation of water, or of specific rivers in their sinister aspect."*

* See Index—' River-deities.'

The circumstance that the scene of this episode in Susa no wo's career is the bank of a river is therefore by no means immaterial. Indeed, we may plausibly conjecture that the description of the serpent with its eight (or many) heads and eight tails, its length extending over eight valleys and eight hills, its body overgrown with moss, pines, and cedars, and its propensity for devouring human beings is nothing more than a fanciful representation of the river, with its serpentine course, its numerous tributaries and branches, its wooded banks, and the danger by drowning in its pools or at its fords.

The poem ascribed to Susa no wo cannot be older than the sixth or seventh century. The word translated "on all sides," is *idzumo*. There is therefore a punning allusion to the province of that name. The "manifold fence," is the "nuptial hut," already referred to.*

**Ohonamochi.**—Susa no wo had numerous children, among whom were Oho-toshi (great harvest), and Uka no mitama† (food-spirit). The most famous of his progeny was a God called Ohonamochi. This is the Great Deity of Idzumo, a place second only to Ise for sanctity.

Ohonamochi's eighty brothers went to pay court to a female deity named Yakami-hime, taking him with them as porter "to carry the bag." On arriving at Cape Keta, they found a naked hare lying on the ground. The brothers maliciously advised the hare to bathe in the sea, and then expose himself to the wind on the slope of a high mountain. The hare did so, with the result that when the sea-water dried, his skin split, and he was weeping with pain, when Ohonamochi came up in the rear of the party. He had pity on it, and taught it remedies which gave relief. The grateful hare promised that he should have the lady Yakami-hime in marriage, and not his brothers. When

---

* See above, p. 90.

† Another authority makes Uka no mitama a daughter of Izanagi and Izanami.

their suit was accordingly rejected, they devised several plans for the destruction of Ohonamochi, which were all unsuccessful. He was then advised to go to the " Nether-distant land," the abode of Susa no wo.

" *In accordance with this counsel, he went to the dwelling of Susa no wo. On arriving there he was met by his daughter Suseri-hime, who married him, and then returning within told her father that a very beautiful deity had arrived. The Great Deity came out, and looking at him said, ' This is the deity called the Ugly-male-deity of the Reed-Plain. Thereupon he invited him in, and made him sleep in the snake-chamber. Now his wife Suseri-hime gave her husband a snake-scarf, saying, ' When the snakes are about to bite thee, drive them away by waving this scarf thrice' He did as she had instructed him, and the snakes were quieted, so that he came forth again after a peaceful sleep. Again, on the night of the next day, he was put into the centipede and wasp chamber ; but as his wife again gave him a centipede-and-wasp scarf, and instructed him as before, he came forth unharmed. Again Susa no wo shot a whizzing arrow into the middle of a great moor, and bid him fetch it. When Ohonamochi went out to the moor, Susa no wo set fire to it all round. Ohonamochi could find no way of escape until a rat appeared, and said, ' Within 'tis hollow-hollow, without 'tis narrow-narrow' Hearing this, Ohonamochi stamped upon the place, and fell in, and hid himself until the fire had burnt past. Then the rat came with the whizzing arrow in its mouth and presented it to him. The feathers of the arrow had all been gnawed by the rat's children. Hereupon his wife Suseri-hime came weeping and bringing the funeral things. Her father, the Great Deity, thinking that Ohona mochi was already dead, went out and stood on the moor. Ohonamochi brought him the arrow and presented it to him. Susa no wo took him into the house, and calling him into a large chamber of many mats, bid him catch the lice on his head. Ohonamochi looked at his head, and saw that it was swarming with centipedes. Then his wife gave him berries of the muku tree and red earth. He chewed up the berries and took the red earth into his mouth. Then he spat them out, and the Great Deity thought that he had chewed up and spat out the centipedes, and feeling fond of him in his heart, fell asleep. Ohonamochi then took hold of the hair of the Great Deity and tied it to the rafters of the chamber. Blocking up the door with a five-hundred-pull rock, he took his wife Suseri-hime on his back and made his escape, carrying with him the Great Deity's live-sword, live bow and arrows, and speaking lute of Heaven. The speaking lute of Heaven brushed against a tree and the earth resounded. The Great Deity was startled out of his sleep by the sound and pulled down the chamber. But while he was unloosing his hair from the rafters Ohonamochi fled a long way off. The Great Deity pursued him to the Even Pass of Yomi, and looking at him from afar, called to him and said, ' With the live sword and live bow and arrows which thou bearest, pursue thy half-brethren till they lie down on the lower slopes of the passes, pursue them till they are swept into the river rapids. Be thou the deity Oho-kuni-nushi (great-land-master) and the deity Utsushi-kuni-dama (real-land-spirit). Make my daughter Suseri-hime thy consort, and basing thy stout palace-pillars on the bottom rock at the foot of Mount Uka, and exalting thy crossbeams to the Plain of High Heaven, dwell there, thou rogue.' When Ohonamochi had driven away and dispersed the eighty deities, he pursued them till they lay down on the lower slopes of every pass, and pursued them till they were swept into the rapids of every river. Then did he begin to make the land."*

He was assisted in doing so by a dwarf deity called Sukuna-bikona, who wore garments of bird skins and came over the sea in a tiny boat. There is probably some echo of real history in the myths of Susa no wo, Ohonamochi, and Sukuna-bikona. Idzumo, the scene of their doings, was one of the earliest centres of civilization and religion in Japan, and its position over against Korea is significant in view of the legends which connect Susa no wo with that country. The incident of Sukuna-bikona's arrival by sea, clothed in bird skins, seems to indicate an acquaintance with some northern tribes, who, like the Kurile islanders at this day, wore garments of this material.

This Ohonamochi myth belongs to a class of stories the main features of which have been thus outlined by Mr. A. Lang : " A young man is brought to the home of a hostile animal, a giant, cannibal, wizard, or malevolent king. He is put by his unfriendly host to various severe trials, in which it is hoped that he will perish. In each trial he is assisted by the daughter of his host. After achieving the adventures, he elopes with the girl and is pursued by the father." Mr. Lang goes on to speak of the articles thrown down by the runaways in their flight. This part of the story belongs in Japanese myth to the history of Izanagi and Izanami.*

**Ninigi.**—The dynasty of Susa no wo was not recognized by the Gods of Heaven. They sent down several other deities to prepare the world for the advent of Ninigi, a grandchild of the Sun-Goddess, as its ruler. Some versions of the story make Taka-musubi the chief actor in these proceedings, in others the Sun-Goddess is more prominent. One of the deities sent down for this purpose was Ame-waka-hiko (heaven-young-prince). The *Nihongi* says :—

" *As soon as he arrived he took to wife Shita-teru-hime, the daughter of Utsushi-kuni-dama. Accordingly he remained, and said: ' I, too, wish to govern the Central Land of Reed-Plains ' He never reported the result of his mission. At this time Taka-musubi, wondering why he was so long in coming and making his report, sent the pheasant Na-naki to*

* See above, p. 93.

*observe. The pheasant flew down and perched on the top of a many-branched cassia-tree which grew before Ame-waka-hiko's gate. Now Ama-no Sagu-me (heaven-spying-woman) saw this, and told Ame-waka-hiko, saying: 'A strange bird has come and is perched on the top of the cassia-tree.' Then Ame-waka-hiko took the heavenly deer-bow and the heavenly feathered arrows which had been given him by Taka-mi-musubi no Mikoto, and shot the pheasant, so that it died. The arrow having passed through the pheasant's breast, came before where Taka-mi-musubi no Kami was sitting. Then Taka-mi-musubi no Kami, seeing this arrow, said: 'This arrow I formerly gave to Ame-waka-hiko. It is stained with blood, it may be because he has been fighting with the Earthly Deities.' Thereupon Taka-mi-musubi no Mikoto took up the arrow and flung it back down (to earth). This arrow, when it fell, hit Ame-waka-hiko on the top of his breast. At this time Ame-waka-hiko was lying down after the feast of first-fruits, and when hit by the arrow died immediately.*

"*The sound of the weeping and mourning of Ame-waka-hiko's wife Shita-teru-hime reached Heaven. At this time Ame no Kuni-dama, hearing the voice of her crying, straight way knew that her son, Ame-waka-hiko, was dead, and sent down a swift wind to bring the body up to Heaven. Forthwith a mortuary house was made, in which it was temporarily deposited. The river-geese were made head-hanging bearers and also broom-bearers, the kingfisher was made the representative of the deceased, the sparrows were made the pounding-women, and the wrens the mourners. Altogether the assembled birds were entrusted with the matter.*

"*For eight days and eight nights they wept and sang dirges.*"

**Futsunushi and Take-mika-tsuchi.**—Finally, the deities Futsunushi and Take-mika-tsuchi* were sent down to prepare Japan for Ninigi's reception.

* See Index—*Futsunushi.*

"*The two deities descended and arrived at the Little Shore of Itasa in Idzumo, and asked Ohonamochi, saying :* ' *Wilt thou deliver up this country to the Heavenly Deity, or not ?* ' *He answered and said :* ' *I will not allow it.*' *Thereupon Futsunushi returned upwards, and made his report. Now Taka-mi-musubi sent the two Gods back again, and commanded Ohonamochi, saying :* ' *Having now heard what thou hast said, I find that there is profound reason in thy words. Therefore again I issue my commands to thee more circumstantially, that is to say : Let the public matters which thou hast charge of be conducted by my grandchild, and do thou rule divine affairs. Moreover, if thou wilt dwell in the palace of Ama no Hi-sumi, I will now build it for thee. I will take a thousand fathom rope of the (bark of the) paper mulberry, and tie it in 180 knots. As to the dimensions of the building of the palace, its pillars shall be high and massy, and its planks broad and thick. I will also cultivate thy rice-fields for thee, and, for thy provision when thou goest to take pleasure on the sea, I will make for thee a high bridge, a floating bridge, and also a Heavenly bird-boat. Moreover, on the Tranquil River of Heaven I will make a flying bridge. I will also make for thee white shields of 180 seams, and Ame no Ho-hi no Mikoto shall be the president of the festivals in thy honour.*' *Hereupon Ohonamochi answered and said :* ' *The instructions of the Heavenly Deity are so courteous that I may not presume to disobey his commands. Let the August Grandchild direct the public affairs of which I have charge. I will retire and direct secret matters.*' *So he introduced Kunado no Kami to the two Gods, saying :* ' *He will take my place and will yield respectful obedience. I will withdraw and depart hence.*' *He forthwith invested him with the pure Yasaka jewels, and then became concealed for ever. Therefore Futsunushi no Kami appointed Kunado no Kami as guide, and went on a circuit of pacification. Any who were rebellious to his authority he put to death, while those who rendered obedience were rewarded. The chiefs of those who at this time rendered obedience were Oho-mono-nushi and Koto-shiro-nushi.*"

Another version adds that—

"*He took the broad spear\* which he had used as a staff when he was pacifying the land, and gave it to the two Gods saying : ' By means of this spear I was at last successful. If the Heavenly Grandchild will use this spear to rule the land, he will undoubtedly subdue it to tranquillity. I am now about to withdraw to the concealment of the eighty road-windings.' Having said these words, he at length became concealed.† Thereupon the two Gods put to death all the rebellious spirits and Deities*"

When Ninigi was about to descend to earth, the Sun-Goddess addressed him, saying :

"'*This Reed-plain-1500-autumns-fair-ears Land is the region which my descendants shall be lords of. Do thou, my August Grandchild, proceed thither and govern it. Go ! and may prosperity attend thy dynasty, and may it, like Heaven and Earth, endure for ever*' *When he was about to descend, one who had been sent in advance to clear the way, returned and said : ' There is one God who dwells at the eight-cross roads of Heaven, the length of whose nose is seven hands, and whose stature is more than seven fathoms. Moreover, a light shines from his mouth and from his posteriors. His eye-balls are like an eight-hand mirror, and have a ruddy glow like the physalis' Thereupon he sent one of his attendant Deities to go and make inquiry. Now among all the eighty myriads of Deities, there was not one who could confront him and make inquiry. Therefore he specially commanded Ame no Uzume, saying : ' Thou art superior to others in the power of thy looks. Thou hadst better go and question him.' So Ame no Uzume forthwith bared her breasts, and, pushing down the band of her garment below her navel, confronted him with a*

---

\* Like Odin, who lends his spear Gungmir to heroes to win victories with.
† *I.e.*, died.

*mocking laugh. Then the God of the crossways asked her saying: 'Ame no Uzume! What meanest thou by this behaviour?' She answered and said: 'I make bold to ask who art thou, that dost thus remain in the road by which the child of Ama-terasu no Oho-kami is to make his progress?' The God of the crossways answered and said: 'I have heard that the child of Ama-terasu no Oho-kami is now about to descend, and therefore I have come respectfully to meet and attend upon him. My name is Saruta-hiko no Oho-kami.' Then Ame no Uzume again inquired of him, saying: 'Wilt thou go before me, or shall I go before thee?' He answered and said: 'I will go before and be his harbinger.' Ame no Uzume returned and reported these circumstances. Thereupon the August Grandchild, leaving the heavenly rock-seat, and thrusting apart the eight-piled clouds of Heaven, clove his way with an awful way-cleaving, and descended to earth."*

He alighted on a mountain in the western island of Kiushiu. He was attended by the ancestors of the five *be*, or hereditary government corporations, viz. : the Nakatomi, the Imbe, the Sarume, the mirror-makers *be*, and the jewellers *be*, to which some accounts add several others.

Ninigi took to wife Konohana-sakuyahime (the lady blooming like the flowers of the trees). Her father Oho-yamatsu mi (great-mountain person) had offered him both his daughters, but the elder was rejected by Ninigi as being too ugly. Her name was Iha-naga-hime (rock-long-lady). The consequences of this choice were disastrous to his descendants. Iha-naga-hime, in her shame and resentment, uttered a curse and said : "The race of visible men shall change swiftly like the flowers of the trees and shall decay and pass away." This is the reason why the life of man is so short.

When the time came for the younger sister's delivery, she shut herself up in a doorless shed, which, on the birth of her three children, she set fire to, with the object of clearing herself from certain suspicions which her husband had entertained of her fidelity. " If," said she, " the children are really the offspring of the Heavenly Grandchild, the fire cannot harm them." The children and their mother came forth unhurt, and were thereupon recognized by Ninigi as his true offspring and wife.

The " doorless shed " here mentioned, is a " parturition house."* It was the custom in ancient Japan for women, when the time drew near for their delivery, to retire to a shed specially constructed to receive them, so that contamination to the dwelling-house might be avoided. This was still the practice in the island of Hachijo in 1878, and even in Japan no longer than a century ago.

The burning of the parturition house represents the ordeal by fire, which, with the ordeal by boiling water or mud, is well known in Japan.

**Ho no Susori and Hohodemi.**—The story concerns itself no further with the youngest of these three children. Of the others, the elder, named Ho no Susori, became a fisher man, and the younger, Hohodemi, a hunter.

Ho no Susori once proposed to his brother to exchange their respective callings. Hohodemi accordingly gave over to his elder brother his bow and arrows and received a fish hook in return. But neither of them profited by the exchange, so Ho no Susori gave back to his brother the bow and arrows and demanded from him the fish-hook.

Hohodemi, however, had in the meantime lost it in the sea. He took his sword and forged from it a number of new fish-hooks which he piled up in a winnowing tray and offered to his brother by way of compensation. But the latter would have none but his own, and demanded it so vehemently of Hohodemi as to grieve him bitterly. Hohodemi went down to the sea-shore and stood there lamenting, when there appeared to him the Old Man of the Sea, by

---

* It was an Arab custom in certain places to build a hut outside the camp, where the parturient woman had to stay for a time. – Welhausen.

whose advice he descended into the sea depths to the abode
of the God of the Sea, a stately palace with lofty towers
and battlements. Before the gate there was a well, and
over the well grew a thick-branching cassia tree, into which
Hohodemi climbed. The Sea-God's daughter Toyo-
tama-hime (rich jewel maiden) then came out from the
palace to draw water. She saw Hohodemi's face reflected
in the well, and returning within reported to her father
that she had seen a beautiful youth in the tree which
grew by the well. Hohodemi was courteously received
by the Sea-God, Toyo-tama-hiko (rich jewel prince)
who when he heard his errand, summoned before him
all the fishes of the sea and made inquiry of them for
the lost fish hook, which was eventually discovered in
the mouth of the Tai. Toyo-tama-hiko delivered it to
Hohodemi, telling him when he gave it back to his
brother to say "a hook of poverty, a hook of ruin, a
hook of downfall," to spit twice and to hand it over with
averted face.

Hohodemi married the Sea-God's daughter Toyo-tama-
hime and remained with her for three years. He then
became home-sick and returned to the upper world. On
the beach where he came to land, he built for his wife, who
was soon to follow, a parturition house which he thatched
with cormorant's feathers. The roofing was still unfinished
when she arrived, riding on a great tortoise. She went
straight into the hut, begging her husband not to look at
her. But Hohodemi's curiosity was too strong for him. He
peeped in, and behold! his wife had become changed into
a *wani* (sea-monster or dragon), eight fathoms long.
Deeply indignant at the disgrace put upon her, Toyo-tama-
hime abandoned her new-born child to the care of her sister,
and barring behind her the sea-path in such a way that
from that day to this all communication between the realms
of land and sea has been cut off, returned hastily to her
father's palace.

The child thus born was the father of Jimmu Tenno, the first human sovereign of Japan.

Hohodemi's troubles with his elder brother were renewed on his arrival home. He was obliged to use against him two talismans given him by his father-in-law. One of these had the virtue of making the tide flow and submerge Ho no Susori and thus compel him to sue for mercy (another account says that Hohodemi whistled and thereby raised the wind and the sea). Then by a second talisman the tide was made to recede and Ho no Susori's life was spared. He yielded complete submission to his younger brother, and promised that he and his descendants to all generations would serve Hohodemi and his successors as mimes and bondservants. The *Nihongi* adds that in that day it was still customary for the Hayato (or Imperial guards), who were descended from Ho no Susori, to perform a mimic dance before the Mikados, the descendants and successors of Hohodemi, in which the drowning struggles of their ancestor were represented.

The castle-gate and the tree before it, at the bottom of which is a well which serves as a mirror, form a combination not unknown to European folk-lore. We may also note the partiality evinced for the younger of two brothers, the virtue of spitting and of set forms of speech to bring good or ill luck, and of whistling to raise the wind.

There are several features in this story which betray a recent origin and foreign influences. A comparatively advanced civilization is indicated by the sword and fish hooks forged of iron (the Homeric fish-hook was of horn). The institution of the Hayato as Imperial Guards belongs to a period not very long antecedent to the date of the *Nihongi* and *Kojiki*. The palace of the sea-depths and its Dragon-king are of Chinese, and therefore of recent, origin. The comparatively modern character of this important link in the genealogy which traces back the descent of the Mikados to the Sun-Goddess confirms the view that the so-called ancestor-worship of the ancient Japanese is a later accretion upon what was in its origin a worship of the powers of Nature.

**Jimmu Tenno.**—Though it is difficult to draw clearly a line which shall divide religious myth from legend with an historical kernel, we may conveniently assume that in Japan the latter begins with the story of Jimmu, as it has in all probability a foundation in actual fact, namely, the conquest of Central Japan by an invading army from the western island of Kiushiu some centuries before the Christian epoch.

Jimmu Tennô is said to have been the youngest of four brothers, who lived in the province of Hiuga.

When he reached the age of forty-five, he addressed his elder brothers and his children, saying: "Of old, our Heavenly Deities, Taka-mi-musubi, and Oho-hiru-me, gave this land of fair rice-ears of the fertile reed-plain to our Heavenly ancestor, Hiko-ho no ninigi. Now I have heard from the old sea-father that in the east there is a fair land encircled by blue mountains. Let us make our capital there." So on the fifth day of the tenth month of the year corresponding to B.C. 607* they sailed northwards, and passing through the Bungo Channel arrived at Usa,† near the Strait of Shimonoseki.

At this time there appeared the ancestors of the local chieftains of Usa, named Usa-tsu-hiko and Usa-tsu-hime, who built a palace raised on one pillar on the bank of the River Usa, and offered them a banquet. Then, by imperial command, Usa-tsu-hime was given in marriage to the Emperor's attendant minister Ama no tane, the remote ancestor of the Nakatomi House.

---

* There was no official recognition of the art of writing in Japan until A.D. 405, and no mention of calendars until A.D. 553. So much for the authenticity of the above date.

† Usa is not on the direct route from Hiuga to Yamato. It was no doubt introduced because this place was anciently a famous centre of Shinto worship.

Proceeding on their voyage eastwards through the inland sea, Jimmu and his brothers arrived at the entrance of the river which falls into the sea near Ôsaka. Here they encountered a swift current, for which reason that place was called *Nami-haya* (wave-swift) or *Nami-hana* (wave-flower) of which *Nani-ha* (a later poetical name of Ôsaka) was thought a corruption.*

The first encounter of Jimmu's forces with the inhabitants of this part of Japan was not to their advantage :—

" *The Emperor was vexed, and said : ' I am the descendant of the Sun-Goddess, and if I proceed against the Sun to attack the enemy, I shall act contrary to the way of Heaven Better to retreat and make a show of weakness. Then sacri ficing to the Gods of Heaven and Earth, and bringing on our backs the might of the Sun-Goddess, let us follow her rays and trample them down.' *"

Subsequently he proceeded southwards to Kumano, in the province of Kiї, where he embarked with his army in the " Rock-boat of Heaven." In the midst of the sea they suddenly met with a violent wind, and Jimmu's ship was tossed about. Then Ina-ihi, one of Jimmu's elder brothers, exclaimed, " Alas ! my ancestors were Heavenly Deities and my mother was a Goddess of the Sea. Why do they harass me by land, and why, moreover, do they harass me by sea." So he drew his sword and plunged into the sea, where he became changed into the God Sabi-mochi.† Another brother of the Emperor, Mike Irino, also indignant at this, said : " My mother and my aunt are both Sea-Goddesses : why do they raise great billows to overwhelm us ? " So treading upon the waves, he went to the Eternal Land.

---

* This is a specimen of the numerous derivations of the Jimmu narrative. The Idzumo Fudoki is also full of infantile etymologies, which have usually a scrap of legend attached to them.

† Blade-holder.

At this time the Gods belched up a poisonous vapour, which paralyzed the energies of Jimmu's troops.

"*Then there was there a man by name Kumano no Takakuraji, who had a dream, in which Ama-terasu no Ohokami spoke to Take-mika-tsuchi no Kami, saying : ' I still hear a sound of disturbance from the Central Land of Reed-Plains. Do thou again go and chastise it.' Take-mika-tsuchi no Kami answered and said : 'Even if I go not, I can send down my sword, with which I subdued the land, upon which the country will of its own accord become peaceful.' To this Ama-terasu no Kami assented. Thereupon Take-mika-tsuchi no Kami addressed Takakuraji, saying : ' My sword, which is called Futsu no Mitama, I will now place in thy store house. Do thou take it and present it to the Heavenly Grand child.' Takakuraji said : ' Yes,' and thereupon awoke. The next morning, as instructed in his dream, he opened the store house, and on looking in there was indeed there a sword which had fallen down (from Heaven), and was standing point upwards on the plank floor of the storehouse. So he took it and offered it to the Emperor. Then Ama-terasu no Oho-kami instructed the Emperor in a dream of the night, saying : ' I will now send thee the Yata-garasu \* make it thy guide through the land.' Upon which the Yata-garasu came flying down from the Void, and served as a guide to the army.*"

The progress of the Imperial troops being again ob structed by the enemy, the Emperor prayed and then fell asleep. The Heavenly Deity appeared to him in a dream, and instructed him to take earth from within the shrine of the Heavenly Mount Kagu, and of it to make eighty heavenly platters. Moreover, he was to make sacred jars, and therewith sacrifice to the Gods of Heaven and Earth,

* *Yata-garasu* means eight-hand-crow. The guidance of conquerors or colonists to their destination by a supernatural bird or beast is a familiar feature of old-world story.

pronouncing at the same time a solemn imprecation. This had the desired effect of dispersing the enemy. The Emperor proceeded to utter a vow, saying: " I will now make *ame** in the eighty platters, using no water. If the *ame* forms, then shall I assuredly, without effort and without recourse to arms, reduce the Empire to peace." The *ame* became formed of itself.

Again he made a vow, saying :—

" ' *I will now take the sacred jars and sink them in the River Nifu. If the fishes, great or small, become every one drunken and are carried down the stream like floating leaves, then shall I assuredly succeed in establishing the land.'  So he sank the jars in the river, with their mouths turned downward, and after a while the fish all came to the surface, gaping and gasping as they floated down the stream."*

The Emperor then commanded Michi no Omi, saying :

" ' *We are now in person† about to celebrate a festival to Taka-mi-musubi. I appoint thee Ruler of the festival, and grant thee the title of Idzu-hime.‡ The earthen jars which are set up shall be called the Idzube, or sacred jars ; the fire shall be called Idzu no Kagu-tsuchi, or sacred-fire-father ; the water shall be called Idzu no Midzu-ha no me, or sacred-water-female; the food shall be called Idzu-uka no me, or sacred-food-female; the firewood shall be called Idzu no Yama-tsuchi, or sacred-mountain-father; and the grass shall be called Idzu no No-tsuchi, or sacred-moor-father.'*

"*In Winter, the 10th month, on the 1st day,§ the Emperor*

---

\* *Ame* is the name of a sweet substance made from millet, of the same nature as our malt extract.

† The Mikado deputed most of his priestly functions to the Nakatomi.

‡ *Idzu-hime* means dread or sacred princess. *Michi no Omi* (minister of the way) seems therefore to have been given a feminine title for the occasion, no doubt because the office was usually held by women.

§ It was at this season of the year that the harvest festival, or rather the festival of tasting the new rice, was celebrated. See Index—*Nihiname.*

*tasted the food of the Idzube, and arraying his troops set forth upon his march."*

Among those who made submission to Jimmu was Nigi-haya-hi, of whom it is told that he was a child of the Heavenly Deity, who had come down from Heaven riding in the " Rock-boat of Heaven," and married the sister of a local chieftain named Naga-sune-hiko (Prince Long-shanks). His name and that of his son appear very fre quently in the *Shôjiroku* genealogies.

Jimmu took to wife a daughter of the God Koto-shiro-nushi, or, according to the *Kojiki*, Oho-mono-nushi, by a mortal woman, and having established his capital at Kashi-habara, in Yamato, B.C. 660,* reigned there until his death, B.C. 585, at the age of 127.

---

* Japanese history is said to begin from this date.   In reality nothing deserving the name existed for nearly one thousand years more.

# CHAPTER VII.

## THE PANTHEON — NATURE DEITIES.

### I. GODS OF INDIVIDUALS AND GODS OF CLASSES.

THE neglect of indications of number in the Japanese language often renders it impossible to say whether a God belongs to an individual natural object or phenomenon or to a class. I therefore take these two classes of deities together, noting the distinction wherever it is possible or desirable.

**The Sun-Goddess.**—The most eminent of the Shinto deities is the Sun-Goddess. Nor is this surprising. If, as Scotus Erigena has well said, "every visible and invisible creature is a theophany or appearance of God," what more striking aspect of Him can there be to the uncultured mind than the Sun? In a later stage of intellectual development men find a fuller revelation of Him in the moral order of the world, in the laws of human progress, and in the spiritual experiences of saints and sages, culminating in a synthesis of all the divine aspects of the universe in one harmonious whole. But, naturally enough, there is little of this in Shinto. The ancient Japanese recognized the divinity of the universe in a very imperfect, piecemeal fashion, and almost exclusively in those physical aspects by which they were more directly affected. Among these the light and warmth of the Sun and the sources of their daily food held the chief place. Sun-worship is specially natural to the Japanese as an agricultural people. Almost all the peasant's doings are in some way dependent on, or regulated by, the Sun.

The application of the term "fetish" to the Sun considered as an object of adoration is to be deprecated. It implies a stigma which is altogether out of place.  Socrates prayed to the Sun; Æschylus's Prometheus appeals to him against the tyranny of Zeus ; in Sophocles's 'Œdipus Tyrannus' the Chorus swears by "the Sun, chief of all the Gods"; Plato says that "the soul of the Sun should be deemed a God by every one who has the least particle of sense"; Goethe admitted his claims to worship; Don Quixote swears by God and by the Sun in the same breath, and Tristram Shandy "by the great God of Day." Milton, in the character of Satan, it is true, addresses the Sun in terms of awe and wonder, and  Swinburne calls him "the living and visible God."  The name of the first day of the week still remains to show what an important place he held in the religion of our forefathers.  The association of the ideas of light, splendour, and brightness with divinity has its origin in a primæval sun-worship.  William the Conqueror swore "by the splendour of God." *Divine* contains the root *div*, brightness.  Milton calls light "of the eternal co-eternal beam."  No doubt so long as a nation is hesitating between sun-worship and a higher form of religion there is a reason for treating the former with contempt and aversion.  No form of faith is so odious —because of the danger of relapse—as that from which we have emerged with painful effort to something higher. But such intolerance is no longer needed.  It is now unnecessary to punish with death the worship of the sun, moon, and stars,* or even to stigmatize it as fetish-worship.

The meaning of the word fetish has become so blurred by indiscriminate use that there is a temptation to discard it altogether.  It is frequently applied to all concrete objects of devotion, including not only great nature-gods, like the earth and sun, but their symbols, images, and seats of their real presence, which have no intrinsic divinity of their own, and are only worshipped by reason of their

* Deuteronomy iv. 19 ; xvii. 3.

association with genuine deities. The same objects, after their association with the God has been forgotten and they are blindly adored as if they were themselves Gods, form a third class of fetishes. The sword of the shrine of Atsuta is an example. Probably originally an offering and then a *shintai*, it is still worshipped, for no known reason except, perhaps, an empiric belief in the efficacy of prayers ad dressed to it. Implements of trade, honoured for the help which they render to man, are a fourth class. To these we may add a fifth, consisting of stones, sticks, feathers, &c., worshipped for their imaginary virtues or for no definite reason at all.

The indiscriminate application of the term fetish to objects of all these five classes is highly inconvenient, especially when we come to discuss the question whether fetishism is a primitive form of religion. The answer depends entirely on the kind of fetish which is intended. If the word is used at all, it would be better to confine it to the last three of these classes.

The Sun-Goddess is described as the Ruler of Heaven and as "unrivalled in dignity." She wears royal insignia, is surrounded by ministers, of whom the Court of the Mikado is the obvious prototype, and is spoken of in terms appropriate to personages of sovereign rank. She is selected as the ancestor from whom the Mikados derive their descent and authority. Yet she is hardly what we understand by a Supreme Being. Her power does not extend to the sea or to the Land of Yomi. Her charge as Ruler even of Heaven was conferred on her by her parents, and did not by any means involve absolute control When grossly insulted by her younger brother, instead of inflicting on him condign punishment, she hid in a cave, from which she was partly enticed, partly dragged, by the other deities. This is not the behaviour of a Supreme Being. The punishment of the culprit and other important celestial matters are determined, not by the fiat of the so-called Ruler of Heaven, but by a Council of the Gods. The celestial constitution, like its earthly counterpart, was far from being an absolute monarchy. The epithet *sumera*, translated "sovran," and derived from a verb *sumeru*, which means "to hold general rule," is applied not only to the Sun-Goddess but to many other deities—the Wind-Gods, for example—and also to the Mikados. The same is the case with *Mikoto*, which corresponds roughly to our "majesty." Of course Japan is not the only country which attributes royalty to the Sun. Milton speaks of the Sun's "sovran vital lamp."

In some parts of the Shinto mythical narrative it is the actual Sun that the author has in view, as when he speaks of her radiance illuminating the universe, or of the world being left to darkness when she entered the Rock-cave. Elsewhere she is an anthropomorphic being, with no specially solar characteristics. She wears armour, celebrates the feast of first-fruits, cultivates rice, &c. Inconsistencies of this kind are inherent in all nature myths, and trouble their authors not a whit. Some of the modern theologians, however, are much perplexed by them. Motoori concludes that "this great deity actually is the Sun in Heaven, which even now illuminates the world before our eyes, a fact which is extremely clear from the divine writings." His pupil Hirata, on the other hand, holds that the Sun-Goddess is not the Ruler of Heaven but the Ruler of the Sun, a distinction which never occurred to the mythmakers. Another modern writer attempts to smooth over difficulties by the explanation that the Sun-Goddess is actually a female goddess, but, owing to the radiance which flows from her, seen from a distance she appears round.

The transparent character of the names by which the Sun-Goddess is known is a formidable obstacle to the tendency to neglect her solar quality and to give prominence to the anthropomorphic side of her character. Her most usual appellation is Ama terasu no Oho-kami, or the

Heaven-shining-great-deity. She is also called Ama-terasu hiru-me, or Heaven - shining sun - female — more briefly Hiru-me, Ama terasu mi oya, or Heaven-shining august parent, and other variants. Of these names European writers have generally adopted Ama-terasu, which, like Phoibos, is in reality a mere epithet, and is applied to other deities. Hirume, or sun-female, is more expressive, and probably older.

In modern times the appellation Ama-terasu no Oho-kami is little used, its Chinese equivalent Tenshodaijin being substituted. Partly under cover of a name which is less clearly intelligible to the multitude, the tendency has become accentuated to throw her solar functions into the background and to conceive of her simply as a general Providence, at the expense of other deities. In other words, she has made a distinct advance towards the posi tion of a supreme monotheistic deity.

Even in ancient times there was some recognition of the Sun-Goddess as a Providence that watches over human affairs, more especially the welfare of the Mikado and his Government. She provided Jimmu with the *yatagarasu*, or Sun-crow, as a guide to his army. The following prayer, addressed to her in 870 by envoys despatched to Ise with offerings, illustrates this conception of her character :—

" *By order of the Mikado we declare with deepest reverence in the spacious presence of (with awe be her name pronounced)* . *the Sovran Great Heaven-shining Deity, whose praises are fulfilled in the Great Shrine, whose pillars are broad-based on the nethermost rocks, and whose cross-beams rise aloft to the Plain of High Heaven on the bank of the River Isuzu in Uji, of Watarahi in Ise, as follows :—*

" *Since the past sixth month reports have been received from the Dazaifu\* that two pirate-ships of Shiraki†️ appeared*

---

\* The Vice-Royalty of Kiushiu.
† In Korea.

*at Aratsu, in the district of Naka, in the province of Chi-*
*kuzen, and carried off as plunder the silk of a tribute-ship of*
*the province of Buzen. Moreover, that there having been an*
*omen of a crane which alighted on the arsenal of the Govern*
*ment House, the diviners declared that it presaged war with*
*a neighbouring country. Also that there had been earth*
*quakes with storms and floods in the province of Hizen by*
*which all the houses had been overturned and many of the*
*inhabitants swept away. Even the old men affirmed that no*
*such great calamity had ever been heard of before.*

" *Meanwhile news was received from the province of*
*Michinoku of an unusually disastrous earthquake, and from*
*other provinces grave calamities were reported.*

" *The mutual enmity between those men of Shiraki and*
*our Land of Yamato has existed for long ages. Their*
*present invasion of our territory, however, and their plunder*
*of tribute, show that they have no fear of us. When we*
*reflect on this, it seems possible that a germ of war may*
*spring from it. Our government has for a long time had no*
*warlike expeditions, the provision for defence has been wholly*
*forgotten, and we cannot but look forward to war with dread*
*and caution. But our Japan is known as the country of the*
*Gods. If the Gods deign to help and protect it, what foe will*
*dare to approach it? Much more so, seeing that the Great*
*Deity in her capacity (with awe be it spoken) as ancestress of*
*the Mikado bestows light and protection on the Under-*
*Heaven which he governs. How, therefore, shall she not*
*deign to restrain and ward off outrages by strangers from*
*foreign lands as soon as she becomes aware of them?*

" *Under these circumstances, we (the names of the envoys*
*follow) present these great offerings by the hands of Komaye,*
*Imbe no Sukune, Vice-Minister of the Bureau of Imbe, who,*
*hanging stout straps on weak shoulders, has purely prepared*
*and brought them hither. Be pleased graciously to hearken*
*to this memorial. But if unfortunately such hostile acts as*
*we have spoken of should be committed let the (with awe be*

*it spoken)* *Great Deity, placing herself at the head of all the aeities of the land, stay and ward off, sweep away and expel the enemy before his first arrow is shot. Should his designs ripen so far that his ships must come hither, let them not enter within our borders, but send them back to drift and founder. Suffer not the solid reasons for our country being feared as the Divine Country to be sodden and destroyed. If, apart from these, there should be danger of rebellion or riot by savages, or of disturbance by brigands at home, or again of drought, flood or storm, of pestilence or famine such as would cause great disaster to the State or deep sorrow to the people, deign to sweep away and destroy it utterly before it takes form. Be pleased to let the Under-Heaven be free from alarms and all the country enjoy peace by thy help and pro tection. Grant thy gracious favour to the Sovran Grand child, guarding his august person by day and by night, firm and enduring as Heaven and Earth, as the Sun and the Moon.*

*" Declared with deep reverence."*

The solar character of Ama-terasu or Tenshodaijin having become obscured, the people have personified the Sun afresh under the names of Nichi-rin sama (sun-wheel-personage) and O tento sama (august-heaven-path-person-age). To the lower class of Japanese at the present day, and especially to women and children, O tento sama is the actual sun—sexless, mythless, and unencumbered by any formal cult, but looked up to as a moral being who rewards the good, punishes the wicked, and enforces oaths made in his name. In his ' Religions of Japan,' Dr. Griffis says : "To the common people the Sun is actually a God, as none can doubt who sees them worshipping it morning and evening. The writer can never forget one of many similar scenes in Tokio, when, late one afternoon, O tento sama, which had been hidden behind clouds for a fortnight, shone out on the muddy streets. In a moment, as with the promptness of a military drill, scores of people rushed out of their houses, and with faces westward, kneeling, squatting, began prayer and worship before the great luminary."

I reproduce a drawing by a Japanese artist of a famous spot on the coast of Ise to which pilgrims resort in order to worship the sun as he rises over distant Fujiyama. The *tori-wi*, which in some prints of this scene is seen in the foreground, fulfils the same function as the great trilithon at Stonehenge, viz., to mark the direction of worship. I have seen the eastern wall of a private courtyard which was pierced with a round hole for the convenience of worshipping the morning sun.

There is a modern custom, called *himachi* (sun-waiting), of keeping awake the whole night of the 5th day of the 10th month in order to worship the sun on his rising. The rules of religious purity must be observed from the previous day. Many persons assemble at Takanaha, Uheno, Atago, and other open places in Tokio to worship the rising Sun on the first day of the year. This is called *hatsu no hi no de* (the first sunrise).

The myths mention several other deities which, although not identical with Ama-terasu or Hirume, are plainly of solar origin. Such is Waka-hirume (young-sun-female), who, according to Motoori, is the Morning Sun. The Ise shrine is sometimes called Asa-hi no Jinja, that is to say, the shrine of the Morning Sun. One version of the names of the three children of Ninigi calls them Ho no akari (fire or sun-light), Ho no susori (fire or sun-advance), and Ho no wori (fire or sun-subside), originally, it may be suspected, names for the rising, noonday, and setting sun. Such a distinction is recognized in Egyptian mythology. The mythical founder of the dynasty which preceded Jimmu in Yamato was called Nigi-haya-hi—that is, gentle-swift-sun—and he is said to have come flying down from Heaven. One myth gives him the epithet *Ama-teru kuni-*

*teru* (Heaven-shining, earth-shining). I am disposed to regard this personage as the Sun-deity of the earlier Yamato Japanese, from whom their chieftains were feigned to be descended. Even in *Shōjiroku* times many noble families traced their descent from him, as the Mikados did from Hirume. There are a good many other names suggestive of solar deities. But here caution is necessary, in view of the habit, common to the Japanese with other nations, of borrowing solar epithets for the adornment of human beings. There is a Take-hi (brave-sun) in the *Nihongi* who is unquestionably a mere mortal. And what could be more solar than Takama no hara hiro nu hime (high-heaven-plain-broad-moor-princess), the last word meaning etymologically "sun-female"? Yet this is indu bitably the name of an historical Empress who came to the throne A.D. 687. The Mikado Kotoku's Japanese name was Ame-yorodzu-toyo-hi (heaven-myriad-abundant-sun).

Although Shinto contains no formal system of ethics, moral elements are not wanting in the character of the Sun-Goddess as delineated in the ancient myths. She exhibits the virtues of courage and forbearance in her dealings with her mischievous younger brother Susa no wo. She is wroth with the Moon-God when he slays the Goddess of Food, and banishes him from her presence. Her loving care for mankind is shown by her preserving for their use the seeds of grain and other useful vegetables, and by setting them the example of cultivating rice. There is a recognition of her beneficent character in the joy of Gods and men when she emerged from the Rock-cave.

The circumstance that, according to one story, the Sun-Goddess was produced from the left and the Moon-God from the right eye of Izanagi is suggestive of the influence of China, where the left takes precedence of the right. Compare the Chinese myth of P'anku : " P'anku came into being in the great waste ; his beginning is unknown. In

F

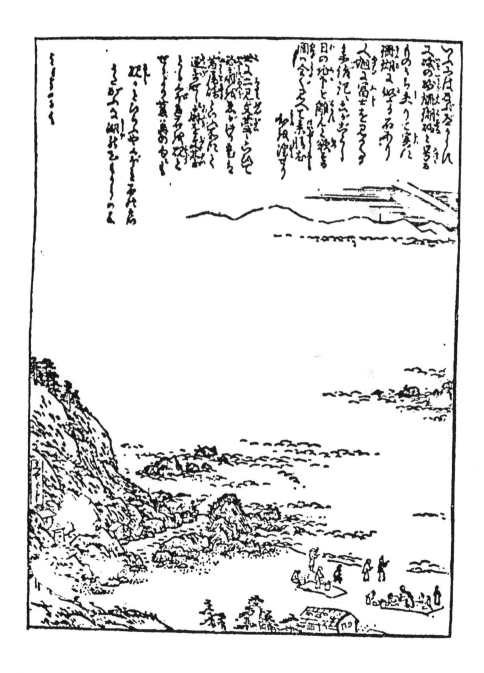

dying he gave birth to the material universe. His breath was transmuted into the wind and clouds, his voice into thunder, his left eye into the sun, and his right eye into the moon." Hirata endeavours to combat the obvious inference from this comparison by pointing out that the sun is masculine in China and feminine in Japan. How little weight is due to this objection appears from the fact that two so nearly allied nations as the English and the Germans differ in the sex which they attribute to the sun, as do also closely related tribes of Australian aborigines and Ainus of Yezo. And does not Shakespeare make the sun both masculine and feminine in the same sentence, when he says, "The blessed sun himself a fair hot wench in flame-coloured taffeta"? There is, moreover, unsuspected by Hirata and his fellow-theologians, an unmistakeable vestige in the old myths of an obsolete or abortive masculine Sun-deity. We are told that the first child of Izanagi and Izanami was Hiruko. Hiru-ko is written with Chinese characters, which mean "leech-child"; and it is stated that when this God had completed his third year he was still unable to stand upright. He was therefore placed in a reed-boat and sent adrift. But the original author of the Hiru-ko was never guilty of such a palpable absurdity as to make a leech the first-born of creation, preceding even the Sun and the Moon. Hiruko is in reality simply a masculine form of Hirume, the Sun-female, just as *hiko*, prince, is of *hime*, princess; *musuko*, boy, of *musume*, girl; and *otoko*, youth, of *otome*, maiden. Egypt had a Sun-God Ra and a Sun-Goddess Rat.

No doubt with the greater development of the Sun-Goddess myth it was felt that there was no room for a male Sun-God. The tag of story which is appended to the leech derivation is one of those perversions of true myth which arise from an ignorant misunderstanding or a wilful misapplication of language.

The leech-child can hardly be reckoned among the

effective deities of Shinto.   In modern times, however, he has, for some inscrutable reason, been identified with a widely worshipped deity of unknown origin called Ebisu. This God has to all appearance nothing in common either with the sun or the leech.   He is a favourite subject of the artist, and is usually depicted with a smiling countenance (*emi* or *ebi* means to smile), in ancient Japanese costume, and holding a fishing-rod while a *tahi* struggles at the end of his line.   He is reckoned one of the seven Gods of good fortune, and is a favourite deity to pray to for success in trade.   Merchants hold a great feast in his honour on the 20th day of the 10th month.

The ascription of the female sex to the most prominent among the Shinto Gods is not owing merely to caprice. Myth-makers have often more substantial reasons for their fancies than might be supposed.   In the present case there is evidence that women played a very important part in the real world of ancient Japan as well as in that of imagi nation.   Women rulers were at this time a familiar pheno menon.   Both Japanese and Chinese history give us glimpses of a female Mikado who lived about A.D. 200, and whose commanding ability and strong character have not been wholly obscured by the mists of legend.   Women chieftains are frequently mentioned.   Indeed the Chinese seem to have thought that feminine government was the rule in Japan, for their historians frequently refer to it as the " Queen-country."   In more historical times several of the Mikados were women.   In some families descent was traced by the female line.   From the *Kojiki* we learn that in Suinin's time it was the custom for the mother to give children their names.

One might think that so obviously solar a Goddess as the Heaven-shining-great-deity, or Sun-female, whose abode is the " Plain of High Heaven," who fills the universe with her radiance and leaves it to darkness when she conceals herself, and who is even spoken of in so many words as the "Deity of the Sun," would have escaped the teme rarious touch of the Euhemerist. Yet I have before me a ' History of the Empire of Japan,' compiled by doctors of the Imperial University, and published in 1893 by order of the Japanese Government, which speaks of the principles of rice-culture and the arts of weaving, mining, and of making swords, hats, and pantaloons being known in the reign of Ama-terasu. Other writers are even more precise. Much to Motoori's indignation, they say bluntly that she was a mortal empress who reigned in a locality on earth called Takama no hara (the Plain of High Heaven).

**Yatakagami.**—The *shintai* of the Sun-Goddess is a mirror,[*] sometimes called the *yatakagami*, or eight-hand-mirror, probably because it had a number of leaves or pro jections round it. It is also called the *hi-kagami* (sun-mirror) or *hi-gata no kagami* (sun-form-mirror). It appears from the *Nihongi* that similar mirrors were honoured in Korea. Ama no hihoko is stated to have brought a sun-mirror from that country in B.C. 27.

The mythical notices of the *yatakagami* represent it in various aspects. It is mentioned in the *Kojiki* among the offerings made to the Sun-Goddess to propitiate her after her retirement to the Rock-cave of Heaven. In the same passage Uzume calls it " a deity more illustrious than thine (the Sun-Goddess's) augustness." When the Sun-Goddess. and Musubi sent down Ninigi to rule the earth they gave him the *yatakagami*, saying : " Regard this mirror exactly as our *mitama*, and reverence it as if reverencing us." The *Nihongi* adds : " Let it be with thee on thy couch and in thy hall, and let it be to thee a holy mirror." The *yata-kagami* is frequently spoken of as if it were the Sun-Goddess herself, and is even called "the Great God of Ise." Another sun-mirror received an independent worship at Kumano. The *Nihongi* says, under the date B.C. 92 :—

" *Before this the two Gods Ama-terasu no Oho-kami and*

---

[*] See above, p. 70 ; also Index—' Mirror.'

*Yamato no Oho-kuni-dama were worshipped together within the Emperor's Great Hall. He dreaded, however, the power of these Gods, and did not feel secure in their dwelling together. Therefore he entrusted Ama-terasu no Oho kami to Toyo-suki-iri-bime no Mikoto to be worshipped at the village of Kasanuhi, in Yamato."*

Here we must understand that it was the sun-mirror which was sent away from the palace. It was subse quently (B.C. 5) enshrined at Ise, where it is to this day preserved with the greatest care and reverence.* It is about eight inches in diameter.

In ancient Peru, the Sun-God was represented by a golden disc, the Moon-Goddess by one of silver.

We find, however, that in A.D. 507 a sacred mirror was still preserved in the Imperial palace as one of the regalia. It was destroyed by fire in the eleventh century, but its successor is to this day transmitted from sovereign to sovereign as a token of royal authority. The religious ceremony in its honour is described below.† Associated with the mirror as regalia were a sword and a jewel. These three objects are presented to the Mikado on his accession with great ceremony. In ancient times there were probably only two regalia, the mirror and the sword. The latter was lost in the sea at the battle of Dannoüra. But such losses are not irreparable.

The Sun-Goddess in her capacity as sovereign is attended by a Court of minor deities who belong to the class of man-deities, and will be dealt with in the next chapter.

---

* "The mirror is kept in a box of chamaecyparis wood, which rests on a low stand covered with a piece of white silk. It is wrapped in a bag of brocade, which is never opened or renewed, but when it begins to fall to pieces from age another bag is put on, so that the actual covering consists of many layers. Over the whole is placed a sort of wooden cage, with ornaments said to be of pure gold, over which again is thrown a cloth of coarse silk falling to the floor on all sides."—Murray's ' Japan,' fifth edition, p. 308.

† See Index—*Naishidokoro.*

**Yatagarasu.**—Like the Greek Phoibos, who had his κίρκος * the Egyptian Ra, who was accompanied by a hawk, and the Peruvian Sun-God, who was attended by a condor, the Sun-Goddess is provided with a bird as her messenger and attendant. This bird is called in Japanese *ya-ta-garasu*, which means "eight-hand-crow." It is not, however, a Japanese invention, but is borrowed from China, where it is called the Sun-crow or Golden Crow, and described as a bird with three claws and of a red colour which roosts in the sun. It is mentioned in a Chinese poem written B.C. 314. Possibly it may be traced even further back. A three-legged bird was figured on coins of Pamphylia and Lycia in very ancient times. In Japan the *yatagarasu*, as a symbol of the Sun, was depicted on the banners set up in front of the Imperial Palace on State occasions as a mark of sovereignty. This custom is known to go back to A.D. 700, and is probably much older.

The Euhemerists have tried their hand on the *yatagarasu.* Mr. Takahashi Goro informs us in his dictionary that this was the name of one of Jinmu Tennô's generals, and Klaproth thinks it probable that the "corbeau à huit pattes designe la boussole dont Zimmu s'est servi pour se guider dans son expedition." A Japanese noble family claimed descent from it, and a shrine in its honour is mentioned in the *Yengishiki*.†

There is a God called Ame no hi-washi (heaven-sun-eagle), which, although not to be identified with the *yatagarasu*, is no doubt a product of the same tendency to associate birds with the Gods. Both are inhabitants of the same celestial region.

**Susa no wo.**—The history of Susa no wo‡ illustrates the tendency of Nature-Gods to have their original character obscured by the anthropomorphic fancies of successive

---

* A kind of hawk.   ' Odyssey,' xv. 525.
† *Vide* ' The *Hinomaru* ' in the *T. A. S. J.*, vol. xxii. p. 27.
‡ See above, p. 65.

myth-makers.  The *Kojiki* and *Nihongi* accounts of him
are extremely vague and contradictory.  Later Japanese
writers have identified him with the Moon-God, with an
Indian Hades deity named Godzu Tennô, and with Emma,
the Rhadamanthus of the Buddhist Hell.  He has also
been made a God of Pestilence, of Love and Wedlock, or
of War.  European scholars have described him as a
" rotating-heavens God " or as " evidently a human being."
Dr. Buckley, of Chicago, was the first to suggest* that he
is the Rain-storm.  We need not adopt every detail of this
scholar's explanations, and indeed no one theory can solve
all the problems presented by the mutually inconsistent
stories related of this deity, but there can be no hesitation
in accepting Dr. Buckley's view as substantially correct.
It is as the Rain-storm that he is " continually weeping,
wailing, and fuming with rage "; that he " weeps the
mountains bare and the seas and rivers dry "; that he is
a lover of destruction ;† that " by reason of the fierceness
of his divine nature he causes a commotion in the sea and
makes the hills and mountains groan aloud " when he
ascends through cloud and mist to visit his elder sister the
Sun-Goddess.  Torrent Goddesses are born from the frag
ments of his sword.  He breaks down the divisions between
the rice-fields and defiles his sister's dwelling, disgusting
her so that she hides in a cave and leaves the world to
darkness.  He is further represented as going down to
earth at the season of continuous rains, and as wearing
a broad hat and a rain-coat.  When he marries, the nuptial
hut to which he retires with his wife is built of thick clouds.
The sword which he takes from the serpent's tail is called
*ama no mura-kumo,* that is to say, " the gathering clouds of
Heaven."  Another appropriate name for the weapon of
a rain-storm deity is *kusa-nagi,* " the herb-queller."  His

---

* ' In the Shinto Pantheon,' in the *New World*, December, 1896.

† Japan is annually visited by destructive typhoons, accompanied by great
darkness and a terrific downpour of rain.

wife's name, Inada-hime (the rice-field lady), is probably not without significance.

But mythology is rarely consistent. An explanation which suits one episode of a story may fail altogether when applied to others. There is nothing of the rain-storm about the Susa no wo who rescues a Japanese Andromeda from the great serpent which comes to devour her, or in the provider of timber and fruit-trees for mankind, or in the names and attributes of his very numerous children. His visit to Korea can hardly have a rain-storm significance. Moreover, it is impossible to pass over the explicit state ment of the *Nihongi* that he was appointed to rule the land of Yomi. A *Kojiki* myth* gives an account of his abode here in which no trace of his rain-storm quality is perceptible.

Dr. Florenz summarily rejects Hirata's theory that Susa no wo is identical with the Moon-God Tsuki-yomi. It must be admitted that if this deity ever had a lunar quality it had become forgotten in the times of the *Kojiki* and *Nihongi*. Both these works distinguish him unmistakably from the Moon-God. Nor is the European student likely to adopt the literal-minded Hirata's notion that the land of Yomi at first situated at the bottom of the Earth, became detached after Susa no wo was made its ruler, and was placed in the sky where we now see it—as the moon. Yet there is something to be said for his contention that the two deities were originally identical. The analogy of other mytho logies† suggests that a God whose relations with the Sun are at one time marital and at another hostile must be the Moon. There is nothing strange in the darkness of night and of the grave being presided over by the same divinity. Persephone, Queen of Hades, was a Moon-Goddess. The original identity of Susa no wo and Tsukiyomi would account for both deities being severally described in dif-

* See above, p. 106.
† Egyptian is one.

ferent myths as the slayer of the Food-Goddess and as the Ruler of the Sea-plain. It would also explain why the diviners at Ise ascribed to a curse from Tsukiyomi a storm of wind and rain which in 772 uprooted trees and destroyed houses. In an old book quoted by Hirata, Susa no wo is called Haya-Sasura no Kami, "swift-banishment-deity." His daughter while in Yomi is called Suseri-hime, probably identical with the Sasura-hime of the *norito** who dwells in the Root-country, and whose business it is to "banish" and get rid of the pollutions of the people. A Manyoshiu poem calls the moon Sasurahe-otoko, that is to say, the banished or vagabond youth. All this establishes a presumption that Susa no wo was at one time a lunar deity. If so he would appear in three closely related aspects, the darkness of the storm, of the grave, and of night. Brinton, writing without any special reference to Japan, observes† :—"Associated with the gloom of night was the darkness of the storm, which in many mythologies is contrasted with the sunshine in some divine struggle. Endless are the tales and rites which bear upon this contest in early religions."

If we remember the attributes of our own "Prince of Darkness," we shall not be surprised to find traces of a tendency to make of Susa no wo a personification of the evil principle. He is the arch offender of Japanese myth. The crimes committed by him against the Sun-Goddess agree closely with the so-called "celestial offences" of the Great Purification Ceremony. Hence his identification with the horned Godzu Tennô, a minister of the Buddhist hell. The *Shinto Miomoku*, which makes of him a Trinity under the name Sampô Kwojin (three-treasure-rough-god), consisting of Kami Susa no wo, Haya Susa no wo, and plain Susa no wo, by the epithet "rough," recognizes the sinister aspect of his character. We may note the same

* See Index—'Sasura-hime.'
† 'Religions of Primitive Peoples,' p. 80.

element *ara*, rough, in the name of the Moon-god's shrine at Ise, namely, Aratama no Miya.

Several of Susa no wo's acts have an unmistakably beneficent character, as his rescue of Inada hime, and his provision of useful trees for man. The modern worship of him as (with his wife) a deity of love and wedlock also recognizes a beneficent aspect of his nature. Hirata explains this contradiction by the theory that he is beneficent when his *nigi-tama* (gentle spirit) is in the ascendant, and malignant when his *ara-tama* (rough-spirit) gets the upper hand, as in the leading case of Jekyll and Hyde, reported by R. L. Stevenson. The female deity of Yomi, Sasura-hime, is called by Hirata a *waki-dama* (side spirit, or double) of Susa no wo, forming with him a dual divinity, as in the case of the Wind-Gods.

Etymology helps us little in determining Susa no wo's character. The ordinary derivation connects his name with the verb *susamu*, to be impetuous. Hence the " Impetuous Male" of English translators. It agrees well with the rain storm conception of this deity. There is at the present day a festival celebrated in his honour at Onomachi in Bingo, described as follows by a Japanese writer : " The procession is a tumultuous trial of speed and strength. Bands of strong men seize the sacred cars, race with them to the sea, and having plunged in breast-deep, their burden held aloft, dash back at full speed to the shrine. There refreshments are served out, and then the race is resumed, the goal being the central flag among a number set up in a large plain. Their feet beat time to a wildly shouted chorus, and they sweep along wholly regardless of obstacles or collisions." The ceremony here described is no doubt intended as a dramatic representation of the impetuous character of the God. The *susamu* etymology derives some support from a comparison of that of Woden, from *vatha* (the modern German *wuthen*), to go violently, to rush, and of Hermes, from ὁρμάω ; but it is after all questionable. It implies a noun *susa*, impetuosity, which does not exist. Moreover, one of Susa no wo's wife's names was Susa no yatsu mimi, where it is not disputed that Susa is the name of a town in Idzumo. There is a legend which represents Susa no wo as giving his name to this place and allowing his *mitama* to rest here. Susa no wo would therefore be simply the male (God) of Susa, a territorial title (of Tsuki-yomi?) for which there are many parallels in Japanese mythology.*

The *shintai* of Susa no wo, or rather of his supposed modern representative, Godzu Tenno, is a *naginata*, or halbert. But there is some reason to think that the great festival of Gorioye, now held in his honour at Kioto, was originally that of the Sahe no kami, and that the *hoko* or *naginata* carried in procession on this occasion is a substitute for an older phallus.

**Tsuki-yomi.**—This God, although worshipped in many places, Ise and Kadono amongst others, is hardly one of the greater gods of Japan. The usual derivation of his name is from *tsuki*, moon, and *yomi*, darkness. It is to be observed, however, that this *yomi* is often written with a character which implies a derivation from *yomu*, to reckon, a word which contains the same root as *yubi*, finger. "Moon-reckoner" is not an inappropriate name for a luminary which is recognized in so many countries as a measurer of time. Tsuki-yomi was represented at Ise as a man riding on a horse, clad in purple and girt with a golden sword. Another *shintai* of his was a mirror. Live horses were offered to him annually. The *Kiujiki* mentions a Moon-God among the suite of Ninigi when he descended to earth, and states that he was the ancestor of the *agata-nushi* (local chiefs) of Iki. This was probably a local Moon-deity.

* I offer, for consideration only, two conjectures: first, that Tsuki-yomi was the Ise Moon-God, and Susa no wo the Idzumo lunar deity; and second, that *Susa* may possibly be an allotropic form of *sasura*, banish,

The phases of the Moon are not recognized in Japanese myth.

*Tsuki-machi* (moon-waiting). On the 17th or 23rd of the lunar month, people assemble to greet the rising moon. Ritual purity must be observed beforehand. This custom illustrates the tendency to revert to the direct worship of nature when the myths have become obscured by time and no longer fulfil their original purpose.

**Star-God.**—There is only one mention of a Star-God in the *Nihongi*. He is called Amatsu mika hoshi (dread star of Heaven), or Ame no Kagase wo (scarecrow male of Heaven), and was one of the malignant deities conquered by Futsunushi and Mika-tsuchi in preparation for Ninigi's descent to earth. The scarecrow is regarded as a sort of deity. He is said to know everything in the empire, though he cannot walk.

The worship of Tanabata (Vega) and of the North Star is also known in Japan. But these cults have been intro duced from China. They are not Shinto.

**Ame no minaka-nushi.**—The Sky is not deified in Japan as it is in China. *Ame* is the region where the Gods dwell, not itself a God. Possibly, however, we should regard Ame no mi-naka-nushi (heaven-august-centre-master), as a personification of the sky, which has already reached that secondary phase in which the God has become distinct from the natural phenomenon. Some have endeavoured to make of him a sort of Supreme Being. But his cult is recent. Motoori says that he was not worshipped in ancient times. In the *Shōjiroku* he is the ancestor of several noble families.

**Earth-Gods.**—Comte calls Earth a great fetish. There are the same objections to calling the Earth a fetish as there are to applying this epithet to the Sun. Æschylus's All-Mother Earth, and Swinburne's Hertha, ought not to be so stigmatized. The Earth is not a factitious (*feitiço,* fetish) object of adoration, but a real divinity. It should not be discarded or neglected, but, along with other primary objects of worship, merged in the supreme synthesis of all the glimpses of the Divine which are vouchsafed to us.

Several phases of earth worship are exemplified in Shinto. The simplest of all is the *ji-matsuri*, or *ji-chin-sai* (earth-festival or earth-calming-festival), which is the ceremony of propitiating the site of a new building, or a piece of ground to be reclaimed for cultivation. Here it is the ground itself that is worshipped, without distinction of sex, or the adjunct of myth, metaphor, or personal name. This prac tice is as old as the *Yengishiki*, and is not extinct at the present day. Many peasants make sacrifice to the *ta no kami*, or rice-field god, when preparing the ground for a. crop, though here we perhaps pass into the next stage, in which the God is something apart from the rice-field itself. A similar phase of thought is implied by the use of such terms as *Iku-kuni** (living country), and *Taru-kuni* (perfect country), though here too the *norito* of Praying for Harvest, has already taken the further step of regarding this deity as a God who " rules " the islands of Japan. *Ikushima* (living island or region), is also used both for the country regarded as a God and for the God of the country.

We have seen above that several of the provinces had two names, one geographical, the other when considered as a God or Goddess, like our Britain and Britannia, Scotland and Caledonia.

A still further stage of progress is illustrated by the terms *kuni-dama* (country spirit), and *iku-dama* (live spirit). *Kuni-dama* is a general term for deified localities. *Iku-dama*, which has the same meaning, is a contraction for *iku kuni-dama*. Motoöri says that any God who has done service by " making " a country or province is worshipped in that province as the Kuni-dama or Oho-kuni-dama. The *Ichi*

---

* " The large, deep love of living sea and land."—Swinburne, ' Kynance Cove.'

*no miya* (No. 1 shrines) of later times represent the old Gods of localities.

The Kunari no kami, or Kunari-hime, were also appa rently local earth-deities. Kunari is for *kuni-nari* (earth-become).

**Ohonamochi.**—In the case of the great Earth-God of Japan, namely, Ohonamochi, the direct worship and personification of the country have already retired into the background. The myths speak of him not as the land itself, but as the maker of the land. His functions are variously described as constructing, measuring out, consoli dating, subduing, and ordering or governing. The *Idzumo Fudoki* frequently calls him the *ame no shita tsukurashishi ,Oho-kami*, that is to say, "the great God who made the Under-Heaven." The spear which he carries is indicative of warlike prowess and political sway, while the mattock given to him by one myth points rather to agricultural development. He is also, along with Sukuna-bikona, the instructor of mankind in the arts of medicine and magic. The usual tendency to enlarge the sphere of nature deities by attributing to them providential powers is illustrated by a poem in the *Manyoshiu* in which he is appealed to for the protection of the ship of an envoy who was about to proceed to China.

He could assume the form of a snake or of a human being.

The name Ohonamochi tells us nothing. It means great-name-possessor, and is simply honorific. An alter native title is Oho-kuni-nushi, or great land-master, Kuni-nushi being perhaps an honorary epithet equivalent to "king." Another name of this deity. Oho-kuni-dama (great land spirit), is more significant. It shows that he was regarded as one of the Kuni-dama or earth-deities mentioned above. His Earth-God quality is also implied by the *alias* Oho-toko-nushi, or great-place-master.

This God belongs mainly to the Idzumo group of myths. He is the son of Susa no wo, also an Idzumo God. The great centre of his worship to this day, and the holiest spot in Japan, next after Ise, is Kidzuki, a town in that province. His shrine here* is known all over Japan as the *Taisha*, or Great Shrine, and was formerly of exceptional magnificence. There is a widespread belief that all the Gods of Japan resort hither in the tenth month, which is therefore called *Kami-na-dzuki*, or the godless month. But Hirata's suggestion that *Kami-na-dzuki* is really for *Kami-name-dzuki*, the divine tasting-month, that is, the month of the harvest festival, is very plausible. Kaempfer transfers this annual visit of the Gods from Idzumo to the Mikado's palace, a blundering account of a myth which itself rests on a blunder.

The story of his deposition† by Take-mika-dzuchi and Futsunushi is probably an echo of a real historical event, when the rulers of Idzumo were compelled to yield up their temporal power to the conquerors of Yamato, retaining however, their control of spiritual matters.

Miwa, in Yamato, was another seat of this deity's worship. To be more exact, it was his *nigi-tama*, or gentle spirit, which was worshipped here. He is also associated with the numerous shrines called Sanno or Hiye. The Sono no kami (garden deity), to whom there was a shrine in the Palace, is also believed to be Ohomononushi, the *nigi-tama* of Ohonamochi. Along with Sukunabikona he is worshipped at Kanda, Tokio, as showing special favour to the inhabitants of that city (*Yedokko no mitama no kami*). These two deities are supposed to grant protection against small-pox.

The *Kojiki* story of Ohonamochi's adventures in Yomi‡ has no apparent connexion with his status as an Earth-God. Dr. Buckley argues that the Ohonamochi of this

* Graphically described in Lafcadio Hearn's 'Glimpses of Unfamiliar Japan.'

† See above, p. 108.

‡ See above, p. 106.

narrative is a Moon-God, and that his eighty brothers are the stars. I think it will be found to contain foreign and later elements, and that the introduction of Ohonamochi's name is merely accidental. The *Nihongi* passes it over in silence. The *shintai* of Ohonamochi is a necklace of jewels. His *nigi-tama*, or gentle spirit, is represented by a mirror, the *shintai* of the *ara-tama*, or rough spirit, being a spear.

**Asuha.**—An obscure deity, called Asuha no kami, said to be the child of Oho-toshi, the Harvest-God, is referred to in one of the *norito*. Motoori fails to identify him or her. Hirata thinks that Asuha is for *ashiba*, that is, foot-place, and that it means the plot of ground on which the dwelling stands. He mentions a practice by persons whose friends were absent on pilgrimages of making a model of a house, with a thatched roof to which they offered tea and rice every morning. They could not tell him what God it was whom they wished to propitiate. Hirata had no doubt that it was Asuha. He quotes an old poem which says : " Until he returns, I will pray to the God Asuha of the middle of the courtyard." Sir E. Satow calls Asuha no kami the "guardian deity" of the courtyard. I do not deny that this conception existed. But we must not lose sight of the earlier phase of thought in which the courtyard is itself the deity.

**Other Earth-Gods.**—Another obscure earth-deity is Haigi no kami, said to be the God of the space between the door of the house and the outer gate. The soil of the earth is deified under the names of Uhijini, Suhijini, and Hani-yasu-hime, personifications of mud, sand, and clay respectively. The two former are just mentioned in myth. *Hani-yasu* means "clay easy," the latter adjective indicating its plastic quality. Clay was probably deified because it forms the material for the Kamado, or kitchen-furnace, and is therefore deserving of gratitude for its service in restraining the unruly element fire. The water-gourd was deified for the same reason.

**Earthquake-Gods.**—The old myths say nothing about earthquakes, and although they are mentioned several times in the historical part of the *Nihongi*, in only one case* is a God of Earthquakes spoken of. In A.D. 684 there was a great earthquake, and a new island was formed at Idzu. A drumming sound was heard, which was thought to be made by the Gods in constructing it. The *Shoku-nihongi*, a con tinuation of the *Nihongi*, states that in the reign of Shomu (724-48), there were shrines to the God of Earthquakes in all the provinces. But any God might cause an earthquake. There is a legend that the God of Kashima (Take-mika-dzuchi) sealed down the Earthquake-God—he has no particular name—by placing over him the *Kaname-ishi*, or pivot-stone, which is still to be seen near his shrine.

The comparative insignificance of this deity in a country so notoriously subject to these convulsions as Japan is an instructive commentary on Buckle's well-known views of their importance in promoting superstition.

**Mountain-Gods.**—Most mountains of importance have their deity, who sometimes belongs to the general pantheon and is at others a specific mountain deity. The Mountain-God sometimes assumes the form of a serpent.

Though Japan has one hundred volcanoes, of which half are more or less active, the feelings excited by volcanic phenomena have left little trace in the religion. The *Kojiki*, *Nihongi*, and *Norito* do not recognize any worship of volcanoes. Perhaps the Aso-tsu-hiko and Aso-tsu-hime of the *Nihongi*† are to be reckoned an exception. These are no doubt personifications of Mount Aso, a remarkable volcano in the province of Higo, which is frequently referred to in later history. The drying up or overflowing of a lake within its crater was supposed to portend famine, pestilence drought, or the death of the sovereign. A ninth-century notice states that the Mikado informed the Sun-Goddess

* *Nihongi*, ii. 366.
† I. 198.

that "the miraculous pond in the district of Aso recently dried up for about four hundred feet, and in the province of Idzu there has been an earthquake. After divination I learnt that a drought, plague, or war would ensue. In order that this land might be peacefully ruled by the Sun-Goddess, I, having chosen a day of happy omen, send out the messengers (named) and present offerings." On another similar occasion, the God Hachiman was appealed to for help. The God (or Gods), however, of Aso itself was not wholly neglected. There were shrines to him on the mountain, with hereditary guardians to attend to them, and we hear of an offering of a horse. But volcano gods were in no high estimation. In 860 a Satsuma volcano received the junior branch of a lower division of the fourth rank, which is much as if Vesuvius were awarded the Italian equivalent for a D.S.O.

A great eruption of a mountain in Deha in the ninth century was attributed to the wrath of Oho-mono-imi (the Food-Goddess), on account of a pollution of the mountain water by dead bodies.

Fuji no yama is worshipped under the name of Sengen or Asama. At the present day nearly every volcano has its deity and a small shrine.

**Mountain Class-Deities.** — The *Kojiki* and *Nihongi* mention a Mountain-God or Gods,[*] called Yama tsu mi (mountain-body), as among the children of Izanagi and Izanami, or as born from the blood of Kagutsuchi when slain by his father. We hear little more of him or them. The Mountain-God was worshipped before cutting trees for shrines or palaces.

**Sea-Gods.** — The chief sea-deities of Shinto are the three Gods produced by Izanagi[†] when he washed in the sea after his return from Yomi. They are named respectively Soko-tsu-wata-dzu-mi (bottom-sea-body), Naka-tsu-wata-dzu-

---

[*] See 'Ch. K.,' p. 33.
[†] See above, p. 95.

mi (middle-sea-body) and Uha-tsu-wata-dzu-mi (upper-sea-body). Their chief shrine is at Sumiyoshi, near Sakai, and they are prayed to for rescue from ship wreck and for fair winds.* These three Gods are frequently spoken of as one. Hirata identifies them with Toyotama-hiko, whose legend is related above.†

With Toyotama-hiko there is associated a fabulous animal called a *wani*, usually written with the Chinese cha racter for crocodile. There can be little doubt that the *wani* is really the Chinese dragon. It is frequently so repre sented in Japanese pic tures. I have before me a print which shows Toyotama-hiko and his daughter with dragons' heads appearing over their human ones. This shows that he was con ceived of not only as a Lord of Dragons, but as a dragon himself. His

* See Index—'Sumiyoshi.'
† See p. 114.

daughter, who in one version of the story changes at the moment of child-bearing into a *wani* as her true form, in another is converted into a dragon.  In Japanese myth the serpent or dragon is almost always associated with water in some of its forms.

We also hear of a Shiho-tsuchi, or brine-father, and of local harbour deities.

**River-Gods.**—The River·Gods have no individual names. They are called generally *midzu-chi*, or water - father. Japanese dictionaries describe the *midzu-chi* as an animal of the dragon species with four legs.   Hepburn, in his ' Japanese-English Dictionary,' calls it a large water-snake. The difference is not material.   The dragon - kings of Chinese myth (of whom Toyotamahiko is an echo) are in India the Naga Raja, or cobra-kings.

The conception of a stream as a snake, serpent, or dragon, or of one of these animals as the embodiment of a water-deity is widespread.   Dennys, in his ' Folk-Lore of China,' quotes from the *North China Herald* the following :  " The River-God is in every case a small water-snake which popular fancy has converted into a deity." Robertson-Smith, in his ' Religion of the Semites,' says that " the living power that inhabits sacred waters and gives them their miraculous or healing quality is very often held to be a serpent, a huge dragon, or water monster."   Reville tells us that " Le serpent joue en effet un grand rôle symbolique dans le culte de Tlaloc (the Mexican Rain and Water God) en tant qu'il représente l'eau qui coule, les nuages, les cours d'eau."   It is easy to understand how a river, with its sinuous course and its mysterious movement without legs, should come to be thought of as a great serpent, especially if we remember the aquatic habits of some of the ophidia. Rivers have their favourable and their maleficent aspects. On the one hand they furnish water for irrigation, and on the other they cause destruction and loss of life by their floods, metaphorically expressed by the serpent's poison.

The River-Gods are prayed to for rain in time of drought.
We hear oftener of their sinister aspect.   The Perseus and
Andromeda incident related above is probably a trace of
former human sacrifices to rivers, of which further evidence
is afforded by the following extracts from the *Nihongi* :—

" *A.D. 379. This year, at a fork of the River Kahashima, in
the central division of the Province of Kibi, there was a great
water-dragon which harassed the people. Now when travellers
were passing that place on their journey, they were sure to be
affected by its poison, so that many died. Hereupon Agata-
mori, the ancestor of the Omi of Kasa, a man of fierce temper
and of great bodily strength, stood over the pool of the river-
fork and flung into the water three whole calabashes, saying :
' Thou art continually belching up poison and therewithal
plaguing travellers. I will kill thee, thou water-dragon. If
thou canst sink these calabashes, then will I take myself away,
but if thou canst not sink them, then will I cut thy body to
pieces.' Now the water-dragon changed itself into a deer
and tried to draw down the calabashes, but the calabashes
would not sink. So with upraised sword he entered the
water and slew the water-dragon. He further sought out
the water-dragon's fellows. Now the tribe of all the water-
dragons filled a cave in the bottom of the pool. He slew them
every one, and the water of the river became changed to
blood. Therefore that water was called the pool of Agata-
mori.*"

" *A.D. 323. In order to prevent the overflowing of the
Northern river the Mamuta embankment was constructed.
At this time there were two parts of the construction which
gave way and could not be stopped up. Then the Emperor
had a dream, in which he was admonished by a God, saying :
' There are a man of Musashi named Koha-kubi and a man
of Kahachi named Koromo no ko, the Muraji of Mamuta.
Let these two men be sacrificed to the River-God, and thou
wilt surely be enabled to close the gaps.' So he sought for*

*these two men, and having found them, offered them to
the River-God. Hereupon Koha-kubi wept and lamented,
and plunging into the water, died. So that embankment
was completed. Koromo no ko, however, took two whole
calabashes, and standing over the water which could not be
dammed, plunged the two calabashes into the mid-stream and
prayed, saying: ' O thou River-God, who hast sent the curse
[to remove which] I have now come hither as a sacrifice ! If
thou dost persist in thy desire to have me, sink these calabashes
and let them not rise to the surface. Then shall I know that
thou art a true God, and will enter the water of my own
accord. But if thou canst not sink the calabashes, I shall, of
course, know that thou art a false God, for whom why should
I spend my life in vain ? ' Hereupon a whirlwind arose
suddenly which drew with it the calabashes and tried to
submerge them in the water. But the calabashes, dancing on
the waves, would not sink, and floated far away over the
wide waters. In this way that embankment was completed,
although Koromo no ko did not die. Accordingly Koromo
no ko's cleverness saved his life. Therefore the men of that
time gave a name to these two places, calling them ' Koha-
kubi's Gap' and ' Koromo no ko's Gap' ''*

These stories, like that of Perseus and Andromeda, and
the Roman legend that Hercules substituted images of
straw for the living men hurled into the Tiber from the
Sublician bridge, belong to a period when the belief in
the efficacy of human sacrifice for propitiating river-deities
had been considerably shaken. The abolition of sacrifices
of living men at the tombs of deceased Mikados is part of
the same movement in the direction of a greater regard for
human life. The decay of the cult of rivers is also to be
inferred from a statement in the *Nihongi* (A.D. 642) that
prayers to the River-Gods for rain were condemned by the
Government as yielding no good result. Reading Buddhist
Sutras was equally ineffectual, but prayers by the Mikado

to the four quarters of Heaven in Chinese fashion were more successful.

There is a superstition at the present day that the mouths and pools of rivers are haunted by monsters called *kappa*, which destroy human beings and domestic animals.

**Rain-Gods.**—Two special Rain-Gods are mentioned in the *Nihongi*, namely, Kura o Kami (valley-august-god) and Taka-o-Kami (height-august-god). Both are often called simply O Kami, and are conceived of as having dragon shape. But praying for rain was by no means confined to them. The *Yengishiki* gives a list of eighty-five shrines to which messengers were despatched by the Court to pray for rain. These included many river and water deities, such as the Yamaguchi (mountain-mouth) and Mi-kumari (water-distributor) Gods ; but the Wind-God, the Rice-God, the Thunder-God, and many others were added. Even deified men like Temmangu might be prayed to for rain. The following is a modern method of causing rain. A procession is formed, a Shinto priest carrying *gohei* at its head. Next to him follows a conch-blower, and then some men carrying a dragon made of straw, bamboo, &c. Two flags inscribed to the Dragon-kings come after. Next follows a drum, then the people in disorderly rout, shouting, " The black clouds of the honourable peak : from the west the rain comes pouring." The ceremony ends by the straw dragon being plunged into a waterfall.

Water from the sacred lake of Haruna is supposed to produce rain. It is carried to the required place by relays of couriers, for if it stopped on the way the rain would fall there instead.

**Well-Gods.**—Sacred wells are known in Japan. They are called *mi-wi* (august well) or *mana-wi* (true well). There is one at Kitsuki, in Idzumo, called the *ama no manawi* (heaven-true-well), whence sacred water is drawn. Wells or well-gods are widely worshipped, usually in association with such household deities as Ashiba no Kami

(the site deity) and Kamado no Kami (the furnace deity).
We hear of an Iku-wi no Kami (live-well-god) and a Fuku-
wi no Kami (luck-well-god). Special wells were sunk for
the water used in the *ohonihe* ceremony, and worship paid
to them.

Well-diggers (*idohori*) at the present day sometimes
purify the ground previously to beginning their operations
and set up *gohei*. In fine weather, at night, they apply
their ears to the ground, when they can hear the water-
veins below. Old wells should not be wholly closed, or
blindness to one of the family will be the result. Hence to
appease the God of the well a bamboo is let down into
it before filling it up. Wells are worshipped at the New
Year.

**Water-Gods.**—The element of water generally is deified
under the name of Midzuha no me (water-female). She is
said to have been produced from the urine of Izanami
when dying, or, according to another account, from the
blood of Kagu-tsuchi when he was slain by Izanagi.* The
Jimmu legend says that the water used in sacrifice to
Musubi was entitled Idzu no Midzuha no me, that is to say,
" sacred-water-female," thus identifying the element with
the deity to whom it belongs.

**Wind-Gods.**—The *Nihongi* speaks of one Wind-God
named Shinatsu-hiko (wind-long-prince). He was produced
from Izanagi's breath when he puffed away the mists which
surrounded the newly formed country of Japan.† The
conception of the wind as the breath of the Gods is also
found in the Vedas and elsewhere. In the latter part of
the *Nihongi* frequent mention is made of embassies to
Tatsuta, in Yamato, to pray to the Wind-Gods for a good
harvest. A *norito* addressed to them‡ makes two Wind-
Gods—one masculine, named Shinatsu-hiko, and one femi-

* See above, p. 92.
† *Nihongi*, 1. 22.
‡ See Index—' Wind-Gods.'

nine, called Shinatobe. They are also referred to as Ame
no Mihashira (august-pillar* of Heaven) and Kuni no
Mihashira (august-pillar of Earth). Hirata supposes that
it was by them that communication was maintained between
earth and sky in the Age of the Gods, and that it is
due to their agency that the prayers of men are heard in
Heaven. Their *shintai* is a mirror.

Another Wind-God is Hayachi, that is, the swift father,
or perhaps swift wind. He is more especially the whirl
wind. He acted as the messenger of the Gods in bringing
up to Heaven the body of Ame no waka-hiko, who had
died on earth.

**Take-mika-dzuchi and Futsunushi.**—There is much
confusion as to the character and functions of these two
deities. They are associated in myth and in worship.†
Their two oldest shrines at Kashima and Kadori are
close to one another, and they are worshipped together
at Kasuga and other places. Indeed Hirata argues that
they are one and the same deity. He points out that
Futsunushi is not mentioned in the *Kojiki* story of the
pacification of Japan in preparation for the advent of
Ninigi, and that the same authority gives Toyo-futsu no
Kami and Take-futsu no Kami as alternative names of
Take-mika-dzuchi. On the other hand, the Jimmu legend
calls Futsu no mitama,‡ apparently a variant of Futsunushi,
the sword of Take-mika-dzuchi, and ascribes a different
parentage to these two deities. There are other features in
the *Nihongi* myths which are inconsistent with the theory
that they are identical.

Take-mika-dzuchi means "brave-dread-father." His
name is frequently written with Chinese characters which
imply that he is identical with Ika-dzuchi, or the Thunder-

---

* In Yucatan there were four Wind-Gods, who upheld the four corners of
Heaven.

† See above, p. 109.

‡ *Nihongi*, i. 115.

God. This is probably correct, although it is to be remem
bered that Ika-dzuchi had in more ancient times the more
general signification " dread father," and is applied to other
than thunder deities.

In Futsu-nushi the latter element admittedly means
" master." But I cannot accept Motoori's explanation of
*futsu* as an onomatopoetic word expressing the sound
made when a thing is cleanly cut or snapped off.

The following facts suggest a different derivation :—

1. The Sun-mirror (*hi-kagami*, which may also mean
" fire-mirror ") is called in one writing* the Ma-futsu no
kagami (true-fire-mirror).

2. Ama no hihoko is said to have brought over with him
from Korea a *hi-kagami.*

3. *Futsu* is the regular Japanese phonetic equivalent of
the Korean *pul*, " fire." In Furu-no mitama and Furu-
musubi (for Ho-musubi) we have an intermediate form
between *futsu* and *pul.* There is a God called Saji-futsu
or Satsu-futsu, for which the Korean phonetic equivalent
would be *Sal-pul.* This would mean " living fire " (Cicero's
" ignis animal "). I have no doubt that Saji-futsu is an
*alias* of Futsu-nushi.

4. Futsunushi was produced from the blood of Kagu-
tsuchi, the God of Fire, when the latter was slain by
Izanagi.

The inference from these data is that Futsunushi is a
Fire-God of Korean origin.†

But while there is a strong probability that Take-
mika-dzuchi and Futsunushi were originally Thunder
and Fire deities, by a tendency which there is for
nature-gods to become credited with providential functions,
to the neglect or oblivion of their proper natural powers,
these two deities have in historical times been universally

---

* *Nihongi*, i. 44.

† Is it possible that Fuji no yama is really for Futsu no yama, the mountain
of fire ?

recognized as war-gods.   The myth which represents them as subduing Ohonamochi and makes Futsu no mitama a sword contains the germ of this view of their character. A poet of the *Manyoshiu* speaks of praying to the God of Kashima when about to start on a warlike expedition. Fencing and horsemanship were under Futsunushi's special protection.   The *shintai* of both Gods, to some worshippers the Gods themselves, were swords.   That of Take-mika-dzuchi was a sword, five feet long, which at the annual Kashima festival was drawn from its sheath and worshipped by the priests,* all the people present wearing swords and drawing them before the shrine.   It is probably as a war-god that he was constituted the Ujigami of the arrow-makers, and that offerings of horses were made to him. When savage tribes were subdued or foreign invaders repulsed these Gods led the van and were followed by the other deities.   They were supposed to extend their special favour and protection to the Mikado, who sent frequent embassies to their various shrines.   They were also prayed to for a calm passage for envoys to China, and for children. Predictions of the quality of the harvest were recently, and probably still are, hawked about by persons in the garb of Shinto priests, called Kashima no koto-fure, that is to say, " notifications from Kashima."   Believers in the ghost and grave theory of the origin of religion will be interested to learn that not far from Kashima there is a large sepulchral mound called Kame-yama (pot-hill).   On the 8th day of the 1st month an Imperial envoy offers *gohei* here and recites a *norito*.   There are dances and music, and the mound is solemnly circumambulated.   Traditions exist of a great battle in this neighbourhood.   Smaller sepulchral mounds are also met with here, as at all ancient centres of authority in Japan.

**Ika-dzuchi.**—Take-mika-dzuchi having been converted into a war-deity and general Providence, the Thunder

---

* The sword was deified in Teutonic myth.

itself continued to be worshipped under the name of Ika-dzuchi, " dread father," which is short for Naru ika-dzuchi, " the sounding dread father." He is also called Naru kami, or " the sounding God." *Kami-nari* (god-sound) is the modern word for thunder.   There are numerous shrines to this deity.   By the Ika-dzuchi, which were generated from the putrefying corpse of Izanami, we must understand not thunders but personified diseases, the word being taken in its etymological signification.   The *Kojiki,* however, in this passage does undoubtedly say " thunders."   The dis-tinction into " eight thunders " is a fancy of the writer, little reçognized in later ritual.   The *Nihongi* ignores it.

The following story from the *Nihongi* illustrates Japanese ideas respecting the Thunder-God :—

" *A.D. 618. This year Kahabe no Omi was sent to the province of Aki with orders to build ships.   On arriving at the mountain, he sought for ship timber.   Having found good timber, he marked it and was about to cut it, when a man appeared, and said : ' This is a thunder-tree, and must not be cut.'   Kahabe no Omi said : 'Shall even the Thunder-God oppose the Imperial commands ? '   So having offered many mitegura, he sent workmen to cut down the timber. Straightway a great rain fell, and it thundered and lightened. Hereupon Kahabe no Omi drew his sword, and said : ' O Thunder-God, harm not the workmen; it is my person that thou shouldst injure.'   So he looked up and waited.   But although the God thundered more than ten times, he could not harm Kahabe no Omi.   Then he changed himself into a small fish, which stuck between the branches of the tree. Kahabe no Omi forthwith took the fish and burnt it.   So at last the ships were built*"

**Other Fire-Gods.**—Futsunushi's quality as a Fire-God had been quite forgotten even in the *Kojiki* and *Nihongi* times.   But there are several other Fire-Gods, or perhaps we should rather say local or occasional variants of the same deity.   Kagu-tsuchi, or "radiant father," is the name given to a Fire-God in the *Nihongi*, where he is said to have caused the death of his mother Izanami.   *Kagu* con tains the same root as *kagayaku*, to shine.   It also occurs in *Kaguyama*, a sacred mountain in Yamato, from which the needful objects for sacrifice were in early times provided. This God is worshipped under the name of Ho-musubi or "fire-growth "* on the summit of Atago, a mountain near Kioto.   There are many hill-shrines to this deity near other cities in Japan.   His business is to give protection against conflagrations.

The Jimmu legend speaks as if fire-worship arose from the deification of the sacrificial fire.   But there must have been other reasons.   The domestic fire renders important services to mankind, and its relation to the sun is unmistak able.   Indeed the Japanese call fire and sun by the same name, *hi*.   Fire has also its terrible aspect, which is recog nized in myth and *norito*.†

Hirata identifies the God with the element.   He is obviously a class, and not an individual God.   There is a festival at the present day called the Hi-taki-matsuri (fire-kindle-festival), when bonfires are lit, and small offerings made to the flames.

**Furnace Gods.**—Along with the Gods of Fire we may place the deities of the domestic cooking furnace, namely Kamado no Kami and Kudo no Kami.   They are barely mentioned in the *Kojiki* and not at all in the *Nihongi*. They have no myth, and although there is a *norito* addressed to them it contains nothing characteristic.   This worship is nevertheless general, from the Mikado's palace to the home of the peasant.   Sometimes we find a single deity, sometimes a married pair called Okitsu-hiko and Okitsu-hime, sometimes as many as eight co-existing fur nace-gods are met with.   The vulgar call him an *aragami*

---

* " So called," says Hirata, " because heat makes things grow."
† See Index—*Ho-shidzume*, Fire-drill.

(rough deity), and represent him with three heads, a notion which, according to Hirata, is taken from Indian myth. Usually the cooking furnace is the deity. The Japanese kitchen wench at the present day calls her cooking range Hettsui-sama, the termination *sama* implying personifica tion and respect. She thinks it unlucky to lay down an edge-tool on it. But the God is also conceived of as detached from the furnace. Thus he is said to have taught the art of cooking to mankind. In that case the *kama*, or pot, is his *shintai*, or material representative. There was a Kama-matsuri (pot festival) at Kioto before the revolution. It was celebrated at the beginning of the year, when Shinto priests read *harahi*. The pot was addressed in song and adjured to bring plenty of customers, usually by dyers and others in whose business caldrons were used.

**Ukemochi (the Food Goddess).**—Cicero, in his treatise 'De Natura Deorum,' asks whether any one is mad enough to believe that the food we eat is actually a God. The modern student of religion has no difficulty in answering this question in the affirmative. "Eating the God" is a well-known institution, from the custom of the Ainus of Yezo, who worship a bear,* caught and caged for the purpose, and wind up the festival in his honour by eating him, up to the most solemn rite of Roman Catholic Chris tianity. An Ainu prayer, quoted by Mr. Batchelor, contains the following words : "O thou God ! O thou divine cereal, do thou nourish the people. I now partake of thee. I worship thee and give thee thanks." Gratitude in the first place to, and then for, our daily bread, is an important factor in the early growth of religion. Without it we should have had no Roman Ceres, no Mexican Maize-God Centliotl, and no Ukemochi. I do not find the direct worship of our daily food in Shinto, though perhaps a trace of an older identification of the food with the God is to be recognized

* As a source of food ?

in the myth which represents the Food-Goddess as pro
ducing from her mouth and other parts of her body viands
for the entertainment of the Moon-God. Hirata is
indignant at the idea that there is anything metaphorical
about this story.

It is usually the offerings of food which are deified.
Jimmu is said to have directed that the food-offerings to
Taka-musubi should be called Idzu-uka no me (sacred-
food-female), which is another name for Uke-mochi. In a
work of the eighth century the Sun-Goddess is said to have
appeared to the Mikado Yuriaku in a dream. She com
plained to him of her loneliness at Ise, and directed that
"Aga mi ketsu no kami" should be sent for to Tamba in
order to keep her company. This was the legendary origin
of the worship of the Food-Goddess in the outer shrine
(Geku) of Ise. As Motoori points out, Aga mi ketsu no
kami means "the deity of the food offered to me." But in
this last instance the offering and the deity of the offering
are no longer identical.

It was usual for the participants in the ceremony to con
sume the food offered to the Gods. We are told that
Jimmu "tasted the food of the sacred jars." The Mikado
at all times followed this rule, notably at the *Nihiname*, or
harvest festival, when he partook of ordinary food with, but
after, the Gods. He does not "eat the God," but only
associates himself with the deity as his table-companion—
a very simple and intelligible form of communion. It is
on the same principle that in modern times pilgrims to Ise
buy from the priests and eat the rice which has been offered
to the Gods.

There is some confusion in regard to Ukemochi. Her
aliases are very numerous, if, indeed, we ought not to reckon
some of them as distinct deities. No doubt food was deified
over and over again in many places. The etymology of
most of her names is sufficiently transparent. They con
tain the element *ke* or *ka*, "food." One of these, namely

G

Uka no mitama, or the spirit of food, should be mentioned, as it embodies a more advanced and spiritual conception of the nature of this deity.

The parentage of the Food-Goddess is variously given in different myths. One story makes her the daughter of Izanagi and Izanami, and another of Susa no wo. The latter is, perhaps, an expression of the idea that the rain storm fits the rice-fields for producing grain.

After the Sun-Goddess, Uke-mochi is, perhaps (especially if we identify her with Inari), the most universally popular deity in Japan. She was one of the eight deities of the Jingikwan, and was worshipped at four of the twenty-two Greater Shrines, of which a list was made in 1039. There is abundant evidence that her cult was not confined to the State ceremonies. Hirata calls her an *ihe no kami*, or household deity.

The Sake (rice-beer) God is sometimes the same as the Food-Goddess, and at others Sukuna-bikona.

**Inari.**—Notwithstanding the difference of sex, and to some extent of function, the Rice-God Inari is generally recognized by the Japanese as identical with Uke-mochi. Inari, it is explained, is only the name of the locality of her best-known shrine near Kiôto, first established in 711. It is not to be doubted that in Japan the name of the place of his worship has frequently been converted into the name of the God. In the present case, however, it may be suspected that the reverse process has taken place. Might not Inari be *ine*, rice in a growing state, and *ri*, a termination implying personality?

Naturally Inari is much prayed to for agricultural prosperity. But, as so often happens, the functions of this God have been enlarged so as to make him a sort of general Providence who watches over all human concerns. In a recent Japanese novel he is supplicated by a wife to make her husband faithful ; by a mother to cause her son to divorce an obnoxious daughter-in-law ; by a wrestler for victory in his contests ; by a *geisha* for a wealthy protector who will give her plenty of money and rich clothes, and, getting tired of her within a month, will dismiss her with a handsome present. He is also appealed to for the resto ration of stolen property, to avert pestilence, to cure colds, to give wealth and prosperity, and to unite friends. The Kiôto Inari is the special patron of swordsmiths and of *joros*. Another Inari is celebrated for his protection of children from small-pox and measles. People who desire his help in this way offer at his shrine a red clay monkey, and take away with them one which has been deposited there by a previous worshipper.

The *shintai* of Inari is a stone, or a wooden ticket with his name inscribed on it. He is represented as an elderly man with a long beard riding upright on a white fox. The fox is always associated with this deity. A pair of these animals carved in wood or stone may usually be seen in front of his shrines. According to the modern theologians, the fox is properly his servant or messenger. But there is a more ignorant current of opinion which takes the animal for the God himself. Klaproth finds in Japanese books that " the people in Japan worship the *inari* (fox) as a tutelar God : little temples are dedicated to him in many houses, especially of the commoner folk. They ask his advice in difficulties, and set rice or beans for him at night. They take him to be a *kami, i.e.*, the soul of a good man deceased." Be it observed that *inari* does not mean fox, and that a *kami* is something quite different from " the soul of a good man deceased." It is just possible, however, that in this case the ignorant multitude are right, and that the fox is a duplicate representative of the rice or rice-deity. Mr. Frazer, in his ' Golden Bough,' adduces many instances of the Corn-God being represented by animals. " In Poitou, the spirit of the corn appears to be conceived in the shape of a fox."

The festival of Inari is held on the first " horse " day of

the second month.    The Shoguns celebrated it with great
ceremony, of which dramatic performances (*no*) were a part.

**Harvest-Gods.**—The Harvest-Gods, of which there are
several, as Oho-toshi no Kami (Great-Harvest-God), Mi-
toshi no Kami (August-Harvest-God), Waka-toshi no
Kami (Young-Harvest-God), are not very clearly distin
guished from the food and grain deities.   A myth relating
to one of these deities will be found below, p. 196.

The liturgy entitled ' Praying for Harvest ' was addressed
to all the chief deities.*

The worship of the Sun and of Grain, Harvest and
Growth deities, which forms so important a part of Shinto,
is characteristic of an agricultural nation.  It is emphasized
by the ancient custom of the Mikado tilling land in person,
and by the Miko at Kasuga planting rice annually with
much ceremony.

**Tree-Gods.**—Individual trees of great age and size are
everywhere worshipped in Japan.   An ancient example of
this cult is mentioned above, p. 158.   At the present day
the sacred trees are often to be seen girt with *shimenaha*,†
and with tiny shrines at the bottom.   The novelist Bakin,
writing in the early part of the nineteenth century, tells of
one which he visited near Uraga.   It was a common-look
ing fir which had been struck by lightning, no doubt,
Bakin says, before the spirit took up its abode there.   This
tree healed diseases of all kinds and brought luck to fisher
men.   People with sore eyes carried away the water which
collected in a hollow part, and washed their eyes with it.
Incense was burned to it.

At the shrine of Kamo in Kiôto there are two *sakaki*
(sacred evergreen) trees, which are joined together by a
branch which has grown from one trunk into that of the
other.   These trees are much visited by women who desire
to live in harmony with their husbands.   A small red

* See Index—*Toshi-gohi.*
† See Index.

*tori-wi* in front of them shows that they are considered sacred.* Here the emblem of unity has come to be regarded as having intrinsic virtue.

A Kami-gi (God-tree) was often planted in front of Shinto shrines. It was sometimes set in a portable box, which could be carried about by the devotees. A case is recorded in which this was done for the sake of protection to the bearers. The sacred tree of Japan is the *cleyera japonica.* It is an evergreen, as the name, derived from *sakayuru*, to flourish, indicates.

There is a modern custom in places where fruit trees are grown for two men to go out into the orchard. One climbs up a tree while the other stands at the bottom with an axe. The latter asks whether it will have a good crop the next season, and threatens to cut it down if it fails to do so. Hereupon the man above answers for the tree, promising that it will bear plentifully. In Hitachi at the time of the Sai (or Sahe) no Kami feast (the first full moon of the year) a gruel is made of rice coloured red† with *adzuki* beans. This is sprinkled on the fruit trees of the neigh bourhood. The man who does so wears the straw covering of a rice-bag by way of hat, and takes with him an axe and the gruel vessel, saying to each tree, " Will you bear— will you bear, of bags 1,000 bags, of sacks 1,000 sacks ? Say that you will bear." " I will bear, I will bear." Then he gives the tree three cuts with the axe, and pours the gruel on it.

Similar customs are found all over the world. M. D'Alviella, in his Hibbert Lectures, quotes as follows: " Ibn al Awam's agricultural treatise recommends the intimidation of trees that refuse to produce fruit. ' You are to flog them mildly and threaten to cut them down if they go on bearing no fruit.' " The Bohemian Slavs used to say to the garden trees, " Bud ! ye trees, bud ! or I will

---

* Murray's ' Japan,' fifth edit., p. 383.
† See Index—' Red.'

strip you of your bark." Brand's 'Popular Antiquities of Britain' records several variants of this custom. "On Christmas Eve," he says, "the farmers and their men in Devonshire take a large bowl of cider, with a toast in it, and carrying it in state to the orchard, they salute the apple-trees with much ceremony, in order to make them bear well the next season." This salutation consists in throwing some of the cider about the roots of the tree, placing bits of the toast on the branches, and then, "en circling one of the best bearing trees in the orchard, they drink the following toast several times :—

> 'Here's to thee, old apple-tree
> Whence thou mayst bud, and whence thou mayst blow,
> And whence thou mayst bear apples enow !
>         Hats-full ! caps-full !
>         Bushel, bushel sacks-full !
> And my pockets full, too ! Hurra !'"

Mr. J. G. Frazer has treated this subject with his usual fulness in 'The Golden Bough.'

I suspect that the pleasure we take in dramatic make-believe has more to do with such practices than any belief in their practical efficacy, and that they rather contain the germ of a religious cult of trees than are a survival of a primitive tree-worship.

**Kukunochi.**—The older records mention a Kukunochi (trees-father), a Ki no mi-oya no Kami (tree-august-parent-deity). There is also a Ko-mata no Kami (tree-fork-deity) and a Ha-mori no Kami (leaf-guardian-deity). These are class-deities.

**Kaya nu hime.**—The deity of herbs and grasses is called Kaya nu hime (reed-lady), or Nu-dzuchi (moor-father) or Kaya no mi-oya no Kami (reed-august-parent-deity). The chief reason for deifying trees and reeds was that they furnish materials for house-building, and are therefore deserving of our gratitude and worship.

**Ko-dama.**—The echo is called in Japan Ko-dama, or tree spirit.

**House-Gods.**—Our knowledge of these deities is chiefly derived from a *norito* in the *Yengishiki.** One part of this ritual speaks of Yabune, which may be either singular or plural ; but further on in the same document we find Ya bune Kukunochi and Yabune Toyo-uke-hime. Perhaps an original single deity has been split up into a wedded pair by a process of which Shinto affords other examples. *Ya* is " house," and *fune*, which usually means " ship," may also be applied to other wooden vessels, such as troughs or tubs. The *ya-bune* is therefore the shell† of the house. Kukunochi, as we have just seen, is the name of the Tree-God. Toyo-uke-hime, which means abundant-food-lady, has been identified with the Food-Goddess ; but it is more probable that the prefix *yabune* was intended to distinguish her from that deity, as the same prefix made of Kukunochi a distinct God from the ordinary Tree-God. The functions of these Gods was to guard the palace building from harm of all kinds. No doubt each household had also its Yabune no Kami. Hirata, in his *Tamadasuki*, gives a prayer to this deity intended for general use.

The Oho-toma-hiko and Oho-toma-hime of the *Nihongi* and the Oho-ya-hiko of the *Kojiki* are also House-Gods. Nothing is known of them.

A certain sanctity attached to the central pillar of the house, called Daikoku-bashira or Imi-bashira (sacred pillar). The Daikoku-bashira is worshipped in some places on the 14th of the 1st month by offerings of rice-ears, flowers, rice bags, &c. The date indicates a connexion with the phallic Sahe no Kami.‡

**Privy-God.**—There is in modern times a God of the privy, who has no particular name, sex, or mythic record.

---

* See Index— *Yabune.*
† Compare our " nave," from the Latin *navis.*
‡ See below, p. 186.

Hirata, in his *Tamadasuki*, has provided a special form of prayer to him. He himself was his devout worshipper. He saluted the God on entering and leaving, and, that people might not forget this duty, recommends that a card be nailed on the door, with the inscription " Ojigi," or " good manners." According to him privies, as well as dunghills and all unclean places, are a favourite resort of evil spirits. They are haunted by flies and maggots, which are the fractional souls of bad men (a Buddhist notion ?). There is, therefore, all the greater need to put ourselves under the protection of the presiding deity of the place. He deprecates spitting into it (which causes ophthalmia) or defiling it, and says that women who sweep it out daily and make offering to the God of a light on the last day of each month will be free from diseases below the girdle.

All this shows that the original identity of demons and diseases has not yet been wholly lost sight of in Japan.

**Gate-Gods.**—Kushi-iha-mado (wondrous-rock-door) and Toyo-iha-mado (rich-rock-door). These two Gods are known to us from the *norito* entitled Mikado no matsuri.* They are obviously personifications of the gates of the Palace. But the difficulty presents itself that these Gods are (apparently) two in number, these two being differen tiated out of one original deity by the honorary epithets *kushi* and *toyo*, while the gates of the Palace were much more numerous. If it is the gate itself, and not the spirit of the gate, which is worshipped, there ought to be as many Gods as gates. Hirata would no doubt explain this by saying that there are really only two Gods, but that each gate is occupied by a *mitama*, or emanation from them. It seems more probable that the ancient Japanese had no very definite ideas on the subject. They conceived of the gates as in some way or another instinct with life and exercising certain protective functions ; but whether there were two deities for each gate or two for all collectively

* See Index, *s.v.*

was a question which did not occur to them. It must be remembered that the Japanese language seldom takes the trouble to distinguish between singular and plural. This is merely another way of saying that the nation is com paratively indifferent to number, whether of Gods or gates. Whether the Gate-divinity is one or several does not trouble them.

### GODS OF ABSTRACTIONS.

**Izanagi and Izanami.**—The conspicuous position given by the mythical narrative* to these personifications of the dual creative powers of the universe has little to correspond with it in cult and ritual. Although they are no doubt to be reckoned among the *Dii majores* of Japan, they occupy a much lower place than the Sun-Goddess and the Food-Goddess.

Izanagi and Izanami are evidently creations of subse quent date to the Sun-Goddess and other concrete deities, for whose existence they were intended to account. I have little doubt that they were suggested by the *Yin* and *Yang*,† or female and male principles of Chinese philosophy. In deed there is a passage in the *Nihongi* in which these terms are actually applied to them. It may be said, and Motoori does say, that the *Yin* and *Yang* are foreign ideas which have found their way into a purely native myth. We must remember, however, that the Japanese myths as we have them date from a period three centuries after the introduc tion of Chinese learning into Japan, and that there was communication with China hundreds of years earlier still. It would, therefore, not be strange if some knowledge of the fundamental principle of Chinese philosophy and science had reached the Japanese long before the *Kojiki* and *Nihongi* were written.

I conjecture that the early part of the *Nihongi*, taken in the order of the original composition of the myths which it

---

* See above, p. 86.
† In Japanese *In* and *Yo*.

comprises, would be somewhat as follows :—First the Sun-myth, which is the nucleus of all, next that of the creation by Izanagi and Izanami, then the more abstract Musubi and a number of ill-defined creations of some idle fancy which precede him. Last of all was composed the philosophic proem with which the book opens.

Izanagi and Izanami belong to that stage of religious progress in which the conception has been reached of powerful sentient beings separate from external nature. Untrue in itself, it has served a useful purpose. It is obviously easier for nations with little scientific knowledge to conceive of the same being as a ruler or parent of the Sun, Moon, and Earth, with all its human concerns, than to recognize in these phenomena a harmonious living whole. The common parentage of Izanagi and Izanami formed a link of union between the different aspects of nature which did not previously exist, and thus was in so far a step towards monotheism.

The manner of creation is variously represented. In no case is anything made out of nothing. The first act of creation was the formation of an island out of the drippings of the brine of the chaos-ocean from a spear. The other parts of Japan and many of the deities were produced by the ordinary process of generation. The functions of Izanagi and Izanami are elsewhere described as " putting in order and fully consolidating " the floating land beneath. This is precisely what Ohonamochi is represented as doing several generations of Gods later. Deities were also pro duced from Izanagi's clothing and staff which he threw down on his flight from Yomi, and from his eyes and nose when he washed in the sea to remove the impurity con tracted by his visit thither. The Wind-God was his breath and the Gods of Water and Clay were formed of the urine and fœces of Izanami when she was about to die. These ideas, though not quite identical with, are closely related to the legends of other countries which describe the creation

of the universe from the fragments of a fabulous anthropo
morphic being. The Chinese myth of P'anku has been
already quoted.* Norse story tells how "the vast frame
of the world-giant Hymi was completely cut up by the sons
of Bor, with Woden at their head. From Hymi's flesh they
made the earth, from his bones the mountains, from his
skull the heavens, from his blood the sea."†

There is nothing spiritual about these two deities. All
their actions are modelled not on those of ghosts, but on
those of living men. Even when Izanami dies and goes
down to the land of Yomi, she does not become a ghost,
but a putrefying corpse.

Their *shintai* is a mirror.

A Japanese writer‡ says: "In the beginning of all
sentient things we have two Supreme Beings, Izanagi and
Izanami." Even if we admit the possible existence of two
Supreme Beings, Izanagi and Izanami hardly realize our
conception of the Supreme. They acted by command of
other pre-existing deities, and their creation is limited. It
does not include all the Gods, and, as is only natural, is
confined to Japan. The creation of mankind is nowhere
accounted for in Japanese myth. There is, however, a
modicum of truth in this writer's statement. Though not
the first sentient beings, Izanagi and Izanami are the first
who stand out with any distinct characterization, and,
although not supreme, they represent a movement. feeble
and abortive it is true, towards the co-ordination of all the
aspects of divinity in one Supreme Being.

Motoori proposed, and most European scholars have
accepted, a derivation of Izanagi and Izanami from *izanafu*,
a verb which means to invite, to instigate, the terminations
*gi* and *mi* meaning respectively male deity and female
deity. Hence the translation "Male who invites" and

---

* See above, p. 129.
† Rhys, 'Celtic Heathendom,' p. 115.
‡ 'In Japan,' edited by Capt. Brinkley.

"Female who invites." There are, however, grave diffi culties in the way of this interpretation. It is scarcely appropriate in the case of the female deity. Moreover, we must take into account the fact that these are not the only pairs of deities in which the terminations *nagi* and *nami* occur. We have also an Aha-nagi (foam-God) and Aha-nami (foam-Goddess), a Tsura-nagi (bubble-God) and Tsura-nami (bubble-Goddess), and a Sa-nagi (rapid-God) and Sa-nami (rapid-Goddess), in all of which *na* does not belong to the first part of the word, but is put for *no*, the genitive particle, by a letter-change of which we have other examples. The first element of Izanagi is, therefore, not *izana* but *iza*, which is met with as an exclamation of incitement. The harshness of making an interjection fol lowed by a genitive particle is obvious. I am disposed to prefer the derivation which takes Iza as the name of a place. The *Nihongi* mentions a " true well " of Isa or Iza. There are two places called Isa in Hitachi, and an Isa no Jinja, or shrine of Isa, in Idzumo. It is even possible that these Gods are simply the Gods of Ise (Ise no gi and Ise no mi). A similar letter-change takes place in *manabuta*, eyelid, for *me no futa*, and *tanasuye* for *te no suye*. The difference between *s* and *z* is of little consequence in Japanese.

**Musubi, the God of Growth.**—Musubi illustrates a dif ferent conception of creation from that of the myths of Ohonamochi and Izanagi and Izanami. This God is the abstract process of growth personified—that is, a power immanent in nature and not external to it. The emotion which prompts this personification—so natural to an agri cultural people—is well portrayed in the words of a Kafir to the French traveller M. Arbrouseille : " Do I know how the corn sprouts ? Yesterday there was not a blade in my field : to-day I returned to the field and found some. Who can have given the earth the wisdom and power to produce it ? Then I buried my head in both hands." But while

the emotion is the same, the Japanese' conception differs.
Musubi means growth or production.  It is connected with
the word *umu*, to bear, to bring forth, and with *musu*, to
grow, to be born.  *Musu* is said of moss growing on a
stone and of ice forming on water.  *Musuko*, a boy, and
*musume*, a girl, contain the same element.  As a God's
name, Musubi is usually found with one of the laudatory
adjectives, *taka*, high, or *kamu*, divine, prefixed to it.  To
these the honorific particle *mi* is commonly added, giving
the forms Taka-mi-musubi and Kamu-mi-musubi.  Even
in the *Kojiki* and *Nihongi* these are recognized as two
distinct deities.  The *Yengishiki* (901-922) enumerates
three more Musubi deities, and to these still others might
be added.  In poetry a single God Musubi is alone met
with, and the *Wamiosho* recognizes but one such deity.
Probably the division into several persons was an esoteric
refinement of which the people took little heed.

Whether we have regard to his name or to the some
what meagre notices in the *Kojiki* and *Nihongi*, there is
nothing spiritual in the Japanese conception of Musubi.
But the scribes learned in Chinese who committed the old
myths to writing sometimes use characters which imply
a spiritual view of his nature.  They mean " producing-
spirit."

He is also called *mi oya*, or august parent.  Hirata thinks
that Taka-musubi and Kamu-musubi are husband and wife,
the Kamurogi (progenitor) and Kamuromi (progenitrix) of
the *norito*, and condemns his master Motoori for holding
that we have in these deities a unity in duality and a duality
in unity.  But his reasons are not quite convincing, and
there is a passage in the *Kojiki* which cannot be reconciled
with his view.  The same author points out the resem
blance of this God to the Hindu Siva, who represents the
fructifying principle, the generating power that pervades
the universe, producing sun, moon, stars, animals, and
plants.  Siva is represented in his temples by a phallus,

and Hirata conjectures that this was likewise the *shintai* of Musubi.

Musubi is sometimes called the Inochi no Kami, or God of life. The creation of mankind is attributed to him in a poem of the *Jiu-i-shiu*, where a rejected lover exclaims :—

> " I hate not thee,
> It is the God I hate,
> Great Musubi :—
> Why did he men create
> Unto so hard a fate ? "

The *Kojiki* speaks of the two deities Taka-musubi and Kamu-musubi as forming the second and third generations of Gods. The original text of the *Nihongi* omits all men tion of them in this part of the narrative, but in a note there is a quotation from " one writing " in which they are named. In the various accounts of the measures taken to prepare the earth for occupation by Ninigi sometimes the Sun-Goddess is represented as giving instructions, some times Taka-musubi, sometimes both together, and some times Taka-musubi alone. Jimmu, in making mention of the two deities, gives precedence to Taka-musubi. This discordance in the various myths seems to indicate a struggle for ascendency between the respective adherents of Musubi and the Sun-Goddess. The *Nihongi* states that in A.D. 487 (a fairly trustworthy date), by request of the Moon-God and the Sun-Goddess, the worship of Taka-mi-musubi, whom these two deities call their ancestor and the Creator of Heaven and Earth, was established in two places, and grants of lands and of peasants made for the maintenance of the shrines. This is possibly the beginning of the official worship of this God. In 859 several Musubi deities were raised to the first grade of the first rank. In the tenth century eight shrines to various Musubi deities existed within the Palace. With the official classes Musubi was a dangerous rival to the Sun-Goddess, more especially during the Augustan age of Japanese literature.

But he was too philosophical for popular favour. His worship is now greatly neglected. The Musubu no Kami of the present day is identified with the Chinese Gekka-rojin (moon-under-old-man), who presides over the fates of lovers. The strips of cloth frequently seen hung on bushes by the roadsides are offerings to him. The second meaning of Musubi, namely, "to tie," has no doubt something to do with this new view of the God's function.

The *Shōjiroku* traces the descent of a large number of the noble families of Japan from the various forms of Musubi. This is a literal rendering of a statement which, in one sense, is true of everybody. We all resemble Topsy.

**Kuni-toko-tachi.**—I place this deity provisionally among the personifications of abstractions. The name means literally "earth-eternal-stand." He is, therefore, apparently a deification of the durability of earth. Motoori and Hirata take *toko* as for *soko*, bottom or limit. This would make this deity a personification of the horizon, or perhaps more accurately Lucretius's "flammantia mœnia mundi." He has no sex and no special characteristics. He is barely mentioned in myth, and his cult, which is comparatively modern, was no doubt, as Hirata suggests, a result of the prominent position given him in the *Nihongi* as the first God in point of time, and as the ancestor of the Sun-Goddess, before whom he was therefore entitled to prece dence. He was identified with the Taikyoku, or "Great Absolute," of the Chinese philosophers, was said to be immortal, and to comprise all the Gods in himself, was called "the name of the nameless, the form of that which has no form," and, in short, erected into a Supreme Being. In the fourteenth century an unsuccessful attempt was made to substitute him for the Food-Goddess as the deity of the outer shrine of Ise. At the present day he is wor shipped at Mount Ontake, in the province of Shinano, a place much resorted to by pilgrims.

O tento-sama (august-heaven-way-personage) was probably originally a personification of the natural order of things—Laotze's *tao*, or Pindar's Νόμος, the βασιλευς of Gods and men. But this is too abstract for the common Japanese. To them O tento sama is the Sun itself, en dowed, it is true, with certain moral attributes.

Drought and Famine deities belong to this class. None of these is of much importance.

# CHAPTER VIII.

## THE PANTHEON, MAN DEITIES.

### I. DEIFIED INDIVIDUAL MEN.

NONE of the *Dii majores* of the more ancient Shinto are deified individual men, and although it is highly probable that some of the inferior mythical personages were origin ally human beings, I am unable to point to a case of this kind which rests on anything more than conjecture.

**Take-minakata**, the deity of Suha in Shinano, may be a real ancestral deity. He is very popular at the present day. This God is not mentioned in the *Nihongi*, but his legend is given in the *Kojiki** and *Kiujiki*. He was a son of Ohonamochi, who, after his father's submission, refused allegiance to the Sun-Goddess and fled to Suha, where he was obliged to surrender, his life being spared. Tradition says that the present Oho-hafuri, or chief priests of Suha, are direct descendants of this deity. The inhabitants hold that the God *is* the Oho-hafuri, and that the Oho-hafuri *is* the God. An oracle of the God is quoted to this effect : " I have no body, the *hafuri* is my body." His house is called the *shinden* or divine dwelling. He never leaves the neighbourhood, and takes precedence of the chief local official. At every change of office the newly appointed high priest formerly received a cap of honour and robes from the Palace of Kiôto. He takes no active part in the ceremonies of the annual festival, but sits on a chair in the middle of the sacred plot of ground and receives the obeisances of the people. This festival is called the *mi-hashira-matsuri* or " festival of the august pillars." It is so

---

* See Ch. K., p. 102.

called because instead of a shrine there is only a plot of ground containing a "rock-cave"* with a great wooden post at each of the four corners.

**Hachiman.**—The War-God Hachiman is one of the most conspicuous of the later Shinto deities. His origin is really unknown, but he is placed provisionally among deified human beings in accordance with the accepted tradition which makes him identical with the very legendary Mikado Ôjin. The ultimate authority for this statement is an oracle of the God himself delivered hundreds of years after Ôjin's death. There is no mention of his worship in the *Kojiki* or *Nihongi*, and the legends which carry it back to A.D. 570 are unworthy of credence. The original seat of this cult was Usa, in the province of Buzen, an old Shinto centre. Hachiman seems to have first come into notice in 720, when he rendered efficient assistance in repelling a descent of Koreans on Japan. Forty years later Kiyomaro, the founder of the great Minamoto family, made use of his oracles to thwart the ambitious projects of a priest named Dôkiô, the Wolsey of Japanese history. The rise of the Minamoto family carried with it that of the God who had been so useful to them. In Seiwa's reign (859-880) a temple was erected to him at Ihashimidzu near Kiôto, where he received Imperial presents, and even visits. In 1039 he was given a high place in the State religion.

Hachiman is nominally a Shinto God. His Shinto quality is recognized in various ways, notably by the erection of the distinctive Shinto gateways known as *torii*, before his shrines. But his cult is deeply tinctured with Buddhism. The numerous inspired utterances ascribed to him are thoroughly Buddhist in character. In several of these he calls himself Bosatsu (Bodhisattwa), which is a Buddhist term something like our saint. He is also credited with giving instructions for the celebration of an annual

---

* Probably a sepulchral dolmen. There are many in this district, said to be the tombs of Minakata's descendants.

festival for the release of living things, which is, of course, a humanitarian Buddhist institution, wholly foreign to the *rôle* of a Japanese War-God.

The *shintai* of Hachiman may be a pillow, a fly-brush, an arm-rest, or a white stone.

Other legendary mortals, who in later times were honoured as War-Gods, are Jimmu, the founder of the Imperial dynasty, Jingo, the conqueror of Korea, Takechi no Sakune, her counsellor, and Prince Yamato-dake, the hero who subdued the east of Japan. None of these are treated as deities in the older Shinto books.

**Temmangu**, the God of Learning and Calligraphy, is undoubtedly a deified human being.

" *There is nobody in the world, high or low, old or young, man or woman, who does not look up with reverence to the Divine power of Temmangu. More especially children who are learning to read and write, and their teachers, all without exception, enjoy his blessings. Every one is therefore desirous of knowing the exact truth concerning him. But there are many false notions handed down by vulgar tradition. Chinese scholars have wantonly done violence to the history of an awful deity by introducing Chinese ideas, while the Buddhists, on the other hand, have been guilty of disfiguring the story by all manner of forced analogies. Sad to say, there is no book in which the real facts have been set down after investigation.*"

The above is the exordium of a preface to a short life of Temmangu, prepared by Shintoists of the Hirata school. Of the work itself the following is a brief summary. The main facts of the story are beyond question. But the reader will see that, notwithstanding the claims put forward in the preface, this work must be taken with not a few grains of salt.

Temmangu's name as a mortal man was Sugahara Michizane. He was born in 845, and came of a family which had a hereditary reputation for learning. Nomi no Sukune, deified as the patron of wrestlers and potters, was one of his ancestors. Through him Michizane traced his descent up to the Sun-Goddess herself. As a child he was fond of study, and at an early age his knowledge of Chinese was such that he was appointed to entertain an ambassador from China. Being ordered by the Mikado to pray for rain, he observed the rules of ritual purity for several days, and then prepared a form of prayer to the God of Hakusan (Izanagi), which had the desired effect. He established a system of national education, and therefore became known as the " Father of letters." On reaching his fiftieth year he received congratulations and a present of gold dust from a genie. Soon afterwards he was made Prime Minister. In 901, owing to the calumnies of a rival statesman, he fell into unmerited disgrace and was banished to Kiushiu. On his departure he addressed the following lines to a plum tree in his garden :—

> When the east wind* blows,
> Emit thy perfume
> Oh thou plum-blossom ;
> Forget not the spring,
> Because thy master is away.

A branch of this tree broke off spontaneously and fol lowed him into exile. There it planted itself in the ground and took root. Two years after, Michizane climbed a high mountain and, standing on tiptoe on the summit, prayed with all his heart and all his body for seven days and seven nights to Tentei (the Supreme Lord of Heaven). Whilst doing so his hair and beard turned white. The Tento (way of Heaven) had doubtless pity on an innocent man, for a cloud overspread the sky and bore up his petition into the Great Void. Michizane, overjoyed that his prayers were answered, made nine obeisances and retired. He died soon after, in his fifty-ninth year, to the great grief of the

---

* The east is in Japan the soft wind —our zephyr.

whole nation.   Two years later, in accordance with a divine
inspiration, a small shrine was erected to him under the
title of Tem-man-ten-jin (the heavenly Kami who fills the
heavens).  In a few years Michizane's calumniator died by a
curse from him.   Other members of his family had the same
fate.  From the ears of one of his enemies small snakes issued
who declared themselves the messengers of Michizane.
When Prince Yasuaki died, in 923, everybody said that his
death was owing to a curse sent by Michizane's spirit.  Then
the Minister of State Kintada died suddenly.   Three days
after, he came alive again, and informed the Mikado that
he had been to the Court of the King of Hades, where he
saw Michizane, ten feet high, present a petition for an
inquiry into the crime committed by the Mikado in banish
ing him unjustly.   Influenced by Kintada's report, the
Mikado burnt the decree of exile, recalled Michizane's
children, and conferred posthumous honours upon him.
But the angry ghost was still unappeased.   In 929 it came
down from Heaven and appeared to a former friend of his.
Terrible storms, inundations, and other portents ensued.
Ministers who tried to stay him from further ravages were
burnt or kicked to death.   Ultimately the ghost appeared
before the Mikado and protested his innocence, after which
the Kami, as he is called, ascended.   From this day forth
the Mikado suffered from a poison which, in spite of
prayers of all kinds, grew worse and worse.   He abdicated
in 930, and died a few days later.

Michizane's ghost continued to plague the nation.   In
943 he appeared to a mean woman of Kiôto, and directed
that a shrine should be erected to him in that city.   In 947
a boy of six years of age delivered an oracle from him to
the following effect : " All the Thunder-Gods and Demons
to the number of 168,000 have become my servants.   If
any one does evil I have him trampled to death by them.
Pestilence, eruptive diseases, and other calamities have
been placed in my hands by the Supreme Lord of Heaven,

and no Kami, however powerful, can control me. But I
will give help to those who piously express their sorrow."
Eight persons who were present took down this revelation
in writing. At this time the shrine of Kitano at Kioto
was erected to him. But his wrath was not yet wholly
stayed. Further honours were therefore awarded and gifts
made to him. In 1004 the Mikado visited Kitano in person.
At the present day Temmangu is one of the most widely
worshipped of Shinto deities. In 1820 there were twenty-
five shrines to him in Yedo and the neighbourhood.

"*He still hates the wicked, who do not keep the way of
filial piety, and withholds his favour from those who dislike
learning. You must therefore attend strictly to the commands
of your parents and the instructions of your teachers. You
must serve your chief with diligence, be upright of heart,
eschew falsehood, and be diligent in study so that you may
conform to the wishes of Temmangu. If you fail to do so,
you will be cursed by him, and sooner or later incur calamity.
For although the Kami cannot be seen by men, they will
know whether their conduct is good or bad, and whether their
hearts are upright or perverted.*"

Although the life of Temmangu, from which the above
account is taken, was compiled by men of the " Pure
Shinto " school, and though in the preface the importation
of Buddhist and Chinese ideas is stigmatized, it is itself
penetrated with elements of this very kind. The " Supreme
Lord of Heaven " is Chinese, and the Hades to which
Michizane descended is not the Shinto Yomi, but the
Buddhist Jigoku. No doubt the authors found these things
in their materials, and were loth to excise edifying inci
dents, however badly they fitted in with Shinto theology.

The acquaintance of the Japanese with the Chinese cult
of Confucius must have greatly promoted, if it did not
originate the worship of a native God of Learning. It will
be observed that the attribution of nature - powers to

Michizane was a substantial part of the process of deifica
tion, which was based on the alternate influence of the
emotions of gratitude and fear.　　　　　　　．

Nomi no Sukune, the Patron-God of wrestlers, was pro
bably a real human being.　Hitomaro, the Poet-God, was
undoubtedly so.　Another muse of poetry, Sotoori-hime,
belongs to more legendary times, but was probably likewise
a real person.　Iyeyasu, the founder of the last dynasty of
Shoguns, was deified under the title of Tosho Gongen, but
this, like many other similar apotheoses, is, in reality,
Buddhist rather than Shinto.

## II. GODS OF CLASSES.

**Ministers and Attendants of the Sun-Goddess.**—The
application of the hereditary principle to Government
offices has had many vicissitudes in Japan.　When the
country emerges into the light of history, both Court
offices and local chieftaincies were usually transmitted
from father to son.　Among the hereditary institutions of
this kind were the Be.　The Be were Government corpora
tions charged with some special branch of service.　There
were Be of weavers, of farmers, of potters, &c., a Be for the
supply of necessaries to the Palace, an executioner's Be,
and others.　If we imagine a dockyard staff in which the
director and officials belonged to a governing caste, the
artisans being serfs, and the whole having a more or less
hereditary character, we shall have a tolerably correct idea
of a Be.

The Gods of five Be are represented as in attendance on
the Sun-Goddess, and as accompanying Ninigi to Earth
when he was sent down to be its ruler.　These were :—

**Koyane**, ancestor of the Nakatomi* House.　The etymo
logy of Koyane is uncertain.　The worship of this deity
had a special importance, from the fact that he was the

* See Index, *Nakatomi.*

Ujigami* of the Fujihara family, a branch of the Nakatomi, which for many centuries supplied a large proportion of the Empresses and Ministers of State. It would hardly be too much to say that the Fujiharas *were* the Imperial House. The *shintai* of Koyane was a jewel or *shaku*, that is, a tablet borne by Ministers as an emblem of office. Hirata identifies with him a deity named Koto no machi no Kami, or God of Divination. The corresponding deity in the Idzumo myth of Ohonamochi was Ama no hohi. The supposed descendants of this deity had charge of the sacred fire which was handed over by one generation to another with great ceremony.

**Futodama.**—Futodama means great gift or offering. The Imi-be,† his reputed descendants, discharged a number of duties connected with the State religious ceremonies, including the provision of sacrificial offerings.

**Uzume** means " dread female." She was the ancestress of the Sarume, or " monkey female," who performed reli gious dances (*kagura*) at Court and delivered inspired utterances. Hirata identifies this deity with Oho-miya no me (great-palace-female), worshipped as one of the eight Gods of the Jingikwan, or Department of Religion. She represents the chief lady officials of the Palace as a class. Uzume, in announcing to the Sun-Goddess the approach of Susa no wo, discharged one of their duties. From another point of view she is a type of the wise woman, sorceress, or prophetess. She was prayed to for long life, for protection from evil by night and by day, for honours, and for posterity. One of the *norito* splits up Oho-miya no me into five separate deities.

**Ishikoridome** means apparently " the stonecutter." Why should the supposed ancestor of the mirror-makers have received this name ? The circumstance that stone moulds

---

* See Index, *Ujigami*.
† See Index, *Imibe*.

for casting bronze objects have been found in Japan suggests a possible answer.

**Toyo-tama,** "rich jewel," the ancestor of the jewel-makers' Be, requires no explanation.

The *Kiujiki* gives a list of thirty-two deities as forming the Court of Ninigi on his descent to Earth, and adds the names of the noble families who were descended from them. A few of these are nature-deities. Of the remainder some *may* be deified real men, but I prefer to reckon them provisionally along with such class conceptions as Tommy Atkins, John Bull, Brother Jonathan, and Mrs. Grundy.

**Koto-shiro-nushi** is one of those secondary formations in which the personification of nature and the deification of man meet and mingle. As the son and counsellor of the Earth-God and Creator Ohonamochi he is related to the class of nature-deities, while as an individualized type of a class of human beings and as the supposed ancestor of certain noble families he belongs to the current of thought which exalts man to divinity.

*Shiro* in this God's name is for *shiru*, " to know," and so to attend to, to manage, to govern. Koto-shiro-nushi is, therefore, " thing-govern-master." The character and func tions of this deity are not well defined. He was one of the Gods who advised Jingô's famous expedition against Korea, on which occasion he described himself as "the Deity who rules in Heaven, who rules in the Void, the gem-casket-entering-prince, the awful Koto-shiro-nushi." In the Ohonamochi myth he is represented as his father's chief counsellor. Owing to his services in persuading him to transfer the Government of Japan to Ninigi without resistance, he was held in great honour at the Mikado's Court, of which he was considered one of the principal protectors. The Jingikwan included him among the eight Gods specially worshipped by them to the neglect of many more important deities, including even his father, Ohona mochi. In the *Manyôshiu* he is called upon by a lover to punish him if he is insincere in his protestations. In modern times the cult of Koto-shiro-nushi has fallen into decay, while that of his rebellious younger brother, the God of Suha, flourishes greatly. The pious Motoori is much per plexed and grieved by this state of things.

**Sukuna-bikona.**—Another God who is associated with Ohonamochi in myth and worship is the dwarf deity,* Sukuna-bikona (little-prince). He is said to have taught mankind the arts of brewing, magic and medicine, and to have provided medicinal thermal springs, where he is still worshipped. But in modern times his cult has been greatly superseded by that of Yakushi the Indian Esculapius, whose avatar he is supposed to be.

I take Sukuna-bikona to be a deified type of medicine man, a "Father of medicine" in the abstract. But the story related of him† may have some foundation in the history of a real person.

### III. GODS OF ABSTRACT HUMAN QUALITIES.

**Sahe no kami.**—The Sahe no kami are phallic deities. In approaching this subject, it behoves me to walk warily. For, to some writers so repulsive that they shirk even its necessary elucidation, it exercises a fascination upon others which is not conducive to sound reasoning. Has not a President of the Anthropological Institute declared that "so soon as a man begins to study phallicism he goes crazy"? With phallicism we may conveniently associate the corresponding cult of the *kteis.*

In Japan, the phallus symbolizes two distinct, although not unrelated, principles. Primarily, it represents the generative or procreative power, and is recognized in this capacity by myth and custom. By a natural transition it

---

* "There lies in dwarfs a special acquaintance with the healing virtues hidden in herbs."—Grimm, ' Teutonic Mythology.'

† See above, p. 107.

has become the symbol of the more abstract conception of lusty animal life, the foe to death and disease. Hence its use as a magical prophylactic appliance. In Shinto, this latter principle is much the more prominent. It is embodied in the name Sahe no kami, which means " preventive deities." The application of this epithet is clear from the circumstance that in a *norito* they are invoked for protection against the " unfriendly and savage beings of the Root Country," that is to say Yomi or Hades. These by no means imaginary personages are the same as the Ugly Females, the thunders generated from Izanami's dead body and the armies of Yomi of myth.* They represent, or rather are identical with, diseases and other evils associated with death and the grave. Epidemic and contagious diseases are specially intended. Hence the Sahe no kami are also called Yakushin, or " Pestilence Deities," meaning the Gods who ward off pestilence, a phrase wrongly taken in later times to signify the Gods who produce pestilence. The use of the *phallus* and *kteis* for this purpose is primarily magical, and rests on the well-known principle that a symbol possesses something of the virtue of the thing which it represents. The deification of these symbols came later.

In the *norito* entitled Michiahe† there are three Sahe no kami, namely, Yachimata-hiko, Yachimata-hime, and Kunado. The first two of these names mean " eight-road-fork-prince " and " eight-road-fork-princess." Kunado is the " come-not-place," and is, therefore, an equivalent to a notice of " no thoroughfare " addressed to any evil beings who might attempt to pass that way. An alternative form of this word is Funado, or " pass-not-place."

There is a good deal of confusion about the Sahe no kami. Yachimata-hiko and Yachimata-hime are not men tioned in the *Kojiki* or *Nihongi*. The *Kiujiki* has a

* See above, p. 93.
† See Index, *Michiahe.*

Chimata no kami (God of the Crossways), which it says is also termed Kunado no kami, and adds two others named Naga-chiha no kami and Michijiki no kami, both of which names imply a connexion with highways. The *Nihongi* makes five of these deities, adding two to the three of the *Kiujiki*. All are associated in some way or another with Izanagi's descent to Yomi, having been produced either from the articles flung down by him during his flight thence, or when he washed in the sea in order to purify himself from the pollutions contracted during his visit.

These deities had no temples. The festivals in their honour took place at crossways on the four sides of the capital, or at the frontier of the metropolitan province, regularly at the close of the sixth and twelfth months, and at other times upon occasions of emergency. Thus in 735, during an epidemic, the Governor of Dazaifu in Kiushiu was ordered to celebrate a *michi-ahe*, or Road festival, and in 839 the Mikado directed that honours should be paid to the Gods of Pestilence. A ceremony in honour of the Sahe no kami was also performed two days before the arrival of foreign envoys in the capital, in order to guard against the danger of their bringing with them infection, evil influences. or demons from abroad.*

A work entitled ' Fusô Ryakki' states that in 938 Gods were carved in wood and set up face to face along the highways and byways, or female forms were made and set up opposite to males. Children worshipped them boister ously, and made reverent offerings of pieces of cloth and fragrant flowers. They were called Chimata no kami, that is to say "Gods of the Crossways," or Mitama (august

---

* "Before strangers are allowed to enter a district certain ceremonies are often performed by the natives of the country for the purpose of disarming them of their magical powers, of counteracting the baleful influence which is believed to emanate from them, or of disinfecting, so to speak, the tainted atmosphere with which they are supposed to be surrounded." — Frazer's ' Golden Bough,' i. 150.

spirits), a term which in its Chinese form Goryo is still preserved in the name of the great festival (Goryoye) of Gion at Kiôto. The Chimata no kami can be no other than Yachimata-hiko and Yachimata-hime. A later notice speaks of the worship of wooden figures, male and female, provided with sexual organs. Similar figures in stone may still, Hirata says, be seen in the eastern provinces, where they are sometimes mistaken for Jizo, the Buddhist children's God, and honoured in the temples.

The third of the Sahe no kami of the *norito*, namely, Kunado, can be nothing but a simple phallus. Its shape, formed of Izanagi's staff, is consistent with this view. In the Tsujiura, or Cross Roads divination, this God was repre sented by a staff. The same inference is suggested by its association with Yachimata-hiko and Yachimata-hime, who, as we have seen, were unquestionably phallic deities; and also with the peach, which, like Kunado himself, was used by Izanagi for his protection against the evil beings of Yomi. Like the apricot in India and the pomegranate in ancient Greece, the peach is in China and Japan the acknowledged representative of the *kteis*, as the pestle and the mushroom are of the phallus. Peach-wood staves were used in the *oni-yarahi* (demon-expelling) ceremony on the last day of the year. A similar interpretation is, perhaps, applicable to the horseshoes nailed over doors in England which, intended at first to keep out evil spirits, are now meant simply " for luck," in accordance with the tendency for the more special functions of Gods and magical appli ances to become obscured and merged in a hazy, general notion of their beneficence or usefulness. Peach-shaped charms from China figure in a London tradesman's cata logue which has just reached me.

There is a custom, called *sammai*, of scattering rice, which was formerly observed at purification ceremonies, and is kept up at the present day in rooms where there is a new-born child. Hirata tells of a case in which the rice so scattered was found marked with blood-stains, showing, as he infers, that the object of this practice was to drive off demons, not to conciliate them by an offering. I have more than a suspicion that the efficacy of rice for this pur pose, and also of the beans used to drive off demons on the, last day of the year,* is due to a resemblance of this kind.†

The *wo-bashira* (male-pillar) is doubtless only a modified Kunado. This term is applied to the end-post of the railing of a bridge or of the balustrade of a staircase, and is so called from its obviously phallic shape and function. It is a post surmounted by a large knob, and its position com manding the thoroughfare shows that it is intended to arrest the passage of evil beings or influences. It is still to be seen everywhere in Japan, but its meaning is now for gotten. The end-tooth of a comb was also called *wo-bashira*. We now see the significance of Izanagi's selection of this object for converting into a torch in order to light up the darkness of Yomi. In Italy even at the present day the phallus fulfils a similar function. ·

The phallus appears in another form at the festival held in honour of the Sahe no Kami on the first full moon in every year. The *Makura no Sōshi*, written about A.D. 1000, tells us that it was then the custom for the boys in the Imperial Palace to go about striking the younger women with the potsticks used for making gruel on this occasion. This was supposed to ensure fertility. It reminds us of the Roman practice at the spring festival of Lupercalia, alluded to by Shakespeare in his ' Julius Cæsar ' :—

> " Forget not in your speed, Antonius,
> To touch Calphurnia ; for our elders say
> The barren touched in this holy chase
> Shake off their steril curse."

The Japanese novelist and antiquary Kioden, writing

---

* See Index, *Tsuina.*

† Eustathius, the commentator on Homer, points out that the barley-corn denoted the vulva with the writers upon the Bacchic Komuses.

about a century ago, informs us that a similar custom was at that time still practised in the province of Echigo. He gives a drawing of the sticks used for the purpose, of the phallic character of which there can be no doubt. They were called *kedzurikake* (part-shaved), and consisted of wands whittled near the top into a mass of adherent shavings, as in the illustration.

*Kedzurikake* of elder or willow are still made in some places. In Harima, on the 14th day of the 1st month, *kedzurikake* are hung up under the eaves in substitution for the *kadomatsu*, or fir trees placed by the entrance gate at the New Year. In Suwo, *kedzurikake*, made of a thorny tree called *tara*, are placed on each side of the front and back doors at this season, no doubt with the object of averting evil influences. When the *kadomatsu* and other New Year's decorations are removed on the 15th day of the 1st month, they are in many places collected by the boys as material for a bonfire. This is called *dondo* or *sagicho*, and the burning of the *kedzurikake* is a feature of it. In the Yamagata ken, wherever there are stone images of Dosojin, the phallic God of Roads,* the boys at this time make a bonfire of fir trees and straw, and build for themselves a hut beside it. When the people assemble, they come out and fire it. If the dumplings made on the 14th are roasted in this fire and eaten, malignant diseases need not be feared during the ensuing half year. In Hitachi this hut is called the " Hall of the Sai no Kami." The embers are used for re-lighting the domestic fires or kept as charms against pestilence.

* I have before me a picture of a Dosojin. It stands at cross-roads, and is a phalloid natural boulder over which depends a *shimenaka* supported by two bamboos. In front of it are little piles of stones, of which the similar offerings to the Buddhist children's God Jizōsama are doubtless a survival. The modern practice of bringing the Jizō of the neighbourhood and dumping them down before the lodging of a newly-married couple is no doubt a similar case of survival. A custom which began with the Dosojin is continued with the Jizō, which now occupy their place at crossways.

Fire, kindled from *kedzurikake* after prayer, was given out to the people by the priests of Gion in Kioto on the last day of the year. It was transferred to a slow match, and used for rekindling the household fires, the object being to prevent pestilence during the coming year.[*] The mythical burning of a *wobashira* (also a phallic emblem) by Izanagi in Yomi was probably suggested by some such custom.[†] It will be observed that the prophylactic virtue of the phallus has not been forgotten in the *kedzurikake*.

The *kedzurikake* are sometimes described as the *shintai* of Dosojin, and are placed on the domestic altar to be worshipped as his representative. They are also, by a known confusion of ideas, presented to the Gods as offerings. The Ainus of Yezo, who have adopted the *kedzurikake* as the general form of offering to their Gods at all times, and attach to it no phallic signification, were no doubt familiar with this use of it by their Japanese neighbours. It is by them called *inao* or *nusa*, the latter being the old Japanese word for offering. The facility with which such offerings could be prepared by savages must have been a recommendation.

The two cylindrical *shingi*, or "divine sticks," eight or nine inches in circumference and one foot long, thrown to the crowd by the priests of Seidaiji, near Okayama, on the night of the 14th day of the 1st month, and called *o fuku* (luck), to keep off pestilence and bring prosperity, are probably of phallic origin.

The gruel partaken of at the Sahe no Kami festival on the 15th of the 1st month was made of rice, and was coloured with an admixture of the small red bean called *adzuki*.[‡] The bean is a well-known synonym in Japan for

---

[*] We may compare with this an old English custom mentioned by Brand of the priests blessing candles at Candlemas and distributing them to the people, "so that the Divil may fly out of the habitation."

[†] See above, p. 93.

[‡] *Phaseolus radiatus.*

13

the *kteis*. The colour red is also significant. It suggests the ruddy complexion of health caused by an abundance of life-giving blood in the lips and cheeks. Children love this colour. Max Nordau says : " As a feeling of pleasure is always connected with dynamogeny or the production of force, every living thing instinctively seeks for dynamogenous sense impressions. Now red is especially dynamogenous." In ' Œdipus Tyrannus,' the Chorus invoke the aid of ruddy-faced Bacchus against pestilence. In Korea red is a terror to devils. A modern Japanese writer says that red is obnoxious to devils on account of its cheerful appearance.

Small-pox being a *Kijin biō*, or demon-sent disease, the colour red is freely employed in combating it. The candles at the bedside are red, and the clothing of the patient and nurse. The God of Small-pox is worshipped with offerings of red *gohei* (there is here some confusion of ideas) and of red *adzuki* beans. Red paper is hung round the necks of the bottles of *sake* offered to him. Red *papier maché* figures of Daruma are placed near the sick-bed. It is explained that red, being a *yō* (male, bright, positive) colour, is fitted to counteract dark, wintry, negative influences. The potency of red as a charm against small-pox is not unknown to European folk-lore.

Phalli are coloured a bright red, or, what comes to the same thing, gilt. Saruta-hiko, a phallic deity, has a bright red complexion. Torii are painted red. Demons and stage villains have red faces, probably as an indication of great animal vigour.

Griffis, in his ' Mikado's Empire,' tells us that "when by reason of good fortune or a lucky course of events there is great joy in a family it is customary to make *kowameshi*, or red rice, and give an entertainment to friends and neighbours. The rice is coloured by boiling red beans with it. If for any cause the colour is not a fine red, it is a bad omen for the family." There is a modern superstition that if, on the 7th day of the 1st month, a male swallows seven, and a female fourteen red beans, they will be free from sickness all their lives.

The *To-yu-ki*, a work published in 1795, has the following :—

"*In many places along the highway at Atsumi, in the province of Deha, where the cliffs stand up steeply on both sides, shime-naha are stretched across from one cliff to another. Below these shime-naha there are placed skilfully carved wooden phalli fronting the road. They are very large, being seven or eight feet in length and perhaps three or four feet in circumference. I thought this too shocking, and questioned the inhabitants why they did so. Their answer was that it was a very ancient custom. They were called Sai no kami\* and were made afresh every year on the 15th day of the 1st month. As they were local Gods, they were by no means neglectful of them, allowing them to remain even when high officials passed that way. They were not at all, I was told, put up for the amusement of the young folks. Moreover, seeing a number of slips of paper attached to the shime-naha, I inquired what they might be. It appeared that they were fastened there secretly by the women of the place as a prayer for handsome lovers. Truly this is one of those old customs which linger in remote parts. Phalli and ktenes of stone are worshipped by the country-folks in many places as the shintai of their ujigami.*"

The selection of a rocky pass for the erection of these objects, and the association with them of *shime-naha*,† show that their original function, namely, to prevent the passage of evil beings or influences, was not forgotten. The prayers of the women betray a misconception of the proper object of this cult.

---

\* The modern spelling *sai* implies an altered conception of the function of these objects. It means good luck, a vaguer and more general idea than *sahe*, which means prevention (of disease).

† See Index.

Near the end of the *Kogojiui* there is a passage which makes mention of the phallus as a magical appliance. As it has some anthropological interest, I quote it at length :

"*Of yore, in the age of the Gods, Oho-toko-nushi no Kami (great-earth-master-deity), on a day that he was cultivating a rice-field, gave his labourers the flesh of oxen to eat. At this time the child of Mi-toshi no Kami (august-harvest-god) went to that rice-field and spat upon the food, after which he returned and reported the matter to his father. Mi-toshi no Kami was wroth and let loose locusts on that field, so that the leaves of the young rice suddenly withered away and it became like dwarf bamboos. Upon this Oho-toko-nushi no Kami caused the diviners to ascertain by their art the reason of this. They replied that it was owing to a curse sent by Mi-toshi no Kami, and advised him to offer a white pig, a white horse, and a white cock in order to dispel his anger. When amends had been made to Mi-toshi no Kami in the manner directed, the latter replied, saying : ' Truly it was my doing. Take bare stalks of hemp, and make of them a reel with which to reel it, take the leaves and sweep it therewith, take "push-grass"\* of Heaven and push it therewith. Take, moreover, crow-fan\* and fan it, and if then the locusts do not depart, take ox-flesh and place it in the runnels, adding to it shapes of the male stem (phalli). Moreover, strew the banks of earth between the fields with water-lily seeds, ginger, walnut leaves and salt.' When these instructions were carried out the leaves of the young rice became thick again, and the harvest was a plentiful one. This is the reason why at the present day the Department of Religion worships Mi-toshi no Kami with offerings of a white pig, a white horse, and a white cock.*"

The facts quoted in the preceding pages show that there was some confusion between the use of the male and female emblems as non-religious magical appliances and

---

\* The names of plants.

their cult as deities. Primarily they were symbols, next objects of magic. Finally Religion intervened, and by her handmaids Personification and Myth raised them to the rank of deities, consecrating this step still further by devoting a formal ritual to their service. The *kteis* has received somewhat less attention than the phallus. It is no doubt identical with the Yachimata hime of the Michiahe *norito*, and in the *Kojiki*, its representative the peach is dubbed *kami*. But the *Nihongi* in the parallel passage merely speaks of its efficacy in repelling evil spirits, and refrains from deifying or even personifying it.

The circumstance that the Sahe no Kami were worshipped by the roadsides and at c.ossways* led to their being looked upon as guide-Gods and the special friends of travellers. Saruta-hiko, a phallic deity, represented as dwelling at the eight crossways of Heaven, is said to have acted as guide to Ninigi on his descent to earth. He is popularly called Dosojin, or Road-ancestor-deity, and is depicted as of gigantic stature, with a portentously long nose, which (the suggestion is not mine) may perhaps have a phallic morphological signification.

The worship of these deities was extremely popular in ancient Japan. They were much appealed to in divination,† and were prayed to by most travellers when starting on a journey. The phrase *chi buri no Kami* (Gods along the road) means the Sahe no Kami. The Sahe no Kami were the *mitama par excellence*. They were also called *tamuke no Kami* (Gods of offerings) because travellers were in the habit of carrying a *nusa-bukuro* (offering-bag) containing hemp leaves and rice, of which a little was offered to each of them when passing. All unforeseen disasters or illnesses on a journey were attributed to a neglect of the worship of these deities.

---

* Crossways had a special sanctity in many countries. The Hermae of ancient Greece stood at crossways.

† See Index, *Tsuji-ura*.

But a very little advance in enlightenment shows that the sexual instincts need restraint* rather than the stimulus which they must derive from such a cult. So early as A.D. 939 a deity of this kind which stood in a conspicuous position in Kioto, and was worshipped by all travellers, was removed to a less prominent situation. Phallicism ulti mately disappeared from official Shinto. But it lingered long in popular customs, and is not quite extinct even at the present day, especially in eastern Japan. I have myself witnessed a procession in which a phallus, several feet high and painted a bright red, was carried on a bier by a crowd of coolies in festal uniform, shouting, laugh ing, and zig-zagging tumultuously from one side of the street to another. In the lupanars they are honoured by having a lamp of simple construction kept burning before them, and are prayed to by the proprietor for numerous clients. The boys' festival of *dondo*, on the 15th of the 1st month, still retains traces of its phallic origin.†

**Oni.**—*Oni*, or demons, have no individual names. It is clear from the *Kojiki* and *Nihongi* mythical narratives that the *oni* exorcised by means of the peach‡ are the same as the "thunders" and the "armies of Yomi." In other words, they are primarily personified diseases.§ They afterwards lost this specific character. Motoori defines *oni* as *ashiki kami*, or "evil deity." He condemns their identification by the *Wamioshō* with the spirits of the dead. There is a story of a tenth-century hero who cut off the arm of an *oni* and brought it home with him, but was tricked out of it by

* Measures were taken in ancient Greece to check the excesses of the Bacchanalian rites.

† For further evidence on this subject, Dr. Buckley's ' Phallicism in Japan ' (Chicago, 1895), the *Nihongi*, i. 11, and Dr. Griffis's ' Religions of Japan ' may be consulted.

‡ *Nihongi*, i. 30.

§ According to St. Augustine, the devils of Scripture are our passions and unbridled appetites.

the owner, who came to his house in the disguise of an old woman.

The *oni* have red faces, hairy persons, horns, and some times only one eye. They are said to devour men. The modern ideas respecting them are mostly borrowed from Buddhist sources.

**Gods of Good and Ill Luck.**—Among deified human properties we may reckon the Gods of Good and Ill Luck produced when Izanagi washed in the sea after his return from Yomi. Their names, Naobi and Magatsubi, contain the elements *nao*, straight, and *maga*, crooked.

Naki-sahame, the Goddess of weeping, Ta-jikara-wo (hand-strength-male), whose *shintai* is a bow, and Omohi-kane, the thought combiner, are rather mythical personages than deities on the effective list. It is doubtful whether Mari no kami, the foot-ball God, who has three faces, is a personification of skill or a hazy, imaginative recollection of some distinguished player.

The very terrible deity known as Bimbo-gami, the God of Poverty, is of later origin.

# CHAPTER IX.

## THE PRIESTHOOD.

SHINTO illustrates the principle enunciated by Herbert Spencer, that " in early stages of social evolution the secular and the sacred are but little distinguished." The Mikado was at the same time high priest and king. There was no well-marked distinction between secular and religious cere monies. The functionaries who performed the latter had no specially sacerdotal character and no distinctive cos tume. The Jingikwan, or Department of Religion, was simply a Government bureau, and the rites celebrated in its chapel were as much Government proceedings as the issuing of decrees or the collection of taxes. Almost any official might be called upon to discharge religious func tions. The local governors on their appointment made a round of visits for worship to all the shrines in their juris diction. All the principal shrines had State endowments. The word *matsuri-goto*, government, is simply *matsuri*, a religious festival, with the termination *koto*, thing, which adds nothing to its etymological significance. Hirata says that the worship of the Gods is the source of Government —nay, it is Government. The same word *miya* (august-house) was in common use both for shrines and palaces. There was, however, a beginning of a differentiation of sacred and secular functions. The Mikado delegated some of his religious duties to the Nakatomi House, and, as we shall see, other religious duties were hereditary in other families. Thus a Sun-worship Be, or hereditary corpora tion, was established in 577. One version of the myth of Ohonamochi represents him as giving up his authority with the words, " Let the august grandchild direct the public affairs of which I have charge : I will retire and direct secret matters." Evidently we have here an echo of some actual separation of civil and religious authority. Far on into historical times the guardians of the "Great Shrine" of Ohonamochi in Idzumo retained a title (*kuni no miyakko*) which, like that of pontifex at Rome, implied the performance of secular duties. In the reign of Kwammu 782-806) it was found that the local nobility (*kuni no miyakko*), many of whom still acted as governors, neglected their civil functions, on the pretence that their time was occupied by religious duties. A decree was therefore issued that in future no local nobles should hold the office of civil governor.

**The Mikado.**—The chief priest of Shinto is the Mikado himself. Jimmu, the legendary founder of the dynasty, is represented as performing sacrifice in person. Jingo is said to have acted on one occasion as *kannushi*. In his torical times Mikados presided personally over the cere monies of Nihiname, Shinkonjiki, Kanname, and other festivals. Even at the present day the Mikado's priestly functions are not entirely obsolete.

**Nakatomi.**—For many centuries most of the Mikado's sacerdotal functions have been delegated. In the Jimmu legend there is mention of the appointment of a Michi no Omi (minister of the way) as ruler of a festival in honour of Taka-musubi. At the dawn of history we find the Nakatomi hereditary corporation the recognized vicars of the Mikado. Tradition traces their descent from the God Koyane. The most probable etymology of Nakatomi explains it as put for *Naka-tsu-omi*, that is to say, the minister of the middle. Hirata understands by this that the Nakatomi were mediators between the Gods and the Mikado, reciting the Mikado's *norito* to the Gods, and com municating to him their instructions received by divination. In Shinto, however, there was no indispensable sacerdotal mediator. There was nothing to prevent the Mikado, or any one, from holding direct communication with the deities.

A branch of the Nakatomi House, which in the seventh century took the name of Fujihara, was famous in later history. Up to 1868 the nominal Prime Ministers and Regents were invariably taken from it. The officials of the Jingikwan, or Department of Religion, were largely Nakatomi, as were also the Chokushi, or Imperial envoys to the local shrines. Yet the Nakatomi were hardly what we should call a priestly caste, like the Levites or Brahmins. The local priesthood were not ordinarily Nakatomi, and many of this House held purely civil appointments.

The Jingikwan took precedence even of the Dajokwan, or Grand Council of State. It was presided over by an official called Haku. He had the supreme control of all the Shinto State ceremonies, and authority over the local priesthood. He was assisted by a vice-president, and had a staff of Imbe, Urabe, and clerks. The Haku took the place of the Mikado when the latter was prevented by illness from offering his daily prayers. From the eleventh century up till quite recently the Haku was one of the Shirakaha family, who trace their descent from the Mikado Kwazan (985-6), and enjoyed the title of *Ó*, or prince. As explained above, the Nakatomi were practically the Imperial family.

**Imbe.**—The Imbe were another hereditary corporation, descended, it was said, from the God Futodama (great-gift). Their chief business was to prepare the offerings, and their name Imi-be (*imi* means avoidance, or religious abstinence) has reference to the care with which they avoided all sources of impurity in doing so. The Imbe, after praying to the Mountain-God, cut down with a sacred (*imi*) axe the trees required for shrines, or at least began the work, leaving it to be completed by ordinary workmen. They also dug the foundations with a sacred (*imi*) mattock. Two of the *norito*, namely, the Ohotono and the Mikado, were read by them. It was also their duty, at least at one period, to deliver the regalia to the Mikado at his coronation.

A Chinese description of Japan, written long before the *Kojiki* or *Nihongi*, gives the following account of what were in all probability the predecessors of the Imbe :—

"*They (the Japanese) appoint a man whom they call an 'abstainer.' He is not allowed to comb his hair, to wash, to eat flesh, or to approach women. When they are fortunate, they make him presents, but if they are ill, or meet with disaster, they set it down to the abstainer's failure to keep his vows, and unite to put him to death*"[*]

This is a description of a typical ascetic. In the Imbe of historical times we have the closely allied idea of scru pulous attention to religious purity. But they were not celibates or vegetarians except *ad hoc* when a festival was impending, and so far from neglecting the care of their persons, strict cleanliness was incumbent upon them.

**Urabe.** — A third hereditary religious corporation in ancient Japan was that of the diviners or Urabe. They are mentioned in the *Nihongi* under the date A.D. 585. They were divided at a later period into four branches, belonging respectively to the provinces of Iki, Tsushima, Idzu, and Hitachi. Twenty of these diviners were attached to the Jingikwan. It was their duty to decide by the deer's shoulder-blade or tortoise-shell divination such matters as were referred to them by the superior officials of the department. Urabe were despatched to the pro vinces to fetch the rice which was used in the Ohonihe ceremony. It was also their duty to take away and throw into a river the *harahe-tsu-mono*, or offerings of purification. For many centuries this office has been in the hands of the Yoshida family, whose exorbitant pretensions fill Hirata with indignation.

---

[*] For an account of similar priests or medicine men in many other countries, see 'The Golden Bough.' The Nazirite (Numbers vi.) is their Jewish counterpart.

The Nakatomi,, Imbe, Urabe, and Ô (princes of the Shirakaha House), constitute what are called the Shi-sei, or four surnames of the Jingikwan.

**Saishu.**—The high-priest at Ise was called Saishu, or worship-master. This office was hereditary in the Fujinami family, a branch of the Nakatomi.

**Daiguji.**—The high-priests of Atsuta, Kashima, Usa, and Aso were termed Daiguji, or great-shrine-functionaries. There was a Dai gu-ji at Ise, subordinate to the Saishu. This office was also hereditary.

**Kannushi.**—Kannushi is for *kami-nushi*, that is, deity-master. It is the most general word for Shinto priest. Properly it is only the chief priest of the shrine who is so designated. The Kannushi are appointed by the State. In early times their duties were performed by officials who already held secular posts. In 820 a decree was made prohibiting this practice, as it was found that such Kannushi neglected the care of the shrines of which they had charge. At the present time many Kannushi combine other avoca tions with their sacerdotal functions. The title may even be 'conferred on a layman by way of honour. The late famous actor Danjuro was an example. Kannushi are not exempted from military service. They are not celibates, and may return to the laity whenever they please. It is only when engaged in worship that they wear the distinc tive dress of their office, which consists of a loose gown, fastened at the waist with a girdle, and a black cap called *eboshi*, bound round the head with a broad white fillet. Even this is not really a sacerdotal costume, but simply one of the old official dresses of the Mikado's Court. No special education is necessary for the discharge of the duties of a Kannushi, which consist in the recital of the annual prayers and in attending to the repair of the shrine.

**Hafuri or Hori.**—The hafuri are priests of an inferior grade. This word, though now written with Chinese cha racters which mean "prayer-official," is connected with the verb *hoburu* or *hafuru*, to slaughter, to throw away. *Homuru*, to bury, is another form of the same word. The *Nihongi* says that in 642, at the bidding of the village hafuri, horses and cattle were killed as a sacrifice in order to procure rain. The high-priest of the God Minagata at Suha is styled Oho-hafuri (great hafuri). At the festival of this God the heads of seventy-five deer are presented as offerings, while the flesh is eaten by the priests. If others than the priests wish to partake of it without pollution, they get chopsticks from the priests which answer this purpose. These facts point to the conclusion that the hafuri were originally sacrificers. Offerings of animal food were common in ancient times.

The term *hafuri-tsu-mono* (flung-away-things) is used as equivalent to *harahi-tsu-mono* (expiatory offerings), and is also applied to funeral offerings.

**Negi.**—This was another name for priests of lower rank. The word is probably connected with *negafu*, to pray. The negi of Miha and Mikami are called imi-bi (fire-avoid) because they are specially careful to avoid impurity in respect to fire. They will not use the same fire for cooking as other people.

**Miyakko.**—The hereditary chief priests of Kitsuki in Idzumo and the affiliated shrine of Hinokuma in Kii were called *miyakko*, a term which originally meant "local governor."

**Priestesses.**—There are several categories of priestesses attached to Shinto shrines. Their mythical prototype is Uzume, the Goddess who danced before the cave into which the Sun-Goddess retired when insulted by her brother Susa no wo.

**Saiwō.**—At the beginning of every reign, an unmarried princess of the Imperial blood was chosen by divination and consecrated to the service of the Sun-Goddess at Ise. For three years previous to taking up her duties she went every first day of the month to an *imi-dono* (sacred-hall) and worshipped towards the Great Shrine of Ise. This was called the *mi-tose no mono-imi*, or "three years' purity." The Saiwo is also called Itsuki no miya or Saigu, sacred or worship-palace—properly the name of her residence. There was a similar appointment to the shrine of Kamo, where the Ujigami of the Mikados was worshipped. She was also called Saiwo, and both herself and her residence were termed Sai-in, that is, "sacred hall." These offices were discontinued early in the thirteenth century.

**Kamu no ko** (God-child).—The Kamu no ko were also called *miko*, august child, or sometimes *mono-imi*, that is, avoiders of (impure) things. They were young girls attached to all the principal shrines for the performance of the kagura dances, and cooking the food for offerings. They also occasionally became the medium of divinely inspired utterances. From the *Yengishiki* we learn that at that time there were a number of kamuko in the palace for the service of the numerous shrines there. They were appointed at the age of seven or upwards from the families of the local nobles (miyakko). Their places were supplied by others when they got married.

At Kumano in Tango there are certain families whose female children are devoted to the service of the Shrine of Susa no wo. When a girl is born, a divine arrow flies down and sticks in the roof-tree of the house. At the age of four or five, the child thus designated is sent to wait on the God. Though the place is among the mountains, such children are never harmed by wild beasts. When they begin to show signs of puberty, a great dragon comes and glares fiercely at them. Thereupon they return home.*

**Ichi-ko.**—The ichi-ko or agata-miko are parish mediums who are called in when communication is desired with the spirits of the dead. They are sometimes called adzusa miko, from their use of a bow of adzusa wood in their

* See Hirata's *Koshiden*, xviii. 23.

conjurations. There are also strolling ichiko of indifferent character, who for a trifling consideration will throw open the gates of the spirit world. These are modern institutions.

**Kamube.**—The peasants who tilled the glebe lands of the shrine and their place of residence were alike termed kamu-be (God-corporation). The present city of Kobe takes its name from one of these. In the times when slavery was a Japanese institution there were slaves attached to some of the shrines.

Recent statistics give the number of Shinto priests as 14,766. Their maximum salary is about £20 per month.

# CHAPTER X.

## WORSHIP.

RELIGIOUS conduct includes worship, morality in so far as it has obtained the sanction of religion, and ceremonial purity.

The term worship applies both to the forms of courtesy and respect towards human beings and of reverence for the Gods. Indeed the latter is not a separate kind of worship, but is composed almost exclusively of the same elements in a new application. Nearly everything in the worship of the Gods is borrowed from the forms of social respect. It is sometimes maintained that these forms, before they become a part of religious ritual, pass through an intermediate stage, namely, the worship of the dead, whether as ghosts or dead ancestors. This view is based on the hypothesis that Gods were originally deceased men. It cannot well apply to Shinto, where all the Great Gods are nature-deities. When a Japanese greets the rising Sun by bowing his head, he does so because that is already with him an habitual form of respect. No doubt he honours the dead in this way as well as the living. But the occasions for the worship of the living so far outnumber those of paying respect to the dead that the latter may be regarded as a negligible quantity in the formation of the habit. There is surely nothing to prevent a man who had never worshipped ghosts or ancestors from transferring direct to nature-deities forms of respect arising out of the relations of living men.

Several practices of worship, such as clapping the hands for joy and the avoidance of contamination by touching a dead body, have no meaning in the case of the cult of the dead.

Worship has a secondary but most important function. It is addressed not only to the Gods but to our fellow-men. It is a means of communicating religious thoughts and emotions from man to man and from one generation to another.

**Obeisance.**—The simplest and most universal mode of showing reverence to the Gods is by bowing. In Shinto it is the custom to bow twice before and after praying or making an offering. The word *ogamu*, to pray or worship, means to bend. Kneeling is also practised—one of the *norito* has the phrase " bending the knee like a deer "—but is less common. Squatting (*kashikomaru*) is another form of obeisance.

**Clapping Hands.**—Clapping hands (*kashihade*), primarily a sign of joy, as it still is in our nurseries, was in ancient times in Japan a general token of respect. The *Nihongi**\* states that the Ministers clapped hands in honour of the Empress when she ascended the throne. More recently, this form was confined to divine worship. One of the *norito* has the rubric, " Offer three cups of sake, clap hands, and retire." The number of hand-clappings was minutely prescribed in the old ritual. In some ceremonies it was done thirty-two times. A silent hand-clapping (*shinobi-te*) was sometimes directed. It seems possible that in Shinto at least this was the origin of the simple folding of the hands in prayer, common to so many nations, and explained by anthropologists as the attitude of an unresisting sup pliant holding out his hands for the cord.

**Other Gestures.**—Respect may also be shown by raising objects to the forehead or placing them on the head (*ita-daku*), as the most honourable and important part of the body. This is done in the case of the implements used in the greater divination. Among less formal gestures used in worship are reverent upward looks (*awogu*), an almost

* II. 395.

instinctive practice, which has its root in the idea that
Heaven is the dwelling-place of the Gods, and has certainly
nothing to do with ghost-worship.

I cannot point to any case of prostration or of uncovering
the feet as a form of Shinto worship. Uncovering the
head is known in modern times, but I do not find it
mentioned in the older ritual.

**Offerings.**—As the attitude of devotees towards myth
varies according to their intelligence and culture, some
distinguishing, more or less clearly, between the truth
which it adumbrates and its fictitious embroidery, and
others accepting it indiscriminately as absolute fact, as
the image is by some regarded simply as an aid to devo
tion and by others as a true representation of the God, or
even as the God himself, so in the case of offerings, a
double current of opinion is to be traced. There are
always worshippers who well know that the God does not
eat the food, drink the wine, or wear the clothing which is
laid upon his altar ; but there are also more literal-minded
people who cling, in the face of cogent evidence to the
contrary, to the idea that in some ill-defined way he does
benefit physically by such offerings. A story in the
*Konjaku Monogatari* tells how a boy, possessed of superior
insight, could see the devils carrying away the offerings of
the purification ceremony. Even Hirata, a highly educated
man, thought that food-offerings lost their savour in a way
that is inexplicable by natural causes. Incense and burnt-
offerings are adapted to the mental capacity of worshippers
of this class.* The true reason for making offerings,
whether to Gods or to the dead, is to be sought elsewhere.
Men feel impelled to do something to show their gratitude
for the great benefits which they are daily receiving, and
to conciliate the future favour of the powers from whom

---

* The old Hebrew idea (Genesis viii. 21) was that the food actually reached
God in the form of the fragrant fire-distilled essence, and thus gratified him as
an agreeable gift. Hastings, ' Dict. of the Bible.'

they proceed.  Offerings are part of the language by which the intention of the worshipper is manifested to Gods and men.  It is in this rather than in any supposed actual benefit that their chief value consists.  The *norito* state explicitly that the offerings were symbolical.  They are called *iya-jiro no mitegura*, or offerings in token of respect.  There is frequent mention of " fulfilling the praises " of the Gods by plenteous offerings.  Symbolic gifts are, of course, not confined to religion.  In ancient Greece a gift of earth and water indicated a surrender of political independence.

It is on the recognition of the symbolical value of offerings that the practice of substituting humaner, cheaper, or more convenient articles rests.  Shinto has many illus trations of this principle.

I shall only mention Herbert Spencer's view that " the origin of the practice of making offerings is to be found in the custom of leaving food and drink at the graves of the dead, and as the ancestral spirit rose to divine rank, the refreshments placed for the dead developed into sacrifices."  It must stand or fall with his general theory of the origin of religion, of which the reader will form his own judg ment.  I would suggest that the earliest offering was rather a portion of the ordinary meal set apart in grateful recog nition of the source from which it came.

I find little or nothing in Shinto to bear out Jevons's opinion that " the core of worship is communion.  Offerings in the sense of gifts are a comparatively modern institution both in ancestor-worship and in the worship of the Gods."  Communion is, of course, out of the question in the case of the various offerings of clothing and implements.  Even in the case of food-offerings there is no evidence in Shinto of a " joint participation in the living flesh and blood of a sacred victim."[*]

The general object of making offerings is to propitiate the God.  There are several cases in the *norito* where they

* Robertson Smith, ' Religion of the Semites,' p. 345.

are made by way of reward for their services or in bargain for future blessings.* Some are expiatory, and are made with the object of absolving the worshipper from ritual impurity. These are called *aga-mono*, or " ransom things."

Offerings were frequently duplicated, no doubt in order that one set at least of the things offered should be free from chance pollution.

Offerings were sometimes personified, and even deified, as in the Jimmu legend,† where the food-offering is styled Idzu-uka no me, sacred-food-female. Most of the *shintai* were originally nothing more than offerings.

Shinto offerings are of the most varied description. The Gods being conceived of as beings animated by human sentiments, it is inferred that anything which would give pleasure to men is suitable for offering to a God.

*Food and Drink.*—The primary and most important form of offering is food and drink. The Jimmu legend, a very ancient document, speaks of none but food-offerings. The word *nihe*, an element in the names of some of the great festivals, means food-offerings. The central feature of the most solemn rite of Shinto, namely, the *oho-nihe*, was the offering of rice and sake to the Gods by the Mikado on his accession to the throne. The *norito* add clothing, and the *Yengishiki* a great variety of other articles. There are several instances in history of the substitution of cloth for an older food-offering. Under food are included rice, in ear and in grain, hulled and in husk, rice cakes, fruit, sea-ear, shell-fish, vegetables, edible seaweed, salt, sake, water, deer, pigs, hare, wild boar, and birds of various kinds. In 642 horses and cattle were sacrificed in order to produce rain. But even at this early period such sacrifices were condemned. They were no doubt a revival in a case of national emergency of a practice which under Buddhist influence had become more or less obsolete. There are

---

* See Index, *Toshigohi*.
† See above, p. 119.

numerous indications that animal sacrifices were very common in the most ancient times. In the *Yengishiki* period offerings of four-footed animals or their flesh were confined to four services, namely, that of the Food-Goddess, of the Wind-Gods, of the Road-Gods, and that for driving away maleficent deities.

There is no evidence in the older Shinto records of the use of incense or of burnt-offerings, nor is any special im portance attached to the blood of slaughtered animals.

White being considered an auspicious colour, white animals were frequently selected for sacrifice.

At the present time the daily offerings made to the Sun-Goddess and the Food-Goddess at Ise consist of four cups of *sake*, sixteen saucers of rice and four of salt, besides fish, birds, fruits, seaweed, and vegetables. The annual offerings at the tomb of the first Mikado, Jimmu, are products of mountain, river, and sea, including *tahi* (a fish), carp, edible sea-weed, salt, water, *sake*, *mochi* (rice-cake), fern-flour, pheasants, and wild ducks.

*Clothing.*—The clothing of the ancient Japanese con sisted of hemp, *yuju* (a fibre made of the inner bark of the paper mulberry), and silk. All these materials are repre sented in the Shinto offerings enumerated in the *Yengishiki*. Silk, however, was at this time still somewhat of a novelty, and, therefore, religion being conservative, it takes a less conspicuous place. But hemp and bark-fibre, with the textiles woven from them, are very common offerings. They were more convenient than perishable articles of food for sending to shrines at a distance from the capital, and as cloth was the currency of the day, it was a convenient substitute for unprocurable or objectionable articles. In the *Yengishiki* so many ounces of fibre or so many pieces of cloth are prescribed, but at a later period a more specialized and conventional form, called *oho-nusa* (great-offering), came into use. The *oho-nusa* (p. 214) consists of two wands placed side by side, from the ends of which depend a quantity of

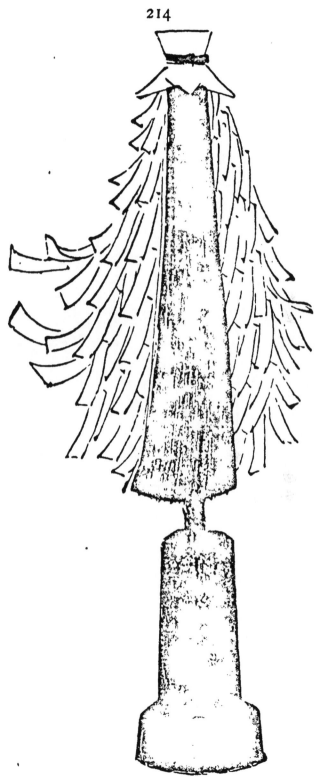

214

hempen fibre and a number of strips of paper.[*]   One of the wands is of the *cleyera japonica*, or evergreen sacred tree.  The other is a bamboo of a particular species.   Their use is con nected with an old Japanese rule of etiquette that presents to a superior should be delivered attached to a branch of a tree, the object being doubtless to mark a respectful aloofness

of the giver from the receiver.  The paper slips represent the *yufu*, or mulberry-bark fibre.   The use of *yufu* for clothing having become more or less obsolete, owing to the introduc tion of cotton, paper, which in Japan is made of the same

---

* Reminding us of Homer's στέμμα θεοῖο, which consisted of tufted wool attached to a wand (σκῆπτρον).   The ancient Jews made offerings of wool.

material, was substituted for it. The *oho-nusa* are still em
ployed on important occasions, but for general use they are
now replaced by the well-known *gohei* (p. 215), in which the
hemp and one of the wands are omitted. Another form of
*nusa*, called *ko-nusa* (little *nusa*) or *kiri-nusa* (cut-*nusa*), con
sists of paper with leaves of the sacred tree chopped up and
mixed with rice. Travellers in ancient times carried this
mixture with them in a bag and made offerings of it to the
phallic deities along their way. It was also used when in
danger of shipwreck. The same system of "accommode-
ments avec le ciel" is further illustrated by the substitution
of the still more inexpensive hemp leaves for the original
hempen fibre or fabric. If, it is argued, the God does not
really eat the food or wear the clothing placed on his altar,
a few grains of rice or a few leaves of hemp will answer
the purpose of expressing the sentiments of the worshipper
just as well as more costly gifts.

There were sometimes sets of coloured *gohei*—blue, yellow,
red, white, and black. The *awo-nigi-te* (blue-soft-articles)
and *shira-nigi-te* (white-soft-articles) consisted of hemp
and bark fibre respectively.

*Tama-gushi* are often mentioned. I take it that in this
combination *tama* means gift or offering, not spirit or jewel,
as is taught by some modern Japanese authorities. *Kushi*
means skewer. The *tama-gushi* are twigs of the sacred
evergreen tree (*sakaki*) or of bamboo, with tufts of *yufu*
attached. They are, in short, a simple form of *nusa* or
*gohei*. They have a striking resemblance to the ἱκτηρίοις
κλάδοισιν (suppliant branches) mentioned in the opening
lines of 'Œdipus Tyrannus' and explained by Jebb as
"olive branches wreathed with fillets of wool." In one
*Nihongi* myth, Susa no wo is said to have planted *kushi* in
the rice-fields of his sister, the Sun-Goddess, "by way of
claiming ownership," says a commentator. Compare with
this the following quotation from Hakluyt's 'Historie of
the West Indies': "Every one [of the Caribs] encloseth his

portion [of ground] onely with a little cotton line, and they account it a matter of sacriledge if any pass over the cord and treade on the possession of his neighbour, and hold it for certayne that whoso violateth this sacred thing shall shortly perish."

Along with the alteration in the form of the *nusa* to the present *gohei* there came a change in the mental attitude of the worshipper. Originally mere offerings, they were at length, by virtue of long association, looked upon as repre sentatives of the deity. Scholars like Motoori and Hirata denounce this view as a corruption of later times, but it is no doubt at present the prevailing conception. Hepburn's Japanese dictionary knows no other. It is illustrated by the fact that instead of the worshipper bringing *gohei* to the shrine, these objects are now given out by the priest to the worshipper, who takes them home and sets them up in his private *Kami-dana* (God-shelf) or domestic altar.

A further step is taken when it is believed that on festival occasions the God, on a certain formula, called the *Kami-oroshi*, or "bringing down the God," being pronounced, descends into the *gohei* and remains there during the cere mony, taking his departure at its close. In the vulgar Shinto of the present day this belief in a real presence of the God is associated with hypnotism.* Akin to the belief in an actual presence of a deity in the *gohei* is their modern use in the purification ceremony, when they are flourished over or rubbed against the person to be absolved of ritual uncleanness or to dispel any evil influences which may have attached themselves to his person. Like the Homeric στέμμα and the host, they were occasionally used for the protection of the bearer. At the present time a *gohei-katsugi*, or *gohei* bearer, is synonymous with a superstitious person.

Skins of oxen, boar, deer, and bear were sometimes offered to the Gods.

* See Index, ' Inspiration.'

*Jewels* (*tama*) were much worn by the ancient Japanese nobility as ornaments for the head or as necklaces and bracelets. They consisted of round beads, tubes (*kuda-tama*), and comma-shaped objects (*maga-tama*) of chalcedony, jasper, nephrite, chrysoprase, serpentine, steatite or crystal. Jewels occur sometimes in the lists of Shinto offerings.

*Mirrors.*—The ancient Japanese mirrors did not greatly differ from those in use at the present day. They were made of a mixed metal, which is described in the myths as " white copper," and were sometimes round and sometimes eight-cornered. The mirror figures frequently in the old records. Mirrors are among the presents made by a female chieftain to a Mikado, and from a King of Korea to another Mikado.* The mirror was primarily an offering, and not to the Sun-Goddess only.† Mirrors were presented to, and even constituted the *shintai* of other Gods as well. In the *Tosa Nikki* (A.D. 935) the author relates that during a storm, an offering of *nusa* having proved unavailing, he bethought him of some more acceptable gift. " Of eyes I have a pair," said he, " then, let me give the God my mirror of which I have only one. The mirror was accordingly flung into the sea, to my very great regret. But no sooner had I done so than the sea itself became as smooth as a mirror."

Mirrors do not appear among the periodical offerings enumerated in the *Yengishiki*, which consisted chiefly of perishable articles. They belonged to a separate class called *shimpō*, or divine treasures, which were not set out on the altar but stored in the treasury of the shrine.

*Weapons.*—Swords were also among the permanent trea sures of the shrine. Wonderful stories are related of them. One which was stolen by a thief is said to have left him and returned to the treasury of its own accord. Swords were

---

* *Nihongi*, i. 193, 251.
† See above, p. 70.

made *shintai*, and even deified.* The God worshipped at Atsuta was the sword Kusanagi, found by Susa no wo in the great serpent's tail, and the God of Isonokami was the sword called Futsu no Mitama (spirit of fire?) given by the Sun-Goddess to Jimmu. I have no doubt that these were originally "divine treasures," which owed their deification to long association with the God. A sword is one of the regalia at the present day.

The principle of substitution is illustrated by the models of swords prescribed as offerings in the *Yengishiki*. I have seen on the top of Ohoyama, sacred to a Goddess named Sekison (Iha-naga-hime?), a pit containing many hundreds of tiny wooden swords which had been deposited there as offerings.

Other weapons which figure as offerings are spears, spear-heads, shields, and bows and arrows.

Agricultural implements, bells, pottery, reels for reeling yarn, are also mentioned. It was the custom, in the case of these and other durable offerings, to offer the same objects again and again.

*Human sacrifices* formed no part of the State Shinto religion as described in the ancient records. But there are several indications of the existence of this practice in still older times. Human sacrifices to river-Gods have been already mentioned. We have seen that when a Mikado died a number of his attendants were buried alive round his tomb, from which it may be inferred that considerations of humanity would not have prevented similar sacrifices to the Gods. Cases are also recorded of men being buried alive in the foundations of a bridge, a castle, or an artificial island. These were called *hito-bashira*, or human pillars. The offerings of *kane-hito-gata* (metal-man-form), so often mentioned in the *Yengishiki*, were perhaps by way of substitution for human victims. It is

---

* Agamemnon's sword was worshipped in Greece in the time of Pausanias.

significant that the Gods of water-distribution (*mikumari*), that is, the river-Gods, are specially distinguished as their recipients. Similar human effigies, gilt or silvered, formed part of the *oho-harahi*, or absolution offerings. In this case they were intended as ransom for the offenders whose ritual guilt was to be expiated. They were touched with the lips or breathed upon before being offered. Peach-wood or paper effigies might be substituted, and in later times articles of clothing or anything which had been in contact with the person to be absolved. These last were called *nade-mono* (rub-thing) or *aga-mono* (ransom-thing). When in danger of shipwreck the hair might be cut off and offered, on the principle of a part for the whole, as ransom to the Dragon-God. The *Kogo-jiui* applies the term *aga-mono* to the hair and nails of Susa no wo, which were cut off by the other Gods. The principle of ransom is also illustrated by the following extract from the *Shinto Miomoku* (1699):—

" *At the festival of Nawoye, held at the shrine of Kokubu in the province of Owari on the 11th day of the 1st month, the Shinto priests go out to the highway with banners and seize a passer-by. They wash and purify him, and make him put on pure clothing. He is then brought before the God. A block, a wooden butcher's knife, and chopsticks for eating flesh are provided. Separately a figure is made to represent the captive. It is placed on the block with the captured man beside it, and both are offered before the God. They are left there for one night. The next morning the priests come and remove the man and the effigy. Then they take clay, and, making it into the shape of a rice-cake, place it on the captive's back, hang a string of copper cash about his neck, and drive him away. As he runs off, he is sure to fall down in a faint. But he soon comes to his senses. A mound is erected at the place where he falls down, and the clay rice-cake deposited on it with ceremonies which are kept a profound mystery by the priestly house. Of late years couriers have been caught and subjected to purification. This was put a stop to. The custom is celebrated yearly, so that nowadays everybody is aware of it, and there are no passers-by. Therefore the priests go to a neighbouring village and seize a man. If they catch nobody on the 11th, they bring in a man on the 12th"*

The *Nawoye* (rectification) festival had probably the same intention as the *Harahi*, namely, to obtain absolution from ritual impurity, and the captive is therefore apparently a scape-goat. As readers of Mr. Frazer's 'Golden Bough' need not be told, the custom has numerous parallels in European folk-lore. There is some difficulty in applying the principle of substitution for an actual human sacrifice to a custom which was in force so recently. It does not appear probable that it could have descended from such a remote antiquity as the time when real human sacrifice was known in Japan. Might not the instinct of dramatic make-believe alone account for it? Confucius condemned the practice of offering effigies of men on funeral occasions because he thought it led to the substitution of living victims.

*Slaves.*—Another form of human offerings was the dedication of slaves to the service of a shrine. Such slaves were called *kami-tsu-ko*, and are to be distinguished from the *kamube*, who were freemen. The gift by the legendary Yamatodake to a shrine of a number of Yemishi (eastern savages) whom he had captured is to be understood in this sense. There is a more historical instance in the *Nihongi,* under the date A.D. 469, when a seamstress was presented to the shrine of Ohonamochi. In 562 a man was allowed to be given over to the *hafuri* as a slave for the service of the Gods instead of being burnt alive for a criminal offence committed by his father.

*Horses.*—Presents of horses to shrines are often men-

tioned.  They were let loose in the precinct.  At the
present day albinos are selected for this purpose, white
being considered an auspicious colour.  Wooden figures
might be substituted by those who could not afford real
horses.  At the festivals of Gion and Hachiman men
riding on hobby-horses (*koma-gata*) or with a wooden
horse's head attached to their breasts formed part of the
procession.  They no doubt represented riding-horses for
the deity.  In more recent times the further step was

taken of offering pictures of horses.  This practice became
so common that special buildings, called *emado* (horse-
picture-gallery) were erected for their accommodation.
But they contained many other pictures as well.  The
*emado* of Kiyomidzu in Kioto and of Itsukushima in the
Inland Sea are very curious collections of this kind.  They
correspond to the *ex-voto* churches of Roman Catholic
countries.

*Carriages.*—The Mikoshi, or carriage of the God (pp. 224,
225), in which his *shintai* is promenaded on festival occa
sions, is usually a very elaborate and costly construction.  It
is carried on men's shoulders to a *tabi no miya* (travel-shrine)

or *reposoir* and back again to the shrine. The confusion in many minds between the *shintai* and the *mitama* is illustrated by the fact that a standard modern dictionary speaks of the Mikoshi as containing the God's *mitama*.

*Shrines.*—A shrine is a species of offering. Whatever may be the case in other countries, in Japan the shrine is not a development of the tomb. They have no resem blance to each other. The tomb is a partly subterranean megalithic vault enclosed in a huge mound of earth, while the shrine is a wooden structure raised on posts some feet above the ground. The Japanese words for shrine indicate that it is intended as a house for the God. *Miya*, august house, is used equally of a shrine and of a palace, but not of a tomb, except poetically, as when the *Manyōshiu* speaks of one as a *toko no miya*, or " long home." *Araka*, another word for shrine, probably means " dwelling-place." In *yashiro*, a very common word for shrine, *ya* means house and *shiro* representative or equivalent. There is evidence* that this word comes to us from a time when the *yashiro* was a plot of ground consecrated for the occasion to repre sent a place of abode for the deity. The analogy of the Roman *templum* will occur to the classical scholar. The *himorogi* (p. 226), a term which has been the subject of some controversy, was probably, as Hirata suggests, at first an enclosure of *sakaki* twigs stuck in the ground so as to represent a house. It is probable that in all these cases the make-believe preceded any actual edifice, and was not a substitute for it.

There is a somewhat rare word, namely *oki-tsuki*, properly a mound, which is applied to both tombs and shrines. Old sepulchral mounds have frequently a small shrine on their summit.

The Shinto shrine is by no means so costly an edifice as its Buddhist counterpart. The *hokora*,† as the smaller

* *Nihongi*, ii. 293.
† See illustration in Chapter XIV.

shrines are called, are in many cases so small as to be easily transportable in a cart. Even the great shrines of Ise (pp. 228, 229) are of no great size and of purposely plain and simple construction. In 771 a "greater shrine" had

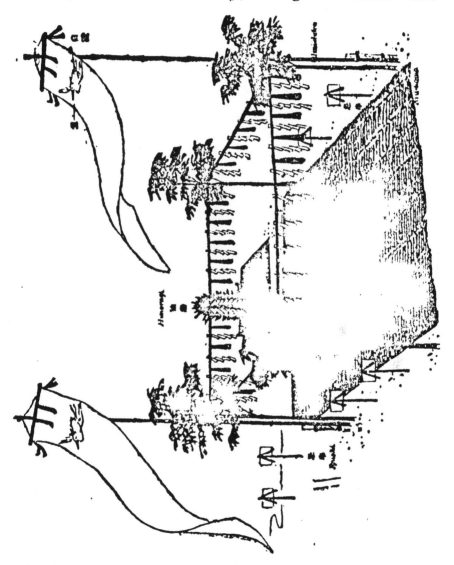

only eighteen feet frontage. Some of the more important *yashiro* have smaller buildings attached to them, such as an *emado*, or gallery of votive pictures; a *haiden*, or oratory, where the official representative of the Mikado performed

his devotions, and a stage for the sacred pantomimic dance.
A number of smaller shrines (*sessha* or *massha*) dedicated
to other Gods are usually to be seen within the enclosure.
No accommodation is provided for the joint worship of the
congregation of believers, which is indeed exceptional.
The individual worshipper stands outside in front of the
shrine, calls the attention of the deity by ringing a gong
provided for the purpose, bows his head, claps or folds his
hands, puts up his petition, and retires. A large box
stands conveniently for receiving such small contributions
of copper cash as he may make.

In many shrines more than one deity is worshipped.
These are called *ahi-dono no kami*, that is to say, deities
of a joint shrine. They may, like Izanagi and Izanami,
have some mythical connexion with each other or they may
not. The *Yengishiki* enumerates 3,132 officially recognized
shrines. Of these 737 were maintained at the cost of the
Central Government. Some had permanent endowments of
lands and peasants. Many minor shrines existed in all
parts of the country. The shrines are classed as great and
small, the respective numbers being 492 and 2,640. They
differed in the quantity of offerings and in the circumstance
that in the former case the offerings were placed on an
altar and in the latter on the ground. Thirty-six shrines
were situated in the palace itself. The most important
deities worshipped here were eight in number, comprising
five obscurely differentiated Musubi, the Goddess of Food,
Oho-miya-no me, and Koto-shiro-nushi. There were also
several Well-Gods, a Sono no Kami, a Kara no Kami
(Korean God), a Thunder-God, a pair of *sake* deities, and
others of whom little is known.

In enumerating the officially recognized shrines through
out the rest of the country the *Yengishiki* unfortunately,
in the great majority of cases, does not name the God, but
only the locality where the shrine was situated, as when
we speak of Downing Street, meaning the collective

I 2

officialdom of the place. This is in accordance with the impersonal habit'of the Japanese mind already referred to. Strange to say, in some even of the most popular shrines, the identity of the God is doubtful or unknown. Kompira is a conspicuous example. According to some he is a demon, the alligator of the Ganges. Others say that Buddha himself became "the boy Kompira" in order to overcome the heretics and enemies of religion who pressed upon him one day as he was preaching. The mediæval Shintoists identified him with Susa no wo. More recently it has been declared officially that he is really Kotohira, an obscure Shinto deity, whose name has a resemblance in sound to that of the Indian God. His popularity has been little affected by these changes.*

In 965 a selection of sixteen of the more important shrines was made to which special offerings were sent. These were as follows :—

| Name of Shrine. | Province. | God or Gods Worshipped. |
| --- | --- | --- |
| Ise. | Ise. | Sun-Goddess and Food-Goddess. |
| Ihashimidzu. | Yamashiro. | Hachiman, Jingo. |
| Kamo. | Do. | ? |
| Matsunowo. | Do. | Thunder-God. |
| Hirano. | Do. | Probably Gods of the Cooking Furnace and New Rice. |
| Inari. | Do. | Food-Goddess. |
| Kasuga. | Yamato. | Koyane and his wife, Take mika-dzuchi, Futsunushi. |
| Ohoharano. | Yamashiro. | Do. |
| Miha. | Yamato. | Ohonamochi. |
| Oho-yamato. | Do. | Do. |
| Isonokami. | Do. | Futsu no mitama (a deified sword). |
| Hirose. | Do. | Food-Goddess. |
| Tatsuta. | Do. | Wind-Gods. |
| Sumiyoshi. | Settsu. | Sea-deities. |
| Nifu. | — | Doubtful. |
| Kibune. | Yamashiro. | Rain-dragon-God. |

* Murray's 'Japan,' fifth edition, p. 50.

In 991 there were added the three following :—.

| Name of Shrine. | Province. | God or Gods Worshipped. |
|---|---|---|
| Yoshida. | Yamashiro. | Same as Kasuga. |
| Hirota. | Settsu. | Sun-Goddess's aratama. |
| Kitano. | Yamashiro. | Temmangū. |

In 994 there was added

| Name of Shrine. | Province. | God or Gods Worshipped. |
|---|---|---|
| Mume no Miya. | Yamashiro. | Ancestor of Tachibana family. |

The next to be added was

| Name of Shrine. | Province. | God or Gods Worshipped. |
|---|---|---|
| Gion. | Yamashiro. | Susa no wo. |

The number was finally raised to twenty-two in 1039 by the addition of

| Name of Shrine. | Province. | God or Gods Worshipped. |
|---|---|---|
| Hiye or Hiyoshi. | Yamashiro. | Ohonamochi. |

Proximity to the capital no doubt influenced this selec tion. Idzumo, Kashima, Katori, Usa, Suha, and other important shrines are omitted. All the principal deities, however, are included in this list.

At the present day there are 193,476 Shinto shrines in Japan. Of these the great majority are very small and have no priests or revenues. Capt. Brinkley, in his ' Japan and China,' gives the following list of the ten most popular shrines in Japan at the present day : " Ise, Idzumo, Hachiman (Kyoto), Temmangu (Hakata), Inari (Kyoto), Kasuga (Nara), Atago (Kyoto), Kompira (Sanuki), Suitengu (Tokyo), and Suwa (Shinano)."

Very many houses have their *kamidana* or domestic shrine, where the ujigami, the ancestor, and the trade-God, with any others whom there is some special reason for honouring, are worshipped.

*Tori-wi.*—The approach to a Shinto shrine is marked by one or more gateways or arches of the special form shown in the illustration (p. 233) and known as *tori-wi.* This word means literally "bird-perch," in the sense of a hen roost. By analogy it was applied to anything of the same shape, as a clothes-horse, or the lintel of a door or gateway. As an honorary gateway, the *tori-wi* is a continental institution identical in purpose and resembling in form the *turan* of India, the *pailoo* of China, and the *hong-sal-mun* of Korea. When introduced into Japan at some unknown date (the *Kojiki* and *Nihongi* do not mention them) the Japanese called them *tori-wi*, which then meant simply gateway, but subsequently acquired its present more specific application. It sometimes serves the purpose of marking the direction of a distant object of worship.*

*Hyaku-do ishi.*—Near the front of the shrine may some times be seen a *hyaku-do ishi*, or hundred-time-stone, from which the worshipper may go back and forward to the door of the shrine a hundred times, repeating a prayer each time.

A *sori-bashi* or *taiko-bashi*, representing the mythical floating bridge of Heaven (the rainbow), is also to be seen at the approach to some shrines.

**Prayer.**—Private individual prayer is seldom mentioned in the old Shinto records, but of the official liturgies or *norito* we have abundant examples in the *Yengishiki* and later works. The authors are mostly unknown, but they were no doubt members of the Nakatomi House. Their literary quality is good. Motoori observes that the elegance of their language is an offering acceptable to the Gods. The Sun-Goddess is represented in the *Nihongi* as expressing her satisfaction with the beauty of the *norito* recited in her honour.

The *norito* are addressed sometimes to individual deities, sometimes to categories of deities, as " the celebrated Gods "

---

* See a contribution by Mr. S. Tuke to the Japan Society's *Transactions*, vol. iv., 1896-7, and a paper by the present writer in the *T.A.S.J.* for December, 1899. Mr. B. H. Chamberlain holds a different view, which is stated in the *Journal* of the Anthropological Institute, 1895, and in ' Things Japanese,' fourth edition.

or " the Gods of Nankaido," and sometimes to all the Gods without exception. They contain petitions for rain in time of drought, good harvests, preservation from earthquake and conflagration, children, health and long life to the sovereign and enduring peace and prosperity to his rule, the safety of his ambassadors to foreign countries, the suppression of rebellion, the repulse of invasion, success to the Imperial arms, and general prosperity to the Empire. Sometimes the Mikado deprecates the wrath of deities whose services had been vitiated by ritual impurity, or whose shrines had suffered from neglect or injury.

The phrase " fulfilling of praises," which occurs frequently in the *norito*, must not be taken literally. It is really equivalent to " show all due honour to," and usually applies to the offerings which were made in token of respect. There is very little of praise in the ordinary meaning of the word. The language of the *norito* presents a striking contrast to the profusion of laudatory epithets and images of the Vedas, or the sublime eulogies of the Psalms of David. The only element of this kind is a few adjectival prefixes to the names of the Gods, such as *oho*, great ; *take*, brave ; *taka*, high ; *haya*, swift ; *toyo*, rich ; *iku*, live ; *yori*, good, and perhaps one or two more.

The *do ut des* principle of offerings is plainly avowed in some of the *norito*.

Besides petitions we find also announcements to the Gods, as of the appointment of a priestess, the bestowal on the deity of a degree of rank, and the beginning of a new reign. The Mongol invasion was notified to Ise in 1277 with the happiest results.

The *Yengishiki* contains no *norito* addressed to deceased Mikados, but several examples of this class, due no doubt to Chinese influence, have come down to us from the ninth century. In 850 Jimmu was prayed to for the Mikado, who was dangerously ill, and who died soon after. In the same year, " evil influences " (the Mikado's illness ?) were attributed to his wrath, and envoys despatched to his tomb, in order to ascertain whether he might not have been offended by some pollution to it. The Empress Jingo was prayed to in 866 under similar circumstances. Other *norito* announce to the preceding Mikado the accession of a new sovereign or the appointment of a Prince Imperial.

The *norito* contain few petitions for which we might not easily find parallels in modern Europe, but a comparison with Christian, Jewish, or even Mohammedan and Buddhist formulæ reveals enormous lacunæ in the ancient Japanese conception of the scope of prayer. Moral and spiritual blessings are not even dreamt of. Such prayers as " that we may live a godly, righteous, and sober life," " to grant us true repentance and His Holy Spirit," are foreign to its character. " Lead us not into temptation " and " Thy will be done " are conspicuously absent. No Shinto God is petitioned to " endue the Sovereign with heavenly gifts," nor that " after this life he may attain everlasting joy and felicity." Indeed, there is no reference anywhere to a future life—a significant fact, in view of the circumstance that human sacrifices at the tombs of great men were at one time common. The commonly received opinion that the latter indicate a belief in a future state is, perhaps, after all, erroneous. Nor does any one beseech a Shinto deity to send down on the priesthood the healthful spirit of his grace.

Numerous specimens of *norito* will be found in Chap. XII. In connexion with the attempted revival early in the last century of the pure Shinto of ancient times, Hirata composed a book of prayer entitled *Tamadasuki*, not for official or temple use, but as an aid to private devotion. It was not printed until some years after his death, and I doubt whether it was ever much used even by Shinto devotees. Notwithstanding the author's professed abhorrence of Buddhism and his condemnation of Chinese religious notions, the *Tamadasuki* owes much to these sources.

He instructs his followers to "get up early, wash the face and hands, rinse the mouth, and cleanse the body. Then turn towards Yamato, clap hands twice, and bow down the head " before offering their petitions.

Prayers to the Shinto Gods, even at the present day, are mostly for material blessings. Anything more which they contain may be confidently set down to Buddhist influence. There are prayers on reclaiming a new piece of ground, building a house, sowing a rice-field, prayers for prosperity in trade and domestic happiness, prayers promising to give up *sake*, gambling, or profligacy (Buddhist), thanks for escape from shipwreck or other danger, &c. Sometimes the prayer is written out on paper and deposited in the shrine, perhaps accompanied by the petitioner's hair or a picture having some reference to the subject of his prayer. When it is answered, small paper *nobori* (flags) are set up at the shrine or its approaches. A common prayer at the present day is for " Peace to the country, safety to the family, and plentiful crops."

**Oaths and Curses.**—The *Nihongi* mentions several cases of Heaven or the Gods being appealed to for the sanction of an oath. Thus in 562 an accused person declares : " This is false and not true. If this is true, let calamity from Heaven befall me." In 581 tribes of Yemishi pro mised submission to the Mikado, saying : " If we break this oath, may all the Gods of Heaven and Earth and also the spirits of the Emperors destroy our race." In 644 the Mikado made an oath appealing to the Gods of Heaven and Earth, and saying : " On those who break this oath Heaven will send a curse and Earth a plague, demons will slay them, and men will smite them." The author of the *Nihongi*, however, is grievously open to the suspicion of adorning his narrative liberally with rhetorical ornaments of Chinese origin. The following is an example of a non-religious oath said to have been made by a Korean king in 249 : " If I spread grass for us to sit on, it might be burnt with fire; if I took wood for a seat, it might be washed away by water. Therefore, sitting on a rock, I make this solemn declaration of alliance." A curse pronounced over a well in 456 has likewise no religious quality. It is simply "This water may be drunk by the people only : royal persons alone may not drink of it." The instructions of the Sea-God to Hohodemi, "When thou givest this fish hook back to thy brother, say, 'A hook of poverty, a hook of ruin, a hook of downfall,'" are a kind of curse. On the whole, oaths and curses of a religious character are rare in Japanese literature. Profanity is almost unknown. A mild appeal to the "three holy things" (of Buddhism) or to the Sun, or a wish that divine punishment (*bachi*) may strike one's enemy, are almost the only things of the kind. And they are infrequent. Probably this is due to the want of a deep-seated sentiment of piety in the Japanese nation. Such expressions as " Thank God," " Good-bye," " Adieu," " God forbid," are also rare, whether in speech or in litera ture. The Mohammedans, with their continual use of the name of Allah, are the antipodes of the Japanese in this respect.

**Rank of Deities.**—A system of official ranks, borrowed from China, was introduced into Japan in the seventh century. There were at one time forty-eight different grades, each with its distinct costume, insignia, and privi leges. The first notice of deities being granted such ranks occurs in 672, when we are told that three deities were "raised in quality" on account of useful military informa tion supplied by their oracles. This practice became systematized in the period 749-757, and was very prevalent for several centuries longer. A rain of volcanic ashes which fell in many of the eastern provinces in 838 was attributed by the diviners to the jealousy of a Goddess, the true wife of a God, and mother by him of five children, at a step of official rank granted by the Mikado to a younger rival. Tantæ ne animis cælestibus iræ! In 851 Susa no wo and Oho-kuni-nushi received the lower third rank and in 859 were promoted to the upper third rank. The Mikado Daigo, on his accession in 898, raised the rank of 340 shrines. In 1076 and 1172 wholesale promotions of deities took place. After this time the custom fell into neglect, owing partly to the circumstance that many of the Gods had reached the highest class and could not be promoted any further. Several of the most important deities were not honoured in this way. The Sun-Goddess and the Food-Goddess were among this number. The same deity might have different ranks in different places. The lowness of the ranks with which the inferior deities were thought to be gratified is rather surprising. It throws a light on the mental attitude of the Japanese towards them. Beings who could be supposed 'to take pleasure in a D.S.O. or a brevet majority must have seemed to them not very far exalted above humanity.              .

**Kagura.**—This word is written with two Chinese cha-racters which mean " God-pleasure." It is a pantomimic dance with music, usually representing some incident of the mythical narrative. Uzume's dance before the cave to which the Sun-Goddess had retired is supposed to be its prototype. Important shrines have a stage and a corps of trained girl-dancers (*miko*), for the purpose of these repre sentations. Kagura was also performed in the Naishidokoro (the chamber in the Palace where the Regalia were kept), and under Chinese influences became a very solemn function, in which numerous officials were concerned. Many kinds of music, song, and dance are included in this term. It was the parent in the fourteenth century of the No, a sort of religious lyrical drama, and less directly of the modern popular drama.

Some authorities say that the music of the Kagura con sisted at first of flutes made by opening holes between the joints of a bamboo, of wooden castanets, and of a stringed instrument made by placing six bows together.

**Pilgrimages.**—Paying visits is a recognized mode of showing respect to Gods as it is to men. The Mikado himself formerly paid frequent visits to the shrines of Kioto and the vicinity, and in all periods of history embassies were continually despatched by him to the great shrines of the Empire. The private worshipper, besides visiting the shrine of his local deity, generally makes it his business, at least once in his lifetime, to pay his respects to more distant Gods, such as those of Ise, Miha, Ontake, Nantai (at Nikko), Kompira, Fujiyama, Miyajima, &c. Intending pilgrims associate themselves in clubs called *Ko*, whose members each contribute five sen a month to the pilgrimage fund. When the proper time of year comes round, a certain number of members are chosen by lot to represent the club at the shrine of their devotion, all expenses being defrayed out of the common fund. One of the number who has made the pilgrimage before acts as leader and cicerone. As a general rule the pilgrims wear no special garb, but those bound for Fuji, Ontake, or other high mountains may be distinguished by their white clothes and sloping broad hats. While making an ascent, they often ring a bell and chant the prayer, " May our six senses be pure and the weather fair on the honourable mountain."* Many thousand pilgrims annually ascend Fuji, and over 11,000 paid their devotions at Ise on a recent New Year's day. Almost all Japanese cherish the hope of visiting this shrine at least once in their lives, and many a Tokio merchant thinks that his success in business depends largely on his doing so. Pilgrimages are an ancient institution in Japan. It is recorded that in the ninth month of 934, 10,000,000 pilgrims of all classes visited the shrines of Ise.

Boys and even girls often run away from their homes and beg their way to Ise. This is regarded as a pardonable escapade.

When an actual visit to a shrine is inconvenient or

* See Index, *Rokkon Shōjo.*

impossible, the worshipper may offer his devotions from a distance. This is called *em-pai*, or distant worship. Special shrines are provided in some places where the God will accept such substituted service. Processions may be joint formal visits of the worshippers to the God's shrine, but they oftener consist in attending him on an excursion from it to some place in the neighbourhood and back again. They much resemble in character the carnival processions of Southern Europe.

**Circumambulation.**—The Brahmanic and Buddhist ceremony of *pradakchina*, that is, going round a holy object with one's right side turned to it, is not found in Shinto. The principle, however, on which it rests—namely, that of following or imitating the course of the Sun—is recognized in the Jimmu legend. Jimmu says :* " If I should proceed against the Sun to attack the enemy, I should act contrary to the way of Heaven......Bringing on our backs the might of the Sun-Goddess, let us follow her rays and trample them down." It is difficult to reconcile with this a passage in the *Kojiki*† where it is counted unlucky for the Mikado to travel from East to West, because in so doing he must turn his back upon the Sun.

Horses presented to shrines were led round them eight times.

* *Nihongi*, i. 113.
† Chamberlain's *Kojiki*, p. 312.

# CHAPTER XI.

## MORALS, LAW, AND PURITY.

In the previous chapter we dealt with the positive side of religious conduct. We have now to examine its negative aspect, namely, those prohibitions which fall under the general description of morality and ceremonial purity.

**Morals.**—Before proceeding to examine the relation of morals to religion in Shinto, let us note some general con siderations. Right conduct has three motives: first, selfish prudence; second, altruism, in the various forms of domestic affection, sympathy with others and respect for their rights, public spirit, patriotism and philanthropy ; and third, the love of God. Conduct which is opposed to these three sanctions is called in the case of the first folly, of the second crime, and of the third sin; to which are opposed prudence, morality, and holiness. With the infant and the savage the first motive predominates. With advancing age in the individual, and civilization in the race, the second and third assume more and more importance. All but the lowest grades of animals have some idea of prudential restraint. Many are influenced by the domestic affections, while the higher, and especially the gregarious species, have some rudiments of the feeling of obligation towards the com munity, on which altruistic morality and eventually law are based. But in the lower animals, and even in many men, the religious sanction is wanting.

Right conduct may usually be easily referred to an origin in one or other of these three classes of motives. The duty of refraining from excess in eating and drinking belongs primarily to the first, the care of children and the avoidance of theft, murder, or adultery to the second, acts of worship and abstinence from impiety and blasphemy to the third. There is, however, a tendency for these motives to encroach on each other's provinces without relinquishing their own. Acts which belong at first to one category end by receiving the sanction of the other motives. Drunkenness, at first thought harmless, is soon recognized as folly, though harming nobody but the drunkard himself. It is eventually seen to be also a crime against the community, and last of all a sin in the eyes of God. Criminal Law is a systematic enforcement of the rights of others by adding prudential motives for respecting them. It also punishes blasphemy and heresy, no doubt for the protection of the interests of the community against the curse which such offences bring down. With ourselves religion condemns not only direct offences against the Deity as in the first three command ments, but selfish folly, and throws its ægis over the rights of our neighbour, by prohibiting theft, murder, adultery, lying, disrespect to parents, &c. Can it be doubted that these were already offences before the ten commandments were delivered from Mount Sinai?

There is no stronger proof of the rudimentary character of Shinto than the exceedingly casual and imperfect sanction which it extends to altruistic morality. It has scarcely anything in the nature of a code of ethics. Zeus had not yet wedded Themis. There is no direct moral teaching in its sacred books. A schedule of offences against the Gods, to absolve which the ceremony of Great Purification was performed twice a year,* contains no one of the sins of the Decalogue.† Incest, bestiality, wounding, witchcraft, and

---

* See Index, *Ohoharahi.*

† I quote here, not from any religious document, but from a poem of the *Manyōshiu,* a solitary instance of a religious stigma being attached to lying :

> " If, while not loving,
> I said that I loved thee,
> The God who dwells
> In the grove of Uneda in Matori
> Will take note of it."

certain interferences with agricultural operations are the only offences against the moral law which it enumerates. The *Kojiki* speaks of a case of homicide being followed by a purification of the actor in it. But the homicide is repre sented as justifiable, and the offence was therefore not so much moral as ritual.* Modern Japanese boldly claim this feature of their religion as a merit. Motoori thought that moral codes were good for Chinese, whose inferior natures required such artificial means of restraint. His pupil Hirata denounced systems of morality as a disgrace to the country which produced them. In ' Japan,' a recent work published in English by Japanese authors, we are told that " Shinto provides no moral code, and relies solely on the promptings of conscience for ethical guidance. If man derives the first principles of his duties from intuition, a schedule of rules and regulations for the direction of every day conduct becomes not only superfluous but illogical."

But although there was little religious sanction of morality in ancient Japan, it by no means follows that there was no morality. We have seen that there are moral elements in the character of the Sun-Goddess as delineated in myth.† Law, which is the enforcement by penalties of a minimum altruistic morality, certainly existed. A Chinese author, in a description of Japan as it was in the later Han period (A.D. 25-220), says that "the wives and children of those who break the laws are confiscated, and for grave crimes the offender's family is extirpated The laws and cus toms are strict." In 490 we hear of two men being thrown into prison for crimes. The Mikado Muretsu (488-506) is said to have been fond of criminal investigation. The *Nihongi* condemns theft, robbery, rebellion, and non-pay ment of taxes, none of which matters is taken formal cognizance of by Shinto. Without some law, unwritten and ill-defined though it was, and unequal and fluctuating

* Ch. K. 291.
† See above, p. 129.

in its application as it must have been, the Japanese could not possibly have reached even the moderate degree of organized government which we find them enjoying at the dawn of their history.

The earliest so-called legislation which we meet with is embodied in a proclamation issued by the Regent Shotoku Taishi in A.D. 604. On examination these "laws" prove to be a sort of homily addressed to Government officials, recommending harmony, good faith, a respect for Buddhism, obedience to the Imperial command, early rising, decorum, disinterestedness in deciding legal cases, fidelity to one's lord, and benevolence to the people. In 645 a "beginning of regulations" was promulgated. It relates to the status of slaves and their children. In the following year a set of rules was issued regulating the construction of tombs forbidding human sacrifice in honour of the dead, &c. In the same year laws were promulgated dealing with dis honesty, retaining slaves belonging to other people, bringing plaints of adultery before the authorities without having the evidence of three credible witnesses, &c. "Severe penalties" are threatened in case of their infraction. In 681 a sumptuary law in ninety-two articles was enacted. In 682 flogging was limited to 100 blows : in 689 a book of laws was distributed to all the local authorities ; and in 701 the code known as the Taihorio was promulgated. The latter was borrowed from China, and no doubt Chinese influences had much to do with the more partial legislation which preceded. Shotoku Taishi's advice to officials is thoroughly Chinese. But the examples quoted show that such enactments were not made without reference to the wants of Japan. It may be inferred from Shotoku Taishi's mention of "legal cases," and from the regulation of pro cedure in cases of adultery, that there was already in existence a body of unwritten common law by which a rude sort of justice was administered. Prisons are men tioned more than once in the seventh-century records.

Dr. Weipert says :* " There are in the *Kojiki* and *Nihongi*
numerous instances of arbitrary punishment inflicted by
rulers, chieftains, &c., or of private revenge, but nothing
shows the existence of fixed punitive laws or conventions.
If we confine ourselves to the prehistoric times of
Japan, we find in them no other traces of conceptions of a
binding law than those handed down to us in the rituals
dedicated to the Gods. It was indeed the power of the
ruler which held the community together, but the idea of
the society being subject to lawful restraint was to be found
only in the religious sentiments of the people. To the
extent of these sentiments alone can it be said that a law
fully regulated community and a consciousness of such
existed in those days. Now since we take criminal law to
be the publicly regulated reaction of a community against
all acts of its members which are detrimental to the common
interest, we can scarcely hesitate to describe the Ohoharahi†
as the first source of Japanese criminal law." This is a
special application to Shinto of the principle laid down in
general terms by Dr. Pfleiderer that " the beginnings of all
social customs and legal ordinances are directly derived
from religion." Max Muller has expressed himself nearly
to the same effect.

I hardly think that the Japanese facts bear out these
views. It may be admitted that before the seventh cen
tury there were no " fixed punitive laws or conventions in
Japan." But between this and mere " arbitrary punishment " or " private revenge " there is a middle term, and I
submit that it was precisely to this stage that the Japanese
nation had arrived at this time. A common law was in
existence, unwritten and ill defined, leaving much room
for arbitrary procedure and punishments, but yet a reality.
It dealt, as there is evidence to show, with matters so
essential to the welfare of the community as treason, rebel-

* Quoted by Dr. Florenz in *T. A. S. J.*, xxvii. p. 56.
† See Index, *s.v.*

lion, and robbery, none of which is so much as mentioned in the Ohoharahi. Indeed we could scarcely expect to find such offences noticed in it, as the application of the criminal law in these cases places the guilty persons far beyond the reach of a purifying process.

In an organized community like the ancient Japanese there must have been many torts recognized by public opinion. We know that adultery and dishonesty were punishable. Yet Shinto takes no notice of them. The only civil wrongs singled out for religious denunciation relate to agriculture. The ancient authorities enumerate, among the misdeeds of Susa no wo, " breaking down the divisions of rice fields," " filling up irrigation ditches,"* " sowing seed over again," with one or two other offences of a similar kind, and the Ohoharahi includes them in its schedule of sins which require absolution. But surely rights of property (we can recognize germs of them in the lower animals) are long antecedent to religion, and offences against them are recognized as offences against man before they became sins against God.

Moreover, the Ohoharahi is wanting in the first essential of a criminal law. It provides no fixed punitive sanction. It is true that the culprit was in some cases obliged to supply at his own cost the necessary offerings for the cere mony, and that practically this amounted to a fine. The original intention, however, was not to punish the offender, but to avert the wrath of the Gods. And it must be remembered that individual cases of purification were exceptional. For the offences of the nation generally, which it was the main object of the Ohoharahi to absolve, no punishment was practicable, or indeed dreamt of. The Ohoharahi fines of purificatory offerings may have contri buted to a system of criminal law, but they were certainly not its main source. The case of Japan seems to prove

* In ancient Egypt, which presents numerous analogies with Japan, inter-ference with the irrigation channels was deemed an offence against the deity.

that, in many cases at least, altruistic morality, even in the crystallized form of law, is in advance of religion. And may we not point to cases in our own country where religion withholds its sanction until the law has become well established? The following extract from the *Nihongi* shows that the distinction between criminal law and offences against the Gods, with their respective punishments, was recognized at an early period :—

"*A.D. 404 Winter, 10th month, 11th day. The Imperial concubine was buried. After this the Emperor, vexed with himself that he had not appeased the divine curse, and had so caused the death of the Imperial concubine, again sought to ascertain where the fault lay. Some one said: 'The Kimi of the Cart-keepers went to the Land of Tsukushi, where he held a review of all the Cart-keepers' Be, and he took along with them the men allotted to the service of the Deities. This must surely be the offence.' The Emperor straightway summoned to him the Kimi of the Cart-keepers and questioned him. The facts having been ascertained, the Emperor enumerated his offences, saying: 'Thou, although only Kimi of the Cart-keepers, hast arbitrarily appropriated the subjects of the Son of Heaven. This is one offence. Thou didst wrongfully take them, comprising them in the Cart-keepers' Be after they had been allotted to the service of the Gods of Heaven and Earth. This is a second offence.' So he imposed on him the expiation of evil and the expiation of good, and sent him away to Cape Nagasa, there to perform the rites of expiation. After he had done so, the Emperor commanded him, saying: 'Henceforward thou mayest not have charge of the Cart-keepers Be of Tsukushi' So he confiscated them all, and allotted them anew, giving them to the three Deities*"

√ **Ceremonial Purity.**—Things displeasing to the Gods are called by the Japanese *tsumi* (guilt), and the avoidance of such things by their worshippers is called *imi* (avoidance). As Motoori points out, the *tsumi* of Shinto comprises three distinct things, namely, uncleanness, sin or crime, and calamity. The distinction between ceremonial impurity and moral guilt (of certain specific kinds) was probably obscure to the ancient Japanese. Certain cala mities are included among *tsumi* because they were looked upon as tokens of the displeasure of the Gods for some offence, known or unknown. All *tsumi* involved religious disabilities or punishments.

Uncleanness holds a far more important place in Shinto than moral guilt. As in the Mosaic law, it assumes various forms. Actual personal dirt was considered disrespectful to the Gods, as we see by the frequent mention of bathing and putting on fresh garments before the performance of religious functions. The Ohoharahi includes the committing of nuisances among the offences to be absolved by it.

**Sexual Immorality and Uncleanness.**—It was probably because the consummation of a marriage was thought to defile the house in which it took place that a special nuptial hut was in the most ancient times provided for this purpose. The same idea is illustrated by the custom which existed until quite recently of sousing with buckets of water on New Year's Day young men who had been married during the preceding year. According to a novel called ' Hino-deshima ' it is now the bride who is thus saluted while on her way to her husband's house. The bridegroom is treated by the boys of the neighbourhood to volleys of stones which break his paper windows. In later times sexual intercourse generally caused temporary uncleanness. Virgins were selected as priestesses and as dancers before the Gods. But there were no vows of perpetual chastity, and they married in due time just like other girls. The *Nihongi* mentions a case of the appointment of a princess as priestess having been cancelled on account of her unchastity. A modern Japanese writer says : " At Ise to-day Laïs opens her doors to the pilgrim almost within sight of the sacred groves. To accept her invitation does not disqualify him in his own eyes nor in the eyes of any one else for the subsequent achievement of his pious purpose. A single act of lustration restores his moral as well as his physical purity." Perhaps this puts the matter too strongly. Those shameless wights Yajiro and Kidahachi, the heroes of the *Hizakurige*, were troubled with scruples in this matter, which were not, however, invincible.

With such ideas of uncleanness it is not surprising that Shinto never had a marriage ceremony. No Shinto or other priest is present. We must, therefore, take with some reserve Max Muller's statement that marriage had a religious character from the very beginning of history. It is to be noted, however, that in modern times Susa no wo and his wife Inadahime are thought to preside over connubial happiness, and that something of a religious flavour is contributed to the marriage ceremony by setting out on a stand (*shimadai*) figures of the old man and old woman of Takasago, spirits of two ancient fir-trees, who are the Darby and Joan of Japanese legend.

Uncleanness includes bestiality, incest of parent and child, of a man with his mother-in-law or stepdaughter,[*] but not of brothers and half-sisters by the father's side. Unions with a sister by the mother's side were unlawful and offensive to the Gods, but they are not specially enumerated in the Ohoharahi schedule.

In 434 Prince Karu, then Heir to the Throne, fell in love with his younger sister by the same mother. At first he dreaded the guilt and was silent. But after a time he yielded to his passion. The next year, in the height of summer, the soup for the Mikado's meal froze and became ice. The diviner said, "There is domestic disorder (incest)." This led to the discovery of Prince Karu's crime, but, as he was successor to the Throne, he was not punished, and his

---

[*] Compare Leviticus xviii. 17.

sister only was sent into banishment. After his father's death, however, the ministers and people refused him their allegiance, and he ultimately committed suicide, or, according to another version of the story, went into exile. It is difficult to say whether the religious or the merely moral element predominates in such a case. The portent by which the Prince's crime was followed and the application to the diviners indicate that the crime was thought offensive to the Gods. On the other hand, banishment is a civil form of punishment, and the idea that the offence might bring disaster on the community was probably at the root of the indignation which it caused. Nor is it to be forgotten that there is another non-religious reason for the law against incest. Consanguineous unions are notoriously unfavourable to the propagation of a numerous and healthy progeny, and therefore to the welfare of the community. The 'Chüen,' a Chinese work written several centuries before the Christian era, says : " When the man and woman are of the same surname, the race does not continue." But in China too, the religious sanction of the prohibition of incest is not absent. It is one of those primarily non-religious sexual taboos, having for their object to place a check on masculine tyranny over the weaker sex and the premature, promiscuous, and excessive indulgence of the sexual passion which even savages find to be fatal to the welfare of the individual and the community, and whose transcendent importance and the difficulty of enforcing them by law lead to be reinforced everywhere by religious terrors. The prohibition of unions between brothers and sisters by the mother's side—that is, practically of the full blood—and not of those of the half-blood by the father's side, may be partly due to the circumstance that the former are more commonly brought up together, and a check on immature and consanguineous intercourse was more necessary in their case. This taboo very likely dates from a period when parentage was reckoned chiefly by maternity.

Vulgar licentiousness is not mentioned in the more ancient books as causing ceremonial impurity.

Interference with the virgin priestesses was not only a source of uncleanness, but was in some cases severely punished. The *Nihongi* states that in A.D. 465

"*Katabu and an Uneme were sent to sacrifice to the Deity of Munagata. Katabu and the Uneme, having arrived at the altar-place, were about to perform the rites, when Katabu debauched the Uneme. When the Emperor heard this, he said, 'When we sacrifice to the Gods and invoke from them blessings, should we not be watchful over our conduct?' So he sent Naniha no Hidaka no Kishi to put him to death. But Katabu straightway took to flight and was not to be found. The Emperor again sent Toyoho, Yuge no Muraji, who searched the districts of that province far and wide, and at length caught and slew him at Awi no hara in the district of Mishima*"

Here it is primarily the offence against the Gods which is reprobated.

As in the Mosaic law, menstruation and child-birth were regarded as sources of uncleanness.* The custom of pro viding a special hut for parturient women has been already noted.† In 811 the wife of a Kannushi was delivered of a child close to the enclosure of the Shrine of the Goddess of Food at Ise. Both husband and wife had to perform an Ohoharahi. After that time no pregnant woman was admitted within the *tori-wi* of this shrine. In 882 a Prince was sent as Envoy to Ise because a bitch had had puppies within the precincts of the Imperial Palace. Several days' religious abstinence had to be observed in consequence. Until recently births and deaths were prohibited on the sacred island of Itsukushima in the Inland Sea.

---

* Leviticus xii. 1 ; xv. 19.
† See above, p. 113. The *couvade* was unknown.

**Disease, Wounds, and Death** caused uncleanness.*
The death of a relation, attending a funeral, pronouncing
or executing a capital sentence, touching the dead body of
a man or beast, even eating food prepared in a house of
mourning, all involved various degrees of ritual impurity.

Before the Nara period of Japanese history it was the
custom on the death of a sovereign to remove the capital
to a fresh site, no doubt for the sake of purity.   The Ainus
of Yezo destroy huts in which a death has taken place.
The modern Japanese custom of turning upside down the
screen which is placed round a corpse is perhaps a much
attenuated survival of the same idea.   In 801 a Great
Purification ceremony was performed, because a dead dog
had been discovered under one of the palace buildings.
The same ritual was celebrated in times of pestilence, when
a death took place close to the palace and on the Mikado's
putting off mourning.   if any one died within the precincts
of a shrine, no festival could be held there for thirty days.
A disability of five days was prescribed in the case of a
dog or other beast dying there.   At the present day lucifer
matches are advertised as "fit for sacred purposes"; that
is, they contain no phosphorus which is made of bones, and
therefore unclean. Leprosy, owing to its reputed contagious
character, is specially mentioned as a cause of uncleanness.†
Wounds, whether inflicted or received, were objectionable,
not so much on grounds of humanity, as because of their
offensiveness.   The *Nihongi* relates that in A.D. 404 the
God Izanagi expressed by the mouth of one of his priests
his dislike for the stench of blood caused by branding some
of the Mikado's escort.   The striking of a Shinto priest
while on duty was a cause of uncleanness.   In grave cases,
however, the offender was handed over to the civil autho
rities.   According to the strict Shinto of a later period, a
man must abstain from worship at a shrine for thirty days

* Compare Leviticus xiii. 2 ; Numbers xix. 11.   See also above, p. 93.
† Numbers v. 2.

if he has wounded somebody, or, if he has accidentally
hurt himself, so that more than three drops of blood have
flowed, for that day. If he has vomited or passed blood,
he must not worship for two days, if he has an abscess,
until it is cured, for seven days after moxa is applied, and
for three days in the case of the operator. At the present
day the common word for wound is *kega*, that is to say,
defilement.

Baldness and emaciation were regarded as disqualifica
tions for the position of Imperial Princess consecrated to
the service of the Gods.*

It was no doubt the fear of contagion and an instinctive
feeling of horror and repulsion which inspired this class of
taboos. Contact with death, disease, and wounds are dis
pleasing to living human beings, and therefore to the Gods.
In ancient Greece it was not *themis* for the Gods to look
on death. There is an obvious absurdity in referring such
incidents of religious ritual to the principle that we must
seek for the origin of forms of divine worship in observances
towards the dead.

**Eating Flesh.**—Eating flesh is not included among the
causes of uncleanness enumerated in the *Kojiki*† or in the
Ohoharahi. A Chinese notice of Japan written centuries
before the dawn of Japanese history says that the "abstainers"
(medicine men) of Japan were not allowed to comb their
hair, to wash, to eat flesh meat, or to approach women.
But this was perhaps asceticism rather than religion. A
prohibition of the eating of the flesh of the ox, the horse,
the dog, the monkey, and the fowl in A.D. 647 was certainly
due to Buddhist influences. The first hint that it was
offensive to the Shinto Gods to eat flesh is found in the
*Kogo-jiui*, where it is stated that when the son of Mitoshi
no Kami saw that Ohotokonushi no Kami had given beef
to his field labourers he spat upon their offering and

* Compare Leviticus xxi. 17 *et seqq.*
† Ch. K. 230.

reported the matter to his father, who was angry and sent a blight upon the rice. But this very passage speaks of a horse, a pig, and a cock as acceptable offerings. In the *norito* things coarse of hair and things soft of hair occur frequently in the lists of offerings. Hirata points out that in sacrifices to the Sun-Goddess no flesh was used. In the most ancient times there was no prejudice against eating the flesh of animals. The Food-Goddess entertained Tsuki-yomi with things soft of hair and things coarse of hair. Hohodemi was a hunter by profession. The ancient Mikados frequently went hunting, and had no scruple in partaking of the products of the chase. Under Buddhist influences, however, there came a change. In the *Jogwan-shiki* (859-877) we find that persons who ate flesh were unclean for one day. In the *Yengishiki* three days are the limit. As time went on the prohibition was extended, until in 1683 we find that to eat the flesh of horse, cow, pig, goat, wild boar, deer, monkey, bear, or antelope caused uncleanness for one hundred days. Birds and fish, it will be observed, are not included in this schedule. Whereas in ancient times the Mikados ate the flesh of deer and wild boar as *ha-gatame* (hardening the teeth) on the third day of the year, from which a person's age was reckoned, fish, fowl, and rice-cake were substituted at a later period.

Persons who are unclean for any cause must have nothing to do with the preparation or serving of the Mikado's food.

Intoxicating liquors are not tabooed in Shinto. There is, however, mention of an embassy to Ise in 749, the members of which were not allowed to take animal life, to eat flesh, or to drink *sake*.

Impure food communicated its uncleanness to the fire with which it had been cooked. Persons who used such a fire (*kegare-bi*) for cooking were unclean for seven days. Hirata suggests that the reason why Izanami was unable to return to the upper world after partaking of the food of

Yomi was because of the unclean fire with which it had been cooked.

On the first day of the sixth month, the Mikado was served with food specially prepared with pure fire (*imu-bi no zen*).

**Buddhist Rites.**— The performance of Buddhist rites incapacitated a man from the service of the Shinto Gods until he had been subjected to purification. For an infringe ment of this rule, Shinto functionaries might be fined or dismissed. The use of Buddhist terms was forbidden to every one concerned in the Shinto ceremonies at Ise and Kamo. A Sutra was called "tinted paper," Buddha the "middle child," a Buddhist temple a "tile roof." Buddhist priests and nuns were ironically styled the "long-haired ones." At Ise Buddhist priests were not admitted to the sacred precincts beyond a certain cryptomeria tree. A separate place was assigned them for their prayers.

Other words of ill omen were "death," for which "recovery" was used; for "disease" the participant in a Shinto festival said "rest"; for "weeping," "brine-dripping"; for "blood," "sweat"; for "strike," "stroke"; for "flesh," "mushroom"; for "tomb," "clod," &c. These are later inventions.

**Calamities.**—We learn from the Ohoharahi that snake bite, being struck by lightning, and other accidents were regarded as *tsumi*, or sources of impurity. At a later time, a fire which destroyed a man's house made him unclean for seven days.

Any neglect or irregularity in the divine services, any interference with the treasures, priests, or slaves of the shrine, or with the sacred grove around it, or failure to repair it whenever necessary, aroused the anger of the God and involved the uncleanness of the culprit.

Magic or witchcraft (*majinahi*) is one of the sources of impurity enumerated by the Ohoharahi.*

---

* Deuteronomy xvii. 11. See Index, ' Magic.'

The above account of Shinto offences must be taken with some qualifications. It is drawn from various sources and different periods of history. Some applied to the whole people, but in most cases it was only the priests and other persons concerned on whom the prohibitions were binding. The *Shinto Miomoku* has an enumeration of the " six pro hibited things " which includes only "mourning for a relative, visiting the sick, eating flesh of quadrupeds, con demnation of criminals, execution of criminals, music, and contact with impure things."

**Imi.**—The avoidance of impurity in preparation for a festival was called *imi* (avoidance). The intending officiator or worshipper remained indoors (*i-gomori*), abstained from speech and noise, and ate food cooked at a pure fire For six days previous to the celebration of a festival at the Great Shrine of Idzumo there was no singing or dancing, no musical performances, the shrine was not swept out, no build ing operations were carried on, and no rice pounded. Every thing was done in stillness. A special *imi* of one month was observed by the priests before participating in the greater festivals. This was called *araimi*. For middle-class festivals three days' *imi* were sufficient, and for those of the third class one day. At the present time *imi* is usually confined to abstinence from meat and from vegetables of the onion class.

By a natural transition *imi* is also used in the sense of sacred, holy. An *imi-dono* is a building in which purity is observed. Sacred (*imi*) axes and mattocks were used in some ceremonies. The Sun-Goddess was in her sacred weaving-hall when Susa no wo outraged her by flinging the hide of a horse into it. A modern derivative of *imi*, namely, *imeimashi*, is the nearest Japanese equivalent for " Hang it ! ' Compare the two meanings of the French *sacré*.

Mourning is also called *imi*, perhaps in the passive sense of something to be avoided in connexion with the service of the Gods.

The following story illustrates the danger of appearing before the Gods while in a state of impurity. In 463 the Mikado Yuriaku desired to see the form of the deity of Mimuro, and ordered one of his Ministers to fetch the God. The Minister brought him before the Mikado in the form of a great serpent. But the Mikado had not practised religious abstinence, and when the God showed his dis pleasure by rolling his thunder and showing his fiery eyeballs, the Mikado covered his eyes and fled into the interior of the palace.

**Fire-drill.**—In order to avoid the risk of using unclean fire in the great Shinto ceremonies, it was the custom at the shrines of Idzumo, Ise, Kasuga, Kamo, and perhaps other places, to make fire afresh on each occasion by means of the fire-drill. Even when not produced in this way, the sacrificial fire was called *kiri-bi* or drill-fire. A description of the Japanese form of the fire-drill will be found in a paper by Sir Ernest Satow, *T. A. S. J.*, vol. vi. pt. ii. p. 223, and a good specimen from Idzumo itself may be seen in the Oxford University Museum. Dr. Tylor, in his ' Early History of Mankind,' has shown how universally this method of producing fire has been employed. It is a natural development of the savage plan of rubbing two sticks together, and no doubt originated independently in many places. It is therefore unnecessary to assume that the Japanese fire-drill was borrowed from India, where it is used for sacred purposes, or even from nearer China, where it is also known. It is frequently mentioned in the old Japanese traditions. The *Kojiki* says that the God Kushiyadama was appointed steward for the service of Ohonamochi (the God of Idzumo), in which capacity he recited prayers, made a fire-drill, and drilled out fire wherewith to cook the heavenly august banquet of fish for the deity.[*] The priests of Idzumo have always used pure fire produced in this way, and pure water from a special well called the

* Ch. K., p. 104. See also Ch. K., p. 211, and *Nihongi*, i. 205.

K

Ama no mana-wi (true well of Heaven). At the present day, when the office is transmitted from one high priest to his successor, they proceed to the " Shrine of the Great Precinct," where the ceremony of " divine fire " and "divine water " is held. The original fire-drill, given by Amaterasu to Ame no hohi and preserved as the chief treasure of the shrine, is carried in a bag slung round the neck of the chief priest, who solemnly delivers it over to his successor. This ceremony is called *hi-tsugi* (fire-continuance). It is curious that the same term (*hitsugi*) is constantly used of the succession to the Mikado's throne, and that the delivery of the sun-mirror formed part of the ceremony used on his accession. *Hi* means either sun or fire.

The old fire-drill was worshipped every New Year's day at Idzumo at a festival called *hi no matsuri* (fire or sun-festival). A fire-drill was among the objects carried in procession at the *Ohonihe*, or coronation ceremony, and was used to produce the fire used for cooking the sacred rice offered on this occasion.

A modern Japanese writer, describing a festival celebrated at Gion in Kioto on the last day of the year, says : " A big bonfire burns within the precincts of the shrine. It has been kindled from a year-old flame tended in a lamp under the eaves of the sacred building, and people come there to light a taper, which, burning before the household altar, shall be the beacon of domestic prosperity. At 2 A.M. the Festival of Pine Shavings takes place. A Shinto priest reads a ritual. His colleagues obtain a spark by the friction of two pieces of wood, and set fire to a quantity of shavings packed into a large iron lamp. These charred fragments of pine wood the worshippers receive and carry away as amulets against plague and pestilence."

A Japanese book written two centuries ago informs us that sticks resembling the wands used for offerings at the purification ceremony were part shaven and set up in bundles at the four corners of the Gion shrine on the last day of the year. The priests, after prayers were recited, broke up the bundles and set fire to the sticks, which the people then carried home to light their household fires with for the New Year.* The object of this ceremony was to avert pestilence. There is here a striking resemblance to the Christian practice mentioned by M. D'Alviella : "The fire which the clergy, on the dawn of Easter, had struck from the flint and steel, served to rekindle the fires of individuals which had all been previously extinguished." The use of such fire to prevent pestilence may also be illustrated from European customs. The need-fire, made by striking flints or by the fire-drill, and used to rekindle all household fires, is one of numerous examples.†

**Removal of Impurity. Lustration.**—With every pre caution, it is not always possible to avoid the pollution of dirt, disease, and sin. In order, therefore, to do away with the offence to the Gods arising from such impure conditions, various expedients are resorted to. The most natural and universal of these is washing or lustration.‡ The Chinese notices of ancient Japan already quoted from inform us that the Japanese, after the ten days' mourning was con cluded, all went into the river and washed. Hirata says that even at the present day, when mourning is over, people go to the bank of a stream or to the sea-beach and cleanse themselves. The mythical account of Izanagi's washing in the sea in order to remove the pollutions of Yomi has been given above. In a fourteenth-century work entitled *Kemmu nenchiu giogi*, the ablutions of the Mikado previous to the ceremony of Shingonjiki are described with great minute ness ; and if this preliminary is usually passed over in descriptions of Shinto ceremonies, the reason no doubt is that it was too well known to require special mention.

---

* See a paper on the Japanese *gohei* in the *Journal* of the Anthropologica Institute, vol. xxxi., 1901. Also a note in *Man*, October, 1892.

† See Grimm's 'Teutonic Mythology,' ii. 603, Stallybrass's translation.

‡ See Dr. Tylor's ' Primitive Culture,' ii. 434.

K 2

Clean garments were put on at the same time. Both the Japanese words for the purification ceremony show by their derivation that washing was originally its cardinal feature. *Misogi* means "body-sprinkling," and *harahi* is probably the same word as *arahi*, "wash."* Penitence is not one of the old Shinto means of purification.

**Salt.**—In Japan, as in other countries, the antiseptic quality of salt has led to its religious use as a symbol for, and means of, purification. In a modern *harahi* ceremony the priest purifies the *himorogi* with salt water. At the entrances to theatres at the present day a saucer of salt is placed on a table in order to keep out evil influences. The *kaname-ishi*, or pivot stones of the earth,† are covered with salt, which is then rubbed on a diseased part in order to obtain relief. " A housewife will not buy salt at night. When obtained in the daytime, a portion of it must first be thrown into the fire to ward off all danger, and espe cially to prevent quarrelling in the family. It is also used to scatter round the threshold and in the house after a funeral for purificatory purposes."‡

**Spitting.**—Spitting, or the ejection from the mouth of any disagreeable substance, is naturally used by analogy as a symbol of dislike and disgust when other senses or feelings than that of taste are offended. The modern writer Fukuzawa tells us that when he left his home for the first time he spat in order to show his disgust with the narrowness and poverty of his life there.§ ,Spitting as a means of symbolical purification is a further corollary from the natural function of this act. In the Izanagi myth a God of the Spittle (Haya-tama no wo) is the result of that

* "Sprinkle the water of expiation on them       and let them wash their clothes."--Numbers vii. 7.

† The "earth-fast" stones of our own folk-lore.

‡ Griffis, ' Mikado's Empire,' p. 470.

§ We have a good illustration of the transition from the physical to the metaphorical use of spitting in Revelation iii. 16 : " Because thou art luke warm and neither hot nor cold, I will spew thee out of my mouth."

deity's spitting during the ceremony of divorce. The " spittle " deity is here associated with another God, who is styled a God of Purification. A commentator on this passage says that " at the present day spitting is essential in the purification ceremony." The ritual, however, does not mention it. Another writer adds that "this is the reason why at the present day people spit when they see anything impure." In the myth of Susa no wo spittle is mentioned along with the nails of the fingers and toes and nose-mucus among the materials for expiatory offerings. When Hohodemi is recommended to " spit thrice " before giving back the lost fish-hook to his brother, a magical effect is probably intended, such as to convey to him any impurity which may have become attached to his own person. Rinsing the mouth as a purifying ceremony before pro nouncing an oath is mentioned in the *Nihongi*.[*]

**Breathing on.**—Ritual impurity may also be conveyed away by the breath. The origin of this practice is the sudden expulsion of air from the mouth when some offensive odour or vapour has found an entrance. This instinctive action[†] is represented onomatopoetically in English by Pooh! Faugh! Pshaw! and in other languages by similar words, which have come to express not only physical repulsion, but dislike and contempt generally.

As a religious practice, breathing away impurity is exemplified by the custom of the Mikado breathing on certain *aga mono* (ransom-objects) of the *harahi* ceremony, thus communicating to them the pollutions of his own person. It is in order to avoid polluting the offerings by their breath that in some ceremonies the assistant priests cover their mouths with a white fillet and hold their arms

---

[*] II. 96.

[†] Hirata says that in books of magic *ibukite harafu* (clearing away by puffing) is a means adopted by men naturally, without teaching, for cleansing away evil influences. See also Darwin's ' Expression of the Emotions,' pp. 258, 261.

outstretched.  Even at the present day the stewards who
prepare the Mikado's food cover their mouths with a white
paper mask.  The *Nihongi* states that when Izanagi washed
in the sea in order to remove the pollutions of Yomi, he
" blew out " and produced a number of deities, among
which were the Great God of Remedy and the Great God
of Offences.  But the action of the Sun-Goddess and Susa
no wo in producing children by crunching various objects
and then " blowing away " the fragments, and of Izanagi's
creation of the Wind-God by puffing away the mists,
requires further explanation.  These myths were probably
the work of a person who had only a vague idea of the
precise nature of the efficacy of this act, and regarded it
simply as attended with some magical power.  Spitting,
primarily a mark of disgust, then practised with the object
of purification, is finally done simply " for luck."

**Ransom.** –The notion of expiating ritual guilt by giving
ransom (*aga-mono*) is familiar to the Japanese.  The more
intimately the objects offered are connected with the person
of the offender, the more effectual is the sacrifice.  Susa
no wo is said to have expiated his offences by the loss of
his hair and of his finger and toe nails.  Among objects of
ransom presented by the Mikado at purification ceremonies
clothing is the most important.  The Mikado was measured
with great ceremony for suits of garments.  Bamboo sticks
were used for this purpose, which were broken to the
required lengths.  Hence the ceremony was called *yo-ori*
(joint-break).  The clothing when made was placed in a
vase, and set before the Mikado by a Nakatomi woman.
He breathed on it thrice, and then returned it to be
taken away by the Urahe (diviners) and thrown into
a stream.  Other ransom offerings were human figures of
iron, wood, or leather, and swords, which were similarly
treated.

A special *mi-aganahi no matsuri* (august-ransom-celebra-
tion) was inaugurated in 814 for the sake of the Mikado,

who was then ill. It was continued annually every sixth and twelfth month, the *miko* officiating.

In the thirteenth century the Onyoshi (diviners of the Chinese school) presented to the Mikado human figures in a box, inscribed with the place and name. The Mikado breathed on them, rubbed them on his person, and then returned them to the box.

The principle of ransom is illustrated in the present day by the custom of *kata-shiro* (form-token) or *nade-mono* (rub-thing). At a shrine of the Sea-Gods in Tokio a purification ceremony is performed twice a year. A few days before, the parishioners and other believers who wish to be purified go to the shrine and obtain from its official a *katashiro*, that is, a white paper cut into the shape of a garment. On this the person to be purified writes the year and month of his birth and his or her sex, and rubs it over his whole body. When he has thus transferred his im purities to the paper he returns it to the shrine. All the *katashiro* which are brought back are packed into two sheaths of reed and placed on a table of unbarked wood. They are then called *harahi tsu mono*, or things of purifi cation. Finally they are put into a boat which is rowed out into the sea, and they are thrown away there.* The bundles of reeds or rushes which are thrown into the sea at the shrine of Gion at Tsushima in Owari, to avert pesti lence, probably represent human figures. It is said that wherever they float to, pestilence breaks out.

A more expeditious form of the same custom is when the *katashiro* or *nademono* are simply bought from the *Kashima-fure*, strolling vendors belonging to the shrine of Kashima, rubbed over the body, and cast into a stream. The object, however, is not so much the removal of ritual pollution as protection against disease. At the present day paper figures, called Ama-gatsu, are made to avert calamity from children. They are prepared before the

* Dr. Florenz, in *T. A. S. J.*, December, 1899.

birth of the child, and are worn up to the age of three. It is thought that evil spirits are diverted into these images from the infant. It is an obvious degradation of these practices when they are used merely to procure good luck instead of to remove impurities offensive to the Gods.

**Chi no wa (Reed-ring).**—In a modern form of the *harahi* ceremony there is a kind of purification which consists in passing three times through a large ring made of reeds (pp. 266, 267), holding in the hands hemp leaves and reeds, and repeating the verse :—

> The sixth month's
> Summer—passing-away—
> Purification
> Who ever doeth
> Is said to'extend his life
> To one thousand years.

Or, according to another version :—

> To the end that
> My impure thoughts
> May be annihilated,
> These hemp leaves,
> Cutting with many a cut,
> I have performed purification.

The *Shinto Miomoku* (1699) says that this ring represents the round of the universe. The same work adds that the object of the ceremony is to avert the dangers connected with the change of summer influences to those of autumn. But these explanations have a tincture of Chinese philo sophy. The purification of the heart from evil thoughts is also a conception foreign to the older Shinto. The injunction to cleanse the inside of the cup and the platter belongs to a later stage of religious development.

The *chi no wa* is subsequently flung into the water.

Another means of purification was to shake a *gohei* over the person or thing to be purified.

The virtue of set forms of speech in absolving from uncleanness is fully recognized in Shinto, as will be seen in the next chapter.

There were various forms of purification at various places for consecrating a new shrine, or new utensils for it, or for reconsecrating a place which had become unclean.

島廻芽輪の道

慶戸田圖

# CHAPTER XII.

## CEREMONIAL.

CEREMONIES are combinations for some specific purpose of the elements of worship described in the two preceding chapters.*

The *Yengishiki* is the chief authority for the following account of some of the more important ceremonies of Shinto. I have also availed myself freely of the results of Sir E. Satow's researches contained in vols. vii. and ix. of the *T. A. S. J.*

**Ohonihe or Daijowe.**—The *Yengishiki* places the Ohonihe in a class by itself, as much the most solemn and important festival of the Shinto religion. *Oho* means great, and *nihe* food offering. It was substantially a more elaborate and sumptuous Nihi-name (new-tasting), or festival of first fruits, performed soon after the accession of a Mikado to the throne, and, like our coronation ceremony, constituting the formal religious sanction of his sovereignty.

A modern Japanese writer explains its object as follows :

"*Anciently the Mikado received the auspicious grain from the Gods of Heaven, and therewithal nourished the people. In the Daijowe (or Ohonihe) the Mikado, when the grain became ripe, joined unto him the people in sincere veneration, and, as in duty bound, made return to the Gods of Heaven. He thereafter partook of it along with the nation. Thus the people learnt that the grain which they eat is no other than the seed bestowed on them by the Gods of Heaven.*"

---

"Un rite est un assemblage de symboles groupes autour d'une idee religieuse ou d'un acte religieux, destine a en rehausser le caractere solennel ou bien à en developper le sens."—Reville, ' Prolegomenes.'

In so far as the motive of the Japanese worshipper is concerned, this is, I think, nearer the mark than Mr. Frazer's : " Primitive peoples are, as a rule, reluctant to taste the annual first-fruits of any crop until some ceremony has been performed which makes it safe and pious for them to do so. The reason of this reluctance appears to be that the first-fruits either are the property of, or actually contain, a divinity." It is gratitude rather than fear which animates the Japanese.

The preparations for the Ohonihe began months in advance. The first step was to designate by divination two provinces from which the rice used in the ceremony was to be provided. These were called respectively *yuki* and *suki*. The most probable meaning of the former term is "religious purity." *Suki* is said to mean next or subsidiary. The object of thus duplicating the offerings was, no doubt, that if any unnoticed irregularity or impurity occurred in one case, the error might not vitiate the whole proceedings. Officers called *nuki-ho no tsukahi* (messengers of the plucked-up ears) were then selected by divination. One of these was called the Inami no Urabe, or rice-fruit diviner, the other the Negi no Urabe, or prayer-diviner. These officers on arriving at the *yuki* or *suki* district performed a purifica tion ceremony in presence of the local officials and people. The site of the *inami-dono*, or rice-fruit-hall, was then chosen by divination and marked out at the four corners by twigs of the sacred evergreen tree (*sakaki*) hung with tree-fibre.* It was 160 feet square. Somewhat more than an acre of rice-field was next set apart, the owner being com pensated by the authorities. Here two *sakaki* twigs hung with tree-fibre were planted, and a guard of four labourers was set over it. Divination was also used for the selection of a local staff of religious functionaries. It consisted of one Saka-tsu-ko, that is, sake-child or brewer-maiden, an unmarried girl of good family, with several other girls as

* See Index, *Yufu.*

assistants, an Inami no kimi, or rice-fruit-lord,* a charcoal-burner, wood-cutters, &c.   A choir of twenty male and female singers was also provided.   Then the site of the Inami-dono was propitiated by prayer and offerings.   A pure mattock and sickle were used in clearing the ground for the buildings, which comprised a shrine to the eight Gods Mi-toshi no Kami (august harvest deity), Taka mi musubi, Niha-taka-hi no Kami (courtyard-high-sun-deity), Mi ketsu no Kami (food-Goddess), Ohomiyanome no Kami, Koto-shiro-nushi, Asuha, and Hahigi.†   A "rice-fruit-store," an office for the envoys from Kioto, and lodgings for the rice-fruit-lord and for the brewer-maiden and her assistants were built of unbarked wood and grass.   The surrounding fence was made of brushwood and the gates consisted of hurdles.

Offerings having been made to the eight Gods above mentioned, the diviners from Kioto, accompanied by the local authorities and by the special staff of the inami-dono proceeded to the rice-field.   The brewer-maiden plucked up the first ears.   She was followed by the rice-fruit-lord and the people.   Songs were sung during the operation. The first four sheaves were reserved for the offering of boiled rice to be made by the Mikado to the Gods.   When all the rice was pulled up, it was carried in procession to the capital, with the four reserved sheaves in the place of honour and the rice-fruit-lord acting as guide.   It arrived at Kioto in the last decade of the ninth month.

Meanwhile a general purification of the whole country had been performed, and to prevent all possibility of error, repeated at a short interval.   As soon as this formality was completed, offerings of cloth and of material for wearing apparel were sent to all the Gods.   The following *norito*‡ was read on this occasion :—

---

* Have we here one of those human representatives of the grain so familiar to us in European folk-lore?   See Mr. Frazer's ' Golden Bough.'

† See Index for these deities.

‡ No. 14 of the *Yengishiki.*

"*He says:* '*Hearken! all ye assembled kannushi and hafuri. I humbly declare in the presence of the sovran Gods, who, according to the command of the dear divine ancestor and dear divine ancestress who dwell in the Plain of High Heaven, bear sway as Heavenly Shrines and Earthly Shrines.*'

"*He says:* '*To the end that on the middle day of the Hare of the 11th month of this year, the Sovran Grandchild\* may partake of the Great Food (ohonihe) as Heavenly Food, as Long Food, as Distant Food, I pray that ye sovran Gods will jointly undertake to bless his reign, to be firm and enduring, and give it happiness as a prosperous reign. Therefore, on behalf of the Sovran Grandchild, who will rule peacefully and serenely for one thousand autumns and five hundred autumns with festive ruddy countenance, do I set forth these fair offerings, namely, bright cloth, shining cloth, soft cloth, and rough cloth.*

"'*Hearken! all of you to this fulfilling of praises as the morning sun rises in glory*'

"*He says:* '*More especially would I enjoin on the kannushi and hafuri with all due ceremony to receive, take up, and present the offerings purely provided by the Imbe, hanging stout straps on weak shoulders.*'"

A special embassy was sent to Ise, consisting of one Prince, one Nakatomi, one Imbe, and one Urabe.

In the third decade of the tenth month the Mikado went in state to a river-bank near Kioto and performed a ceremonial ablution (*misogi*).

For one month before the Ohonihe lesser abstinence (*ara-imi*) was enjoined, and for three days greater abstinence (*ma-imi*). Buddhist ceremonies, and the eating of impure food, were interdicted throughout the five home provinces. Purity of language† was also necessary. During the three days of *ma-imi*, no official was allowed to do any work except that connected with the ceremony.

---

\* The Mikado.
† See above, p. 255.

Special buildings were erected for the Ohonihe at Kitano, a suburb of Kioto. After a purification ceremony, a site 480 feet square was marked out by twigs of *sakaki* hung with tree-fibre. On the arrival of the *yuki* and *suki* rice from the provinces, this site was propitiated. The Brewer-maidens then with a pure mattock turned the first sod and dug the holes for the four corner posts. The Urabe went to the mountain where the timber was to be cut, and wor shipped the God of the mountain. The Brewer-maiden struck the first blow with a pure axe, and wood-cutters completed the work. Similar formalities were practised in cutting the grass for thatch and in digging wells.

The sacred enclosure (*yu-niha*) was divided into two sections, an inner and an outer, and contained numerous buildings, such as shrines to the eight Gods already men tioned, storehouses for the rice and other necessaries, lodgings for the Brewer-maidens and their assistants, kitchens, &c.

The site of the principal building, or Ohonihe no Miya, measured 214 feet by 150 feet. It was erected after the others and was in duplicate, one being for the *yuki*, the other for the *suki*. Each was forty feet long by sixteen feet wide. The roof-tree ran north and south. Undressed wood was used for the erection, which was covered by a roof of thatch. The floor was strewn with bundles of grass over which bamboo mats were placed. In the centre of the sleeping-chamber (the sanctum) several white *tatami* (thick mats) were laid down and upon them the *Saka-makura*, which was a cushion three feet broad by four feet long, for the use of the God or Gods.* This was called the " Deity seat." The Mikado's seat was placed to the south of it.

The preparation of the *sake* for the ceremony was pre ceded by worship of the Well-God, the Furnace-God, and

---

* Sir Ernest Satow says that sleeping in a house being regarded as the sign of ownership, a pillow (*makura*) is often placed in the shrine as a symbol of the God's presence.

the Sake-God. The first fire was produced by a fire-drill. The Brewer-maiden began to turn it and the Rice-fruit-lord continued the work. A third official blew the fire and the attendants then kindled a torch with it. All the utensils had been provided by the Imbe with great care, performing *harahi* and worship at every step.

The Mikado himself practised lesser abstinence for a month and greater abstinence for three days before the ceremony. The procedure at the Ohonihe is too elaborate to describe in detail. It included the recitation before the Mikado of "old words" (myths and legends?) by the Kataribe, or corporation of reciters, and songs by the women who pounded the rice for the offerings, wishing him long life and prosperity. The rice was presented to him by the Nukiho no tsukahi, with the words, "We bring a thousand and five hundred auspicious ears which we offer as divine food of a million loads." Old-fashioned music was performed and the regalia were delivered to him by the Urabe.

The cardinal feature of the Ohonihe was the offering of food to the God (or Gods) by the Mikado in person. With his own hands he sprinkled rice with *sake* which he then placed before the "Deity-seat." No one else was present but the Uneme, or ladies-in-waiting, who repeated the formula, " Let that which ye should clip first be clipped afterwards. Moreover, whatever faults there be, receive these offerings with divine amendment, with great amend ment." The Mikado then bowed his head slightly, clapped his hands, and said *Ô* (amen), after which he joined the God in partaking of the food. When the *yuki* ceremony was completed the Mikado went to his retiring-room, washed and changed his clothes, after which he proceeded to the *suki* chamber and repeated the same ceremonial.

It is not quite certain what God or Gods were worshipped. Some say that the offerings were to the Sun-Goddess, others think that all the Gods were included. The haziness on this point is highly characteristic of Shinto.

The following *norito*, No. 27 of the *Yengishiki*, was pronounced by the Idzumo no miyakko on this occasion. They were the reputed descendants of Ama no hohi, who holds the same position in the Ohonamochi myth that Koyane does in that of the Sun-Goddess. They were originally the hereditary Governors—perhaps even kings— of the province and had also sacerdotal functions. They retained the latter after all lay jurisdiction had been taken from them.

"*The words of blessing of the Miyakko of Idzumo.*

"*Among the many tens of days that be, on this day, this living day, this perfect day, do I* [*here insert name*], *Miyakko of the Land of Idzumo, humbly declare with deepest reverence, to wit:* '*With the object of pronouncing a blessing on the great august reign of our Sovran Lord, who rules the Great-eight-island country as—with fear be it said—a wise manifest deity, and blessing it as a long and great reign, did I, hanging stout straps on weak shoulders* \* *fastening the cords of the sacred offerings, wearing the celestial cap, shearing and spreading the coarse grass as a sacred mat in the sacred house, blackening the sacred vessels, dwelling in pure retirement by the celestial sake-jars, calming the deities in their calm shrines by the avoidance of impurity, did service first to the Great God of Kumano, Kushi mikenu,†  our divine ancestor, the Great-Grandchild of Izanagi, and to Ohonamochi, the maker of the land, for whom within the blue hill-confines of the province of Idzumo the temple pillars have been stoutly planted on the rock-roots below, while the projecting cross beams of the roof are exalted to the Plain of High Heaven. Thereafter I did worship to the Sovran Gods who dwell in the one hundred and eighty-six shrines*'

"*Then, as the morning sun went up in glory, there came these good words of divine blessing, to wit:* '*When Taka-*

---

\* That is, wearing the garb of a priest who makes offerings.

† Probably the same as Ame no hohi, from whom the Miyakko claimed descent.

*mi-musubi* and *Kami mi-musubi, the High-Heaven divine ancestors, bestowed upon the Sovran Grandchild this sub-celestial Great-eight-island country, Ama no hohi, the remote divine ancestor of the Omi\* of Idzumo, was sent by them to view the condition of the land. Forcing his way through the eight-fold clouds of Heaven, soaring across the sky, soaring over the earth, he surveyed the Under-Heaven on all sides, and made report that the Fair-Ear-Land of the Rich-Reed-Plain was a savage land where there were Gods who in the daytime swarmed like flies in the fifth month, and at night shone like fire pots, and where the rocks, trees, and blue water foam had power of speech. However, he promised that it should be subdued so that the Sovran Grandchild might rule it serenely as a peaceful land. Therefore his son Ame-hiva-dori, and with him Futsunushi were sent down from Heaven. They drove out and subdued the savage deities, and persuaded the Great God who made the Land† to divide off the visible outward things‡ of the Great-eight-island Country.'*

" *Then Ohonamochi said: ' In the land to be governed by the Sovran Grandchild and called Great Yamato I will make my own gentle spirit (nigi-tama) to be attached to an eight-hand mirror, and, enshrined in Miha, under the title of Yamato no Oho-mono-nushi kushi-mika-tama no mikoto (great-thing-master-wondrous-awful-spirit), the spirit of my son Ajisuki-taka-hikone to be enshrined at Kamo in Katsuraki, that of Kotoshironushi at Unade, and that of Kaya-narumi at Asuka, dedicating them to dwell there divinely as near guardian deities of the Sovran Grandchild.' He then went to rest in the shrine of fertile Kitsuki.§ Thereupon the Sovran dear divine ancestor and ancestress (of the Mikado ?)*

---

\* The same as the Miyakko.

† Ohonamochi.

‡ That is, to surrender the civil jurisdiction.

§ It is to be understood that after he had enshrined his *nigi-tama,* or gentle spirit, in Yamato, Ohonamochi himself, or perhaps his *aratama,* or rough spirit, retired to Idzumo.

*gave command, saying : ' Do thou Hohi no Mikoto bless the Sovran's long age so that it may be firm and enduring, and make it happy as a prosperous age '*

"*In accordance with this injunction, I (his successor) perform this service of blessing, and as the morning sun rises in glory, bring tribute of congratulatory divine treasures in token of the God's (Hohi) regard and in token of the Omi's (his own) regard.*

"*(These) white jewels are (a prognostic of) the great august white hairs (to which your majesty will reach). The red jewels are the august, healthful, ruddy countenance, and the green-estuary jewels are the harmonious fitness with which your Majesty will establish far and wide, as with a broad sword-blade, his lasting great august reign over the Great-eight-island-country which he governs. As (this) white horse plants firmly his fore hoofs and his hind-hoofs, so will the pillars of the Great Palace be set firmly on the upper rocks and frozen firmly on the lower rocks. The pricking up of his ears is a sign that Your Majesty will, with ears ever more erect, rule the Under-Heaven. [Here follows a passage too corrupt for translation. It continues to allude to the emblematic character of the offerings.] As a token that the visible deity (the Mikado) shall peacefully and serenely rule the Great-eight-island country as long as Heaven and Earth, the Sun and Moon endure, I offer these congratulatory divine treasures by way of respect from the God, and by way of respect from the Omi, with profound awe, and pronounce these auspicious words of divine congratulation delivered to me from Heaven*"

The offerings were sixty jewels, white, red, and green, a sword with mountings of gold and silver, a mirror, two pieces of cloth, a horse, a swan, and fifty trays of eatables.

The similar formula used by the Nakatomi in 1142, in voking the blessing of the Gods on the new sovereign, is given in Dr. Florenz's German translation of the *Nihongi,* Book xxx., Appendix.

The above is the merest outline of a ceremony to a de
scription of which Hirata devotes 480 pages of his *Koshiden*.
It varied a good deal at different times, and was altogether
discontinued for eight reigns (1465-1687) no doubt because
it was found too heavy a burden on the people.

**Nihi-name.**—The Nihi-name or new tasting, when the
rice of the new harvest was first partaken of, was the same
as the Ohonihe, except that it was simpler and was cele
brated annually. The festival is frequently referred to in
the *Kojiki* and *Nihongi*. The Sun-Goddess is said to have
celebrated a Nihi-name in a New Palace. It was accom
panied by songs and dances and was followed by feasting
in holiday dress and presents to the Court and officials.

At shrines not officially recognized, the local official in
charge conducted this ceremony. It was then called *o-hi-
taki* (august-fire-kindling) because a courtyard fire (*nihabi*)
was made, the ceremony taking place at night. Strict
Shinto devotees would not eat the new season's rice until it
had been performed.

It appears from allusions in poetry and legend that there
was also a household Nihi-name. It was celebrated with
closed doors, no stranger being admitted, apparently in
order to prevent pollution by impure persons. The follow
ing legend from the *Hitachi Fudoki* illustrates this point.

"*When the God called the 'Divine Ancestor' went to
the places of the various deities, he came to the Peak
of Fuji in Suruga. The sun went down and he asked for
a lodging, but the God of Fuji refused, saying that he was
that day performing the* Nihi-name, *and his household were
therefore practising abstinence. So he ascended the Peak
of Tsukuba, and asked for a lodging. The God of Tsukuba
said: 'Although I am this night celebrating the Nihi-name,
why should that prevent me from acceding to your august
behest?'*"

**Nanakusa.**—There was in later times a corresponding

spring festival called Nana-kusa (seven herbs), in which wild potherbs of seven different kinds were gathered and eaten.

**Ahi-name or Ahimbe.**—This word means "joint-tasting." It was a harvest festival not essentially differing from the Nihi-name, and was so called because the Mikado joined the Gods with himself in tasting the new season's rice and *sake.* Hirata thinks, however, that the expression "joint-tasting" refers to the association of certain inferior Gods with the greater Gods directly worshipped at this time. It was celebrated on the first Hare day of the eleventh month, and was in honour of the deities of seventy-one shrines.

**Kan-name** (divine-tasting).—This was another harvest festival, distinguished from the preceding by being cele brated in the ninth month, and being confined to the deities of the Ise shrines. An embassy of high officials was specially dispatched to Ise for the purpose, after an elaborate ceremonial in the Palace, in which the Mikado himself took part.

The *norito* (Nos. 20, 21, and 22) used on this occasion are preserved in the *Yengishiki.* They contain nothing of interest.

When a princess was dedicated to the service of the shrines, the following formula (No. 23) was added :—

"*More especially do I humbly declare : ' The offering of a Sacred Princess of the Blood Imperial to serve as the Deities' staff, having first, according to custom, observed the rules of religious purity for three years, is to the end that thou mayst cause the Sovran Grandchild to live peacefully and firmly as long as Heaven and Earth, the Sun and Moon, may last. I, the Great Nakatomi, holding the dread spear by the middle,\* with deepest awe pronounce this dedication of her by the Mikado to the end that she may serve as an august staff.'* "

---

\* Explained to mean "in the discharge of my mediatory function."

**Kamu-ima-ge or Shingonjiki.**—This festival was cele brated in the palace at night after the Tsukinami. The name means literally God-new-food. It consisted in the Mikado in person or by deputy making an offering of food to the Sun-Goddess. The forms resembled those in use for the Ohonihe or Nihi-name, and included laying down a cushion (*saka-makura*) to represent the Deity, the use of a fire-drill, &c.

**Hirano no Matsuri.**—Festival of Hirano, a village in the province of Settsu. There is much doubt as to the deities in whose honour this service (No. 5 of the *Yengishiki*) was first instituted. It is believed that it was originally cele brated in honour of Image no Kami (the God of New Food) and of Kudo no Kami and Kobe no Kami, the Gods of the kitchen-boiler and of the cooking-pan. The *Image* was probably, as explained by Sir E. Satow, freshly hulled rice offered monthly to the Gods.

After the Mikado Kwammu founded the shrine of Hirano, about the end of the eighth century, it became the custom for all the branches of the Imperial family to be represented at the two annual celebrations. It was Kitabatake Chika-fusa (1293-1359) who first invented the popular account of the Gods worshipped here. Knowing that they were in some manner family deities, he proceeded to allot as *uji-gami* to the Tahira, Minamoto, Ohoye and Takashina families, ancient members of the Imperial line taken here and there at random, and comprising the Sun-Goddess, Yamato-dake, and the Mikados Chiuai and Nintoku. This is an instructive example of the intrusion of ancestor-worship so-called into the older Shinto.

The *norito* read at this festival affords no clue to the identity of the Gods worshipped. It mentions the founding of the shrine at the behest of the Sovran Great God (or Gods) and makes offerings in acknowledgment of his (or their) preserving the Mikado's life and prospering his reign.*

**Kudo and Kobe no Matsuri.**—This service (No. 6 of the *Yengishiki*) is practically identical with the last, which is natural, if, as is probable, the Gods worshipped are really the same.

**Toshigohi no Matsuri** (harvest-praying service).—This festival (No. 1 of the *Yengishiki*) was in honour of the deities of the 3,132 official shrines, in other words, the entire Shinto Pantheon. It was celebrated on the 4th day of the 2nd month (when the seed rice is sown) in the *Sai-in*, or sacred precinct, a courtyard in the Palace measuring 230 feet by 370 feet, with offices opening on to it on all sides. On the west were the shrines of the eight deities† in a row, surrounded by a fence to the interior of which three sacred archways gave access. In the centre of the court a temporary shed was erected in which the altars were placed. Early on the morning of the festival day, the offerings, prepared by the Imbe, were set out here. They are minutely described in the *Yengishiki*, and consisted of silk and cloth of various kinds, some of the raw materials for the same, models of swords, shields, spear-heads, bows, quivers, stags' horns, mattocks, sake, fish of various kinds, edible seaweed, salt, and matting. In the case of the Ise temples, a horse was added. A white horse, cock, and boar were sent to Mitoshi no Kami, the special deity of Harvest, and a horse to each of nineteen others, including the God of Growth and the water-deities of Yamato.

When everything was ready, the officials of the *Jingikwan*, accompanied by the *miko*, or virgin priestesses, entered by the middle gate and took their places in the western offices with their faces to the east, the north being the upper (or more honourable) end. The Ministers of State and their

---

* For a more detailed discussion of this ritual, see Sir E. Satow in *T. A. S. J.*, vol. ix. pt. ii. p. 183.

† See above, p. 270.

subordinates entered by the north gate and took their places in the north office, the Ministers facing the south, the others east or west. The priestesses occupied seats below the office. The other officials entered by the south gate and sat facing the north. The subordinate Shinto functionaries and *hafuri* stood in the courtyard south of the west office.

Then the Jingikwan officials came down and took their places in front of their office. They were followed by the Ministers of State. A Nakatomi read the *norito*, the *hafuri* responding with $\hat{O}$ ("Yes" or "Amen") at the end of every paragraph. It is as follows :—

" *He** says : ' Hearken all ye assembled Kannushi and Hafuri.'*

" *He says : 'I humbly declare in the presence of the Sovran Gods, whose praises are fulfilled as Heavenly Deities and as Earthly Deities, by command of the Sovran, dear, divine ancestor and ancestress who divinely dwell in the Plain of High-Heaven.*

" *' In the second month of this year the Sovran Grandchild is graciously pleased to pray for harvest, and I, therefore, as the morning sun rises in glory, offer up his plenteous offerings, thus fulfilling your praise' [Here the Kannushi and Hafuri of the shrines concerned remove this set of offerings.]*

" *He says : 'I humbly declare in the presence of the Sovran Gods of the harvest.*

" *' If the Sovran Gods will bestow in ears many a hand's breadth long and ears abundant the latter harvest which they will bestow, the latter harvest produced by the labour of men from whose arms the foam drips down, on whose opposing thighs the mud is gathered, I will fulfil their praises by humbly offering first fruits, of ears a thousand, of ears many a hundred, raising up the tops of the sake-jars, and setting in rows the bellies of the sake-jars, in juice and in ear will I*

* The Nakatomi.

*present them, of things growing in the great moor-plain, sweet herbs and bitter herbs, of things that dwell in the blue sea-plain, the broad of fin and the narrow of fin, edible seaweed, too, from the offing and seaweed from the shore, of clothing, bright stuffs and shining stuffs, soft stuffs and coarse stuffs —with these I will fulfil your praises. [In the meantime] having furnished a white horse, a white boar, and a white cock, with things of various kinds before the Sovran Gods of the Harvest, I fulfil their praises by humbly presenting these plenteous offerings of the Sovran Grandchild.'*

*" He says : ' I humbly declare in the presence of the Sovran Gods whose praises the chief priestess fulfils, and I fulfil your praises, namely, Kami-musubi, Taka-mi-musubi, Iku-musubi, Taru-musubi, Tama-tsume-musubi, Oho-miya no me, Oho-mi-ketsu no kami, and Kotoshironushi. Because you bless the Sovran Grandchild's reign as a long reign, firm and enduring, and render it a happy and prosperous reign, I fulfil your praises as our Sovran's dear, divine ancestor and ancestress by making these plenteous offerings on his behalf.'*

*" He says : 'I humbly declare in the presence of the Sovran Gods, whose praises the priestess of Wigasuri fulfils. I fulfil your praises, repeating your names, to wit, Live Well, Blessing Well, Long-rope Well, Asuha, and Hahigi.\* Whereas, on the nethermost rock-roots ruled by the Sovran Gods (just named) the palace pillars have been raised stout and high, and the projecting cross-beams exalted to the Plain of High-Heaven, furnishing a fair abode for the Sovran Grandchild, wherein, finding shelter from the rain and shelter from the sun, he serenely governs in peace the world on all sides, I fulfil your praises by making these plenteous offerings on his behalf.'*

*"He says : 'I humbly declare in the presence of the Sovran Gods, whose praises are fulfilled by the priestess of the Gate. Repeating your names, to wit, Kushi iha-mado (wondrous-*

---

\* See Index for these two deitie

*rock-gate) and Toyo-iha-mado (rich-rock-gate), I fulfil your praises. Whereas you guard the gates of the four quarters by night and day, obstructing the passage like manifold piles of rock, and whether you open them in the morning or close them in the evening, guard below against unfriendly things coming from below, and guard above against unfriendly things coming from above, I fulfil your praises by making these offerings on behalf of the Sovran Grandchild.'*

*"He says: 'I humbly declare in the presence of the Sovran Gods, whose praises the priestess of Ikushima (live-island or region) fulfils. Repeating your names, to wit, Iku-kuni (live country) and Taru-kuni\* (perfect country), I fulfil your praises. Because you the Sovran Gods, who rule the islands many tens in number wherever the frog of the valley finds his way, wherever the ocean foam extends, making wide the narrow regions and the steep regions level, have granted these many islands to him every one, I fulfil your praises by making these plenteous offerings on behalf of the Sovran Grandchild.'*

*"He says: 'More especially do I humbly declare in the mighty presence of the Great Heaven-shining Deity who dwells in Ise. Because the Great Deity has bestowed on him the lands of the four quarters over which her glance extends as far as where the wall of Heaven rises, as far as where the bounds of Earth stand up, as far as the blue clouds are diffused, as far as where the white clouds settle down opposite, by the blue sea-plain, as far as the prows of ships can go without letting dry their poles and oars; by land, as far as the hoofs of horses can go, with tightened baggage-cords, treading their way among rock-roots and tree-roots where the long road extends, continuously widening the narrow regions and making the steep regions level, drawing together, as it were, the distant regions by throwing over them (a net of) many ropes,—therefore will the first-fruits for the Sovran Great Deity be piled up in her mighty presence like a range of hills, leaving the remainder for him tranquilly to partake of.'*

\* See Index.

"'*Moreover, whereas you bless the Sovran Grandchild's reign as a long reign, firm and enduring, and render it a happy and prosperous reign, I plunge down my neck cor morant-wise in reverence to you asour Sovran's dear, divine ancestress, and fulfil your praises by making these plenteous offerings on his behalf.'*

"He says: '*I humbly declare in the presence of the Sovran Gods who dwell in the Crown lands and name your august names, to wit—Takechi, Katsuraki, Tohochi, Shiki, Yamanobe and Sofu* * Whereas the Sovran Grandchild partakes of, as his long food, his distant food, the sweet herbs and bitter herbs which grow in and are brought from the six Crown lands aforesaid, I fulfil your praises by making these plenteous offerings on his behalf.'*

"'*I humbly declare in the presence of the Sovran Gods who dwell in the mountain-mouths and name your august names, to wit—Asuka, Ihare, Osaka, Hatsuse, Unebi, and Miminashi.† Whereas the great trees and the small trees which grow on the near mountains and on the far mountains are cut at the root and at the top, and brought to furnish a fair abode for the Sovran Grandchild, wherein, sheltered from the rain and sun, he serenely governs in peace the lands of the four quarters, I fulfil your praises by making these plenteous offerings on his behalf.'*

"He says: '*I humbly declare in the presence of the Gods who dwell in the water-partings, and, naming your august names, to wit—Yoshinu, Uda, Tsuge, and Katsuraki, fulfil your praises. If you, the Sovran Gods, will bestow in ears many a handsbreadth long, and ears abundant the latter harvest which you will bestow, I will fulfil your praises by offering first-fruits in ear and in juice, raising up the tops of the sake-jars and filling and setting in a row the bellies of the sake-jars. The Sovran Grandchild will then partake with ruddy countenance of that which remains as the corn of*

---

* These are names of places. The Gods seem to have had no others.
† These are names of mountains.

*his august morning meals and his august evening meals, for his long food, and for his distant food. Therefore do I now fulfil your praises by making these plenteous offerings on his behalf.*

*" ' Lend ear, all of you.'*

*" He says : ' More especially, let the Kannushi and Hafuri, having received the offerings which the Imbe, hanging stout straps on weak shoulders, have prepared with purity, take them away and offer them in all due form.' "*

It will be observed that this *norito* contains paragraphs—possibly later accretions—which have nothing to do with the harvest. In some of the petitions the *do ut des* principle is very thinly disguised.

**Tsukinami no Matsuri.**—This festival was in honour of the Gods of the "Greater Shrines." The name means monthly festival, but it was really celebrated only twice a year, on the eleventh day of the sixth and twelfth months. The *norito* (No. 7 of the *Yengishiki*) is almost identical with the Toshigohi. The *Jingishiriō*, a modern history of Shinto, describes it as a thanksgiving service for the protecting care of the Gods.

Another Tsukinami ceremony was performed at Ise by a Nakatomi despatched thither as special envoy in connexion with the Toshigohi and also in the sixth and twelfth months of every year. The *norito* (No. 16) read on these occasions was as follows :—

*" He says: ' By the great command of the Mikado, I humbly declare in the mighty presence of the Great Deity whose praises are fulfilled (in the shrine built) upon the nethermost rock-roots on the bank of the River Isuzu in Watarahi. I, of such a rank, of such a name, humbly repeat his commands, as his envoy to convey hither and make offering of the customary great offerings of Praying-for-Harvest in the second month (or as the case may be).' "*

A similar service (No. 17) was performed at the same time in honour of the Goddess of Food. The phraseology is somewhat less honorific.

On the two latter occasions, the Chief Priest of Ise read the following *norito* (No. 19).

" *He says:* ' *Hearken, all ye kannushi and mono-imi to this celestial, this great norito, which I humbly pronounce in the mighty presence of the Heaven-Shining Great Deity, whose praises are fulfilled in Uji of Watarahi, where on the bank of the River Isuzu the pillars of the Great Shrine are stoutly erected, and the projecting cross-beams are exalted to the Plain of High-Heaven. (Here the Negi and Uchi-bito, priests of lower rank, answer "Ô," that is, "Yes," or "Amen") Bless the life of our Sovereign as a long life, let his reign be prosperous, firm and enduring as a pile of multitudinous rocks, and show thy favour to the princes born of him. As to the functionaries of every rank, down to the peasants of the four quarters of the Under-Heaven, make the five grains which they long and peacefully cultivate to flourish abund antly. Favour them with thy protection, and grant them thy blessing.*

" ' *On this seventeenth day of the sixth month (or as the case may be) as the morning sun rises in glory, I fulfil thy praises, setting before thee in ample measure, like seas and mountains, the tribute yarn and the great food-offerings of holy rice and sake, provided according to custom by the con secrated peasants of the three districts, and the various localities of the various provinces, while the Great Nakatomi himself is hidden in offering-branches.* .

" ' *Hearken, all ye kannushi and mono-imi.*'

" *He says : ' This service is likewise addressed to the Ara-matsuri shrine and to the Tsukiyomi (Moon-God) shrine.'* (*The kannushi again answer ' O.'*)"

**Ki-u no Matsuri** (praying for rain). No *norito* of this ceremony is given in the *Yengishiki.* It was performed in

honour of the Gods of eighty-five shrines, and was accom
panied by the usual offerings of cloth-stuffs. To a few out
of the number a black horse was offered in addition. The
choice of a black animal for this purpose belongs to the
magical pre-religious stage of thought. Black is the colour
of the rain-clouds, and therefore, on the principle that what
suggests a thing will actually produce it, the exhibition of a
black horse is thought likely to make the clouds collect and
rain to fall. A white horse was offered when fine weather
was desired.

Mr. Weston, in his 'Mountaineering in the Japanese
Alps,' describes the sacrifice of a black dog "symbolical of
the wished-for storm-clouds" in order to cause rain.

**Kamu miso no matsuri** (divine-clothing-service).—This
ceremony consisted in presenting offerings of clothing to
the Sun-Goddess at Ise. It was celebrated twice a year, in
the fourth and ninth months. The *norito* (No. 18) is very
short and uninteresting.

**Service for the Removal of the Ise Shrine.**—The *norito*
(No. 24) is a very short formula. It announces to the Sun-
Goddess the rebuilding of her shrine, which took place every
twentieth year. A similar form was used in the case of the
Food-Goddess.

**Oho-tono hogahi** (luck-wishing or blessing of the Great
Palace).—This ceremony was performed on the morning
after the Kamu image and the Nihi-name. It was in honour
of three deities, namely, the two Yabune no Kami, or
House deities, and Oho-miya no me, a personified Lady
Chamberlain.

I quote from Sir Ernest Satow's 'Ancient Japanese
Rituals' in the *T. A. S. J.*, vol. ix. pt. ii., a ninth-century
description of this ceremony :—

"The Jingikwan took four boxes containing precious
stones, cut paper-mulberry bark, rice and sake in bottles,
and placed them on two eight-legged tables, which were
then borne by four attendants, preceded by Nakatomi and

Imbe functionaries, all wearing wreaths and scarfs of paper-mulberry bark, walking in double line, the rear being brought up by virgin priestesses. On the procession arriving in front of the Palace gate, the tables were deposited under the arcade which ran along the outside of the wall. A servant called out for admittance, and the porter having announced the procession by saying that an officer of the Imperial Household had asked for admission in order to pronounce the Luck-wishing of the Great Palace, the order, 'Let him pronounce it,' was transmitted back from the Mikado. The porter thereupon called out 'Let him declare his name and surname,' in reply to which the officer advanced to a spot previously marked out by a wooden ticket with his name on it, and said: 'It is so and so, of the Jingikwan, who wish to perform the Luck-wishing of the Great Palace.' To this the Mikado's answer was 'Call them.' The officer of the household replied 'Ô,' and retiring called the functionaries of the Jingikwan, who in their turn replied 'Ô.' The Nakatomi and Imbe then put on their wreaths of paper-mulberry, to which the latter added straps of the same material, and advanced ahead of the tables up to the 'Hall of Benevolence and Long Life.' The virgin priestesses had meanwhile entered by another gate, and were waiting in the Palace enclosure. They now followed the tables, and came up to the verandah on the east side of the building, where they took charge of the boxes of offerings. The procession then entered the build ing. One virgin priestess went to the Hall of Audience and scattered rice about it, while another proceeded to the gate on its south side and performed the same ceremony there. The Imbe took out the precious stones and hung them at the four corners of the Hall, and the priestesses withdrew, after sprinkling sake and scattering rice and cut paper-mulberry fibre at the four corners of the interior. The Nakatomi stood on the south side of the building while the Imbe turned to the south-east, and in a low voice read the ritual. The whole company next went to the Mikado's bath-room, and hung precious stones at its four angles, and the same at his privy, while the priestesses scattered rice and sprinkled sake as before."

The *norito* (No. 8) of this ceremony, as appears from the archaic forms of language which it contains, is probably very ancient. It is quoted in the *Kogojiui ;* and the *Nihongi* describes as " an ancient saying " a sentence which forms part of it.

The reader will note the confusion—of a kind inherent in all mythologies—between the house considered as a deity and the protecting deity of the house.

"*When by command of the dear, divine ancestor and ancestress who divinely dwell in the Plain of High Heaven, the Sovran Grandchild\* was made to take his seat on the high august throne of Heaven, and the Heavenly Emblems, namely, the mirror and the sword, were delivered to him, these words of blessing were pronounced : ' Let our sovran great offspring, the Sovran Grandchild, receiving over the celestial Sun-succession on this high throne of Heaven, rule tranquilly for myriads of thousands of autumns, for long autumns, over the Great-Eight-islands, the Rich Reed-plain, Land of fair rice-ears, as a peaceful country.' With these words they delivered it unto him. Then, celestial counsel having been held, they put to silence the rock-roots and tree-roots, even to the smallest blades of grass, that previously had power of speech.*

"*And for the Sovran Grandchild who in Heavenly Sun-succession rules the Under-Heaven, to which he had descended, trees are now cut down with the sacred axes of the Imbe in the great valleys and the small valleys of the secluded mountains, and sacrifice having been made of their tops and bottoms to the God of the mountains, the middle parts are brought forth and set up as sacred pillars with sacred mattocks to form a fair*

---

\* Ninigi. Below the same term means the Mikado.

*Palace wherein the Sovran Grandchild finds shelter from the sky and shelter from the sun. To thee, therefore, Ya-bune no Mikoto [the Palace treated as a God] I address these heavenly, wondrous, auspicious words of calm and blessing.*

" *He says : ' I humbly declare the names of the Gods who calmly and peacefully watch so that this Great Palace where he holds rule, as far downwards as the lowermost rock-roots, suffer no harm from reptiles among its bottom-ropes* * as far upwards as the blue clouds are diffused in the Plain of High Heaven, may suffer no harm from flying birds in the celestial smoke-hole,† that the joinings of the firmly planted pillars, and of the crossbeams, rafters, doors, and windows may not move or make a noise, that there may be no slackening of the tied rope-knots and no dishevelment of the roof-thatch, no creaking of the floor-joints or alarms by night. I humbly praise your honoured names, to wit, Yabune Kukunochi no Mikoto and Yabune Toyo-uke hime no Mikoto [House-tree God and House-food Goddess].‡ And inasmuch as you humbly preserve the Sovran Grandchild's reign to be firm and enduring, and humbly bless it as a lasting, prosperous, and perfect reign, the Imbe no Sukune [name], adding shining cloth and lustrous fine cloth to the countless strings of fair jewels prepared by the sacred jewel-makers with observance of purity and avoidance of pollution, and hanging stout straps on weak shoulders [will offer them to you], with words of blessing and calm. And let the Gods Kamu-nahobi and Oho-nahobi peacefully and tranquilly exercise their office, correcting, whether in things heard or in things seen, any omission which he may make in so doing'*

" *More especially does he humbly declare : ' Naming her as Oho-miya-no-me I humbly fulfil her praises because, within the same Palace as the Sovran Grandchild, she blocks the way and takes cognizance and makes choice of the persons who go*

---

* The ancient Japanese houses had their timbers lashed together with ropes.
† The translation is doubtful.
‡ See above, p. 167.

*in and out, with words amends and mollifies the hurry and roughness of the Gods, keeps from error the hands and feet of the scarf-wearing attendants and the strap-wearing attend-ants\* who serve the morning meal and the evening meal of the Sovran Grandchild, preventing the Imperial Princes, Princes, Ministers of State, and all the functionaries from indulging their several inclinations and causing them, pure of evil intents and base hearts, to attend in the Palace with a Palace-attendance, and to serve in the Palace with a Palace-service, and amending to eye and ear all faults and errors, so that their duties may be performed peacefully and tranquilly.'"*

**Naishi-dokoro or Kashiko-dokoro.**—Every new moon offerings were presented in the *naishi-dokoro* (*naishi*-place) or *kashiko-dokoro* (place of reverence†) by the *naishi* or female attendants of the Palace to the sacred mirror which represented the Sun-Goddess. They consisted of rice, cakes, paper, cloth, egg-plant, fish, shellfish, &c. Twice a year *Kagura* was performed. The ceremonies used on these occasions were regulated in Uda's reign (889-898) and closely resembled those of the Great Shrine of Ise. The *Yengishiki* has not preserved the *norito* belonging to it.

A Japanese writer thus describes the modern form of this ceremony :—

"Within the palace there is a large hall, the *kashiko-dokoro*, or place of reverence, constructed of milk-white, knotless timbers, exquisitely joined and smooth as mirrors, but absolutely devoid of decoration. At one end stands a large shrine, also of snow-pure wood, with delicately chased mountings of silver gilt. It encloses models of the divine insignia, and a number of long, narrow tablets of pine, on which are inscribed the posthumous titles of all the

---

\* Male and female attendants.

† These terms are often used as synonymous with the regalia, of which the Sun-mirror was the chief.

Emperors since the days of Jimmu. Within the folding doors of the shrine hangs a curtain woven of bamboo threads. At the appointed hour, generally the grey of morning, *sakaki* boughs are laid beside the shrine and provision of incense is made ; after which the officials of the Bureau of Rites and those of the Imperial Household file in and seat themselves on either side of the hall. The doors of the shrine are then opened and offerings of various kinds—vegetables, fish, cloth, and so forth—are carried in and ranged before it, solemn music in Japanese style being performed the while. Thereafter the princes of the blood and all officials of the two highest ranks as well as the peers of the ' musk-chamber ' and the ' golden-pheasant chamber' enter, and when they are seated the Emperor himself appears and, proceeding slowly to the shrine, bows his head, takes a branch of *sakaki* with pendant *gohei*, and having waved it in token of the purification of sins, ignites a stick of incense* and places it upright in the censer, thereafter repeating a ritual (*norito*). So long as his Majesty is present in the hall, all the officials remain stand ing. His Majesty then retires, and, on his departure, worship of the same kind, but without any prayer, is per formed by a representative of the Prince Imperial," and subsequently by the other members of the Court.

**Mitama Shidzumuru no matsuri** (ceremony for settling or calming the august spirit).

There was an ancient ceremony called *mitama furishiki* that is, shaking the august jewels, which is referred to in the *Kiujiki*. We are there told that when the Sun-Goddess sent down Ninigi to rule the world, she gave him " ten auspicious treasures, namely, one mirror of the offing, one mirror of the shore, one eight-hands-breadth sword, one jewel (*tama*) of birth, one jewel of return from death, one perfect jewel, one road-returning jewel (that is, a jewel which has the property of making evil things return by the road they came),

---

* The incense is Buddhist.

one serpent-scarf (a scarf which has power when waved to keep away serpents), one bee-scarf, and one scarf of various things," saying : " In case of illness shake these treasures and repeat to them the words, ' One, two, three, four, five, six, seven, eight, nine, ten.' If thou doest so the dead will certainly return to life."

The *Nihongi* states that in A.D. 685 the ceremony of calling on the spirit (*mitama*) was performed for the Mikado's sake. An ancient gloss identifies this ceremony with that of the *mitama furishiki* just described. The object of the two ceremonies was, no doubt, the same, but it is to be noted that *mitama*, which in the one case means jewel or talisman, in the other means spirit—a rare case in the older Shinto records of this word being applied to the human soul. The phrases " calling on the spirit " and "settling the spirit " are of Chinese origin, *mitama* being in this connexion simply a translation of the Chinese *hun* (pronounced *kon* in Japanese). The same ceremony is known in China, and some features of its Japanese form were probably borrowed from that country. Its object, according to a modern writer, was to summon back to and settle in the body the volatile *kon*. It was performed every year in the eleventh month in the Chapel of the Jingikwan, and also at one time in connexion with the coronation ceremony.

The *norito* (No. 15 of the *Yengishiki*) begins with a recital of the Mikado's divine claims to sovereignty. Then the offerings are enumerated. It concludes with a prayer to the eight Gods of the Jingikwan to grant the Mikado a long and prosperous reign, and that he may dwell peace fully in his Palace during the ensuing year. It says nothing of the Mikado's spirit, an expression found only in the heading, which may be supposed to be a later addition.

A performance by the Miko resembling that of Uzume before the Rock-cave of Heaven, and comprising the repeti-tion of the magic words one, two, three, &c., formed part, no doubt the oldest part, of the ceremony. It is now usually called by the Chinese name *Chinkonsai.*

There is a story of a thief having stolen the clothing presented on this occasion, and also the string which tied the Mikado's *mitama,* whatever that may mean.

**Oho-harahi** (Great Purification).*—This ceremony in cludes a preliminary lustration, expiatory offerings, and the recital of a *norito* or formula—not a prayer, as it is some times called—in which the Mikado, by virtue of the autho rity transmitted to him from the Sun-Goddess, declares to his ministers and people the absolution of their sins and impurities. This formula is often referred to as if it constituted the whole ceremony. It is known as the *Nakatomi no Oho-harahi,* because in ancient times it was usually read by the Nakatomi as representatives of the Mikado.

The myths which represent Izanagi as flinging down his garments during his flight from Yomi, and washing away in the sea the pollution contracted by his visit there, and describe the expiatory offerings exacted from Susa no wo, presume an acquaintance with the ceremony of which the Oho-harahi *norito* forms a chief part. The *Nihongi* informs us, under the legendary date A.D. 200, that after the sudden death of the Mikado Chiuai, his widow and successor Jingo commanded her ministers "to purge offences and to rectify transgressions," while in the parallel passage of the *Kojiki*† details are given of these offences, which, as far as they go, are identical with those enumerated in the Oho-harahi itself. Great Purifications are mentioned as having been performed in 676, 678, and 686. The Japanese scholar Mabuchi ascribes the present Oho-harahi *norito* to this last-named period. In substance it must be very much older.

---

* I am much indebted to Dr. Florenz's exhaustive monograph on this rite in vol. xxvii. of the *T. A. S. J.*

† Ch. K., p. 230.

The chief ceremony was performed in the capital twice yearly, on the last days of the sixth and twelfth months. These dates are not chosen arbitrarily. There is a natural impulse at the close of the year to wipe out old scores and to make a fresh start with good resolutions. The *tsuina*,[*] or demon-expelling ceremonies, of the last day of the year, described below, are prompted by a similar motive. Tenny son gives expression to this feeling in his ' In Memoriam ':—

> " The year is dying in the night,
> Ring out, wild bells, and let him die.
>
> &ast; &ast; &ast; &ast;
>
> Ring out the false, ring in the true,
>
> &ast; &ast; &ast; &ast;
>
> Ring out the want, the care, the sin,
>
> &ast; &ast; &ast; &ast;
>
> Ring out old shapes of foul disease."

The summer celebration of the Oho-harahi is analogous to the custom of lustration, or bathing on St. John's Eve, formerly practised in Germany, Italy, and other countries.

The Chinese had an Oho-harahi, defined by Mr. Giles in his ' Chinese Dictionary ' as " a religious ceremony of puri fication performed in spring and autumn, with a view to secure divine protection for agricultural interests." The Ainus of Yezo have a similar ceremony.[†]

The Oho-harahi was not confined to the last days of the sixth and twelfth months. It was performed as a pre liminary to several of the great Shinto ceremonies, notably the Ohonihe, and on other emergencies, such as an outbreak of pestilence,[‡] the finding of a dead body in the Palace (865), the officiating of a Nakatomi who had performed Buddhist rites (816), &c.

---

[*] See Index, *sub voce.*

[†] See Mr. Batchelor in *T. A. S. J.*, xxiv. 46.

[‡] It will be remembered that it was on an occasion of this kind that Agamemnon ordered an Oho-harahi to be performed :—

> ......λαους απολυμαίνεσθαι ανωγεν.
>
> Ὁι δ' ἀπελυμάινοντο καὶ εἰς ἅλα λύματ' ἔβαλλον.
>
> ' Iliad,' I. 313.

We learn from the regulations of the period Jogwan (859-876) that at that time the ceremony was performed at the southern gate of the Kioto Palace, in front of which there was a canal. The purification offerings were set out before this gate. The officials took their seats in due order, the women being separated off by a curtain. The officials of the Jingikwan then distributed *kiri-nusa*\* among the audience, upon which the Nakatomi took his place and recited the ritual, the officials responding *Ô* after every paragraph. When the purification was finished, the Oho-nusa ceremony was performed. It had also a purifying influence, and consisted, according to Dr. Florenz, in bran dishing the Oho-nusa over the assembly, first to left, then to right, and then again to left.

The *norito* (No. 10 of the *Yengishiki*) is as follows :—

"*He†* says: '*Give ear, all ye Imperial Princes, Princes, Ministers of State, and functionaries who are here assembled, and hearken every one to the Great Purification by which at this year's interlune of the sixth (or twelfth) month he deigns to purge and absolve all manner of faults and transgressions which may have been committed by those who serve in the Imperial Court, whether they wear the scarf or the shoulder-strap, whether they bear on their back the quiver or gird on them the sword, the eighty attendants of the attendants, including, moreover, all those who do duty in the various offices of State.*'

"*He* says: '*Hearken, all of you. The Sovran dear ancestors,‡ who divinely dwell in the Plain of High Heaven, having summoned to an assembly the eight hundred myriads of deities, held divine counsel with them, and then gave command, saying: "Let our August Grandchild§ hold serene*

---

\* See Index.

† "He" is the officiating Nakatomi, speaking on behalf of the Mikado.

‡ Usually said to be Taka-musubi, Kamu-musubi, and the Sun-Goddess.

§ Ninigi.

*rule over the fertile reed-plain, the region of fair rice-ears\**
*as a land of peace."*

"'*But in the realm thus assigned to him there were savage
deities. These were called to a divine account and expelled
with a divine expulsion. Moreover, the rocks, trees, and
smallest leaves of grass which had power of speech were put
to silence. Then they despatched him downward from his
celestial everlasting throne, cleaving as he went with an awful
way-cleaving the many-piled clouds of Heaven, and delivered
to him the Land. At the middle point of the lands of the four
quarters thus entrusted to him, Yamato, the High-Sun-Land,
was established as a peaceful land, and there was built here for
the Sovran Grandchild a fair Palace wherewithal to shelter
him from sun and sky,† with massy pillars based deep on the
nethermost rocks and upraising to the Plain of High Heaven
the cross-timbers of its roof.*

"'*Now of the various faults and transgressions to be
committed by the celestial race destined more and.more to
people this land of his peaceful rule, some are of Heaven,
to wit, the breaking down of divisions between rice-fields,
filling up of irrigation channels, removing water-pipes, sow
ing seed over again,‡ planting skewers,§ flaying alive,*

---

\* Poetical expressions for Japan.

† That is, rain.

‡ Sowing wild oats was one of the misdeeds of Loki, the Scandinavian
mischief-God. Compare also Matthew xiii. 24: "The kingdom of Heaven
is likened unto a man that sowed good seed in his field: but while men
slept, his enemy came and sowed tares also among the wheat." See above,
p. 97.

§ Motoori says that this is with the malicious intention of injuring the feet
of the owner of the ground. I prefer the explanation suggested by the *Shiki*,
an ancient commentary on the *Nihongi*. It says: "Planting rods (or skewers)
in the rice-fields with words of incantation is called 'skewer-planting.' The
object is the destruction of any one who should wrongly claim that field.
The present custom of planting skewers in a field whose ownership is disputed
is probably a survival of this." *Kushi*, or skewer, is the word used for the
wand to which offerings are attached. See Florenz's 'Ancient Japanese
Rituals' in *T. A. S. J.*, p. 32.

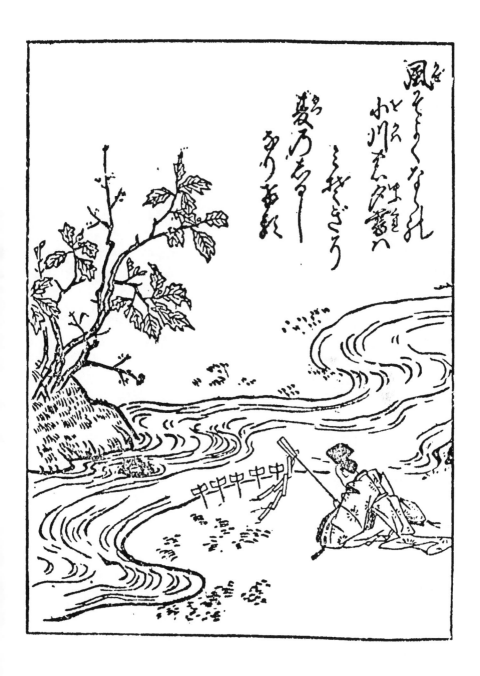

風をいたくなれそ
とて
　小川名を打越へ
　　　み麦とそろ
麦乃たて
あり其を

*flaying backwards. These are distinguished as Heavenly offences* *

"*' Earthly offences which will be committed are the cutting of living bodies, the cutting of dead bodies, leprosy, kokumi,†† incest of a man with his mother or daughter, with his mother-in-law or step-daughter, bestiality, calamities from creeping things, from the high Gods‡ and from high birds, killing animals, bewitchments.§*

"*' Whensoever they may be committed, let the Great Naka-tomi, in accordance with the custom of the Heavenly Palace, cut Heavenly saplings at the top and cut them at the bottom, and make thereof a complete array of one thousand stands for offerings.‖*

* The native commentators point out that the "Heavenly Offences" are so called because they were first committed by Susa no wo in Heaven. This passage of the *norito* was therefore suggested by the myth. (See above, p. 83.) The object of the myth-maker, however, was simply to enhance the dramatic quality of his story by attributing to the boisterous Rain-storm God misdeeds whose odious character would forcibly strike his audience, a nation of agriculturists. In the *norito* the further step is taken of recognizing the same acts, committed on earth, as offences not only against men, but as sins before the Gods. He may have argued that the Sun-Goddess has a tender care for the rice-fields of her beloved race of men as well as for her own, and that any interference with them is therefore hateful to her. The "skewer-planting" above mentioned points to a still earlier attempt to bring agriculture under religious protection. There is no substantial basis for the distinction between Heavenly and Earthly offences. The author's real object in making it was no doubt rhetorical. He wished to break up the long list of offences into two balanced sentences, after a fashion common in Japanese poetry and poetical prose composition. I suspect that the "flaying alive" and "flaying backwards" were magical practices of the same class as the "witchcraft" condemned just below. The flaying was objected to, not for its cruelty, but on account of the malicious use to which the skins so procured were put. See Index, *Inugami.*

† A disease which has not been clearly identified. Dr. Florenz renders "afflicted with excrescences."

‡ Especially being struck by lightning.

§ Another rendering is "killing animals by bewitchments." The Chinese character used implies that it is for an evil purpose.

‖ Dr. Florenz, following Motoori, renders "and deposit [upon them] in abundance [the purification offerings]." The character of these offerings is indicated by a passage in the *Nihongi* (A.D. 676): "The Mikado commanded,

"' *Having trimmed rushes of heaven at the top and trimmed them at the bottom, let him split them into manifold slivers.**

"' *Then let him recite the mighty ritual words of the celestial ritual.*†

"' *When he does so, the Gods of Heaven, thrusting open the adamantine door of Heaven and cleaving the many-piled clouds of Heaven with an awful way-cleaving will lend ear. The Gods of Earth, climbing to the tops of the high mountains and to the tops of the low mountains, sweeping apart the mists of the high mountains and the mists of the low mountains, will lend ear.*

"' *When they have thus lent ear, all offences whatsoever will be annulled, from the Court of the Sovran Grandchild to the provinces of the four quarters of the Under-Heaven.*

"' *As the many-piled clouds of Heaven are scattered by the breath of the Wind-Gods ; as the morning breezes and the evening breezes dissipate the dense morning vapours and the dense evening vapours ; as a huge ship, moored in a great harbour, casting off its stern moorings, casting off its bow moorings, drives forth into the great sea-plain ; as yonder*

saying : ' Let a Great Purification (Oho-harahi) be held in all quarters. The articles needed for this purpose are to be forwarded to the shrines of purifica tion by the governors of each province, to wit, one horse and one piece of cloth. The other things are to be supplied by the governors of districts, namely, each one sword, one deerskin, one mattock, one smaller sword, one sickle, one set of arrows, and one sheaf of rice in the ear. Further, let each house provide a bundle of hemp.'" This Oho-harahi was doubtless celebrated in consequence of the appearance of a comet at this time. On another occa sion (681) each local governor supplied a slave as a purification offering. In later times the Harahi-tsu-mono, or purification offerings, were furnished by the central Government.

* The meaning of this clause is doubtful. The object seems to be to pro vide a brush for brushing away (*harahi*) offences. Sir E. Satow says, with regard to a different ceremony : " The high priest waves before the company a sort of broom made of grass, to symbolize the sweeping away of their offences."

† In later times it was thought, without sufficient reason, that the " ritual words" here spoken of were a special form of incantation distinct from the *norito* itself.

*thick brushwood is smitten and cleared away by the sharp sickle forged in the fire, so shall all offences be utterly annulled. Therefore he (the Mikado) is graciously pleased to purify and cleanse them away. The Goddess called Se-ori-tsu-hime who dwells in the rapids of the swift streams whose cataracts tumble headlong from the tops of the high mountains and from the tops of the low mountains will bear them out into the great sea-plain. Thereupon the Goddess called Haya-aki-tsu-hime, who dwells in the myriad meetings of the tides of the myriad brine-paths of the myriad ways of the currents of the boisterous sea will swallow them up. And the God Ibuki-do nushi, who dwells in the Breath-blowing-place,\* will puff them away to the Root-country, the Bottom Country.†  Then the Goddess Haya-sasura-hime,‡ who dwells in the Root-country, the Bottom-country, will banish and abolish them. When they have been so destroyed, every one, from the servants of the Imperial Court to the four quarters of the Under-Heaven, will remain void of all offences whatsoever.*

"'Attend, therefore, all of you to this Great Purification, by which he is graciously pleased at sunset on this interlunar day of the sixth (or twelfth) month of this year to purify and cleanse you, having led hither a horse as an animal that pricks up its ears to the Plain of High-Heaven.'§

"He says: ' Ye diviners (Urabe) of the four provinces, remove them to the great river-way and abolish them.' "‖

---

\* See above, p. 261.

† Yomi or Hades.

‡ Swift-banishment-lady.

§ A horse was one of the expiatory offerings. It seems here to typify the attentive attitude of the audience, or perhaps of the deities concerned.

‖ *Harahi-zare.* There is some confusion here between the offences and the expiatory offerings. The *harahi-tsu-mono* were then taken away and thrown into some convenient river. I suspect, however, that most of them were not thrown away, but went to provide a fund for the expenses of the ceremony. It is not clear what became of the horse or of the slaves. The *harahi-tsu-mono* were not gifts to any particular Gods, but rather, like the scape-goat of the Mosaic law, vehicles by which the transgressions of the people were conveyed away. But it is better not to put this too sweepingly. There is reason to

In addition to the Oho-harahi, or National Purifications, there were local and individual celebrations. In the latter case, of which Susa no wo's punishment is the mythical type, the *harahi-tsu-mono* were naturally furnished by the person for whose benefit they were performed, and so amounted practically to a fine on the offender. The *Nihongi* (A.D. 646) mentions a number of cases in which travellers and others were compelled by the country people to do *harahi*, that is, to pay a fine, under various pretences. For example, when a man returning from forced labour fell down by the roadside and died, the villagers of the place said, "Why should a man be allowed to die on our road?" and detained the companions of the deceased until they had done *harahi*. Cases of drowning were followed by similar claims, and even the cooking of rice by the roadside or the upsetting of a borrowed pot. An Imperial decree was issued prohibiting these extortions, which are described as habitual with the unenlightened vulgar.

The application of the *harahi* to the purpose of a fine was regulated by an ordinance which was issued in 801. Those who were guilty of neglect in connexion with the celebration of the Ohonihe, or who, during the month of special avoidance of impurity, contracted mourning, visited the sick, were concerned with capital sentences, ate flesh, or touched anything impure were mulcted in an *oho-harahi*, which in this case meant simply a heavy fine. It consisted of one horse, two swords, two bows, and a long list of other sundries. Other offences of the same classes were fined in a *naka-harahi*, or medium *harahi*.

Dr. Florenz describes a more modern form of *harahi* as follows: "As a third species of *harahi* we may mention the purification preceding every greater festival of a Shinto shrine, through which the priests and others taking part in

think that by some they were thought to be offerings to Se-ori-tsu-hirhe and the other deities mentioned. At the present day they consist of a few pieces of cloth.

the Matsuri are purified. This ceremony takes place in a
hall or open place specially prepared for the purpose, called
*harahi-dokoro* (purification-place). It consists in the *Kami-
oroshi* (bringing down the spirits of the purifying deities)
Into the *himorogi*, which stands on an eight-legged table in
the middle of the *harahi-dokoro*, the recitation of the purifi
cation prayer, various subsequent symbolic ceremonies, and
the *Kami-age*, or sending back the Gods to their abodes.
Thereupon the priests are considered to be pure, and the
Matsuri proper can begin. The prayer addressed to the
Gods is as follows :—

"*In reverence and awe : The great gods of the purification
place who came into existence when the Great God Izanagi
deigned to wash and purify himself on the plain of Ahagi
[east] of Tachibana [near] the River Woto in Himuka in
Tsukushi, shall deign to purify and deign to cleanse whatever
there may be of sins and pollutions committed inadvertently
or deliberately by the officials serving here to-day. Listen ye
to these my words. Thus I say reverentially.*"

In later times there were many abuses and perversions of
the harahi, due mainly to Buddhist influence. The
formula was much modified, and is found in numerous
versions. Some of these are wholly Buddhist, such as the
well-known "Rokkon shojo" (may the six senses be pure),
so constantly in the mouths of pilgrims at this day. Others
include a prayer for purity of heart, which is an idea quite
foreign to the ancient Shinto. *Harahi-bako* (*harahi*-boxes)
were sold at Ise with inscriptions half Buddhist and half
Shinto. In imitation of a similar Buddhist practice, these
boxes contained a certificate that the *harahi* had been
recited one thousand or ten thousand times for the
purchaser's benefit. Pieces of the *gohei* wand used by the
priests at the Oho-harahi of the sixth and twelfth months
were enclosed with these certificates. Sometimes a small
fragment of the old shrine, which was broken up every

twentieth year and a new one erected, was compressed between two thin boards and called an *o-harahi*. Pilgrims received these in return for their offerings. The devout could even purchase them from hawkers, who went about the country (like the sellers of indulgences in Luther's time) disposing of them for the benefit of the shrine. This practice is now prohibited.*

The ideas associated with the *harahi* ceremony also underwent a change. Some writers speak of it as intended "to propitiate evil deities." The *harahi* sold by the priests of Ise were set up in the *Kami-dana*, or domestic shrine, and worshipped as the *shintai* of the deity. They were supposed to be indestructible by fire or water, to keep away robbers, to heal diseases, to make the old young, and to protect against calamity of every kind.

In some later forms of the *harahi* the purifying Gods are besought to cleanse from evil, sin, and pollution. This marks a different attitude from that of the Nakatomi no Oho-harahi, where they are merely a part of the machinery of purification.

**Invocation by the Hereditary Corporation of Scholars of Yamato and Kahachi.**—This *norito* (No. 11 of the *Yengi-shiki*) was read previous to the performance of the Oho-harahi. The two corporations named were descendants, or, at least, successors of the Korean scholars who in the fifth century introduced Chinese learning into Japan The language, thought, and sentiment of this *norito* are Chinese. The Sun, Moon (not Hirume and Tsukiyomi) and stars, the High Emperor of Supreme Heaven (Shangti), the five Emperors of the five cardinal points, the King-father of the East, the King-mother of the West, the four influences of the four seasons, and other Chinese divinities are invoked to grant prosperity to the Mikado. An offering

---

* See 'Notes of some Minor Japanese Religious Practices,' by Mr. B. H. Chamberlain, in the *Journal* of the Anthropological Institute, May, 1893, and Sir E. Satow's 'Visit to the Shrines of Ise,' *T. A. S. J.*, 1874.

was made of a silver man in order that calamity might be averted from him, and of a golden sword so that his reign might be lengthened. The sword, really of wood gilt, was called the *harahi-tsu-tachi*, or sword of purification, and was breathed upon by the Mikado before being taken away. The silver man was also for use as an *aga-mono*, or ransom-object.

**Michi-ahe no Matsuri.**—The object of this ceremony was to invoke the aid of the Sahe no Kami in preventing evil spirits, that is to say, pestilences, from entering Kioto.* The *norito* (No. 13 of the *Yengishiki*) read on this occasion is as follows :—

"*I humbly declare in the presence of the Sovran Gods, whose functions first began in the Plain of High Heaven, when they fulfilled the praises† of the Sovran Grandchild by guarding the great eight-road-forks like a multitudinous assemblage of rocks.‡*

"*Naming your honoured names, to wit, Yachimata-hiko, Yachimata-hime, and Kunado, I fulfil your praises. When ever from the Root-country the Bottom-country there may come savage and unfriendly beings, consort not and parley not with them, but if they go below, keep watch below, if they go above, keep watch above, protecting us against pollution with a night guarding and with a day guarding.*

"*The offerings I furnish in your honour are bright cloth, shining cloth, soft cloth, and rough cloth. Of sake I raise up the tops of the jars and fill and range in order the bellies of the jars. [Grain] in juice and in ear I offer you. Of things that dwell in the mountains and on the moors I offer the soft of hair and the coarse of hair. Of things that dwell in the blue sea-plain, the broad of fin and the narrow of fin, even to the weeds of the offing and the weeds of the shore. Peacefully*

---

* See above, p. 187.

† That is, "did honour to."

‡ These deities were worshipped at cross-roads, and were called the eight-cross-road deities.

*partaking of these plenteous offerings, which I lay before you
in full measure like a cross range of hills, hold guard on the
highways like a multitudinous assemblage of rocks, preserving
from pollution the Sovran Grandchild firmly and enduringly,
and bless his reign to be a prosperous reign.*

"*Also be pleased peacefully to preserve from pollution the
Imperial Princes, the Princes, the Ministers of State, and all
the functionaries, including, moreover, the people of the Under-
Heaven.*

"*I, as official of the Department of Religion, humbly fulfil
your praises by this celestial, this great pronouncement.*"

The offerings included hides of oxen, boar, deer, and
bear, in addition to those above enumerated.

**Sagi-cho.**—This is a modern ceremony, which was also
intended to repel evil influences. The Wakan-Sansai-
dzuye (1713) gives the following description of it as
practised in the Imperial Palace :—

"*On the fifteenth day of the first month\* green bamboos
are burnt in the courtyard of the Seiryoden, and happy reports†
sent up to Heaven therewith. On the eighteenth also bamboos
are dressed up with fans attached to them, which are burnt
at the same place. There is a reader of spells called Daikoku
Matsudaiyu, who has four followers, two old men and two
old women. These wear devil-masks and 'red-bear' wigs.
The two old women carry drums, and the two old men run
after them trying to beat the drums. There are two boys
without masks, but with 'red-bear' wigs, who beat double
cymbals. Moreover, there are five men in dress of ceremony
who stand in a row and join in with cries of 'dondoya,' while
one costumed somewhat differently calls out 'Ha!'*"

The Wakan Sansai does not know the origin of this
ceremony, which is said to expel demons. There is a

---

\* The date of one Sahe no Kami festival.
† Written on paper and thrown into the flames.

similar Chinese practice, though on a different date, namely, the first day of the year. Its object is said to be to drive away mountain elves.

**Mikado matsuri.**—This ceremony was in honour of two Gate Gods named Kushi-iha-mado (wondrous-rock-gate) and Toyo-iha-mado (rich-rock-gate).* The *Yengishiki* contains a *norito* (No. 9) in which their praises are fulfilled, because they prevent the entrance to the Palace of noxious things and exercise a superintendence over the persons who come in and go out.

**Tsuina** or **Oni-yarahi,** that is to say, demon expelling, is a sort of drama in which disease, or more generally ill-luck, is personified, and driven away with threats and a show of violence. Like the Oho-harahi, it was performed on the last day of the year. This association is only natural. The demons of the *tsuina* are personified wintry influences, with the diseases which they bring with them, while the Oho-harahi is intended to cleanse the people from sin and uncleanness, things closely related to disease, as well as from disease itself. Though probably of Chinese origin, the *tsuina* is a tolerably ancient rite. It is alluded to in the *Nihongi* under the date A.D. 689. It was at one time performed at Court on an imposing scale. Four bands of twenty youths, each wearing a four-eyed mask, and each carrying a halberd in the left hand, marched simultaneously from the four gates of the Palace, driving the devils before them. Another account of this ceremony says that a man disguised himself as the demon of pestilence, in which garb he was shot at and driven off by the courtiers armed with peach-wood bows and arrows of reed. (See illustration, p. 310.) Peach-wood staves were used for the same purpose. There was formerly a practice at Asakusa in Tokio on the last day of the year for a man got up as a devil to be chased round the pagoda there by another wearing a mask. After this 3,000 tickets were

* See above, p. 168.

scrambled for by the spectators. These were carried away and pasted up over the doors as a charm against pestilence. At the present day, the popular form of *tsuina* consists in scattering parched beans with the cry, "*Oni ha soto: fuku ha uchi*" that is, "Out with the devils and in with the luck." The former phrase is uttered in a loud voice, the latter in a low tone. This office should properly be discharged by the head of the family, but it is frequently delegated to a servant. The performer is called the *toshi-otoko*, or year-man. In the Shogun's palace a specially appointed *toshi-otoko* sprinkled parched beans in all the principal rooms. These beans were picked up by the women of the palace, who wrapped them in paper in number equal to the years of their age, and then flung them backwards out of doors. Sometimes *tsuina* beans were gathered by people who had reached an unlucky year (*yaku-toshi*), one for each year of their age and one over, and wrapped in paper with a small copper coin, which had been rubbed over their body to transfer the ill-luck. These were placed in a bamboo tube and flung away at cross roads. This was called *yaku-sute* (flinging away ill-luck). Other people pass under seven *tori-wi* as an antidote.

The significance of the peach and bean in this ceremony has been already explained.[*] The vulgar notion is that the beans hit the devils in the eye and blind them. A more philosophical theory is that the beans dispel the *in-aku no ki*, or female evil influences, and welcome in the *sei-yo*, green male influences. By the female influences are here meant wintry influences; by male influences those of spring.

Mr. J. G. Frazer, in 'The Golden Bough,' iii. 67, second edition, gives an interesting account of another Japanese form of this custom.

The *tsuina* is only a special form of a world-wide ceremony. We may compare with it the Roman Lemuria, a

* See above, pp. 189, 190.

festival for the souls of the dead, in which the celebrators threw black beans nine times behind their backs, believing by this ceremony to secure themselves against the Lemures. Some of my readers may have witnessed the Scotch Hog manay, when the house is thrice circumambulated on the last day of the year in order to frighten away devils. In Lady Burton's life of her husband she tells us that at Trieste on St. Sylvester's Eve, the servants went through a very usual ceremony of forming procession and chevying the evil spirits with sticks and brooms out of the house, inviting the good spirits and good luck to come and dwell there. This is curiously like the Japanese formula just quoted. At Chæronea, in Bœotia, the chief magistrate at the town hall and every householder in his own house, as we learn from Plutarch, had on a certain day to beat a slave with rods of *agnus castus*, and turn him out of doors, with the formula, "Out hunger! in health and wealth." The "expulsion of winter" of Teutonic and Slavonic folk lore belongs to the same class of customs. It should be remembered that the Japanese New Year was later than our own, and was recognized as the beginning of spring.

I must not quote further from the extensive literature of this subject. The reader is referred to 'The Golden Bough,' second edition, vol. iii. pp. 39 *et seqq.*, for a rich collection of evidence relating to it.

**New Year in Modern Japan.**—Although most of the New Year's observances in modern Japan belong to the province of popular magic rather than of Shinto, some general account of them may not be out of place here. The preparations begin on the thirteenth day of the last month, which is therefore called *koto-hajime* (beginning of things). On this day people eat *okotojiru*, a kind of stew, whose ingredients are generally red beans, potatoes, mushrooms, sliced fish, and a root called *konnyaku*. Presents of money are made to servants at this time. About the same date there is a partly real, partly ceremonial house-cleaning called *susu-harahi* (soot-sweeping). The other preparations for the New Year consist in decorating the front entrance by planting at each side of it small fir-trees, with which bamboos are frequently joined. Both of these symbolize an ever-green prosperity. A *shimenaha* is hung over the door or gate, attached to which are fern leaves, and *yudzuri-ha* (*Daphniphyllum macropodum*) with *daidai* (a kind of bitter orange). *Daidai* also means ages, generations, so that this is a sort of punning prayer for long life and the continuance of the family. The prawn, which forms part of the decorations, is supposed by its curved back to suggest old age. Sometimes holly leaves, of which the prickles are thought, as in Europe, obnoxious to demons, bean pods, and a head of a salt sardine (*ihashi*) are added. On the domestic shrine is placed an offering of unleavened cakes of glutinous pounded rice, the preparation of which is a matter for much fun and excitement. These cakes are called *kagami-mochi*, or mirror-cakes, on account of their shape, which is that of a flattened sphere. There are two of them. One is said to represent the sun, the *yō*, or male principle of Chinese philosophy, the parent and the husband, while the other is put for the moon, the female principle, the child and the wife. The *kagami-mochi* is also called the *ha-gatame mochi* (tooth-hardening cake) because it fortifies the constitution. The explanation given is that the Chinese character for *ha*, " tooth," also means " age."

The *tsuina* on the last day of the year is described above.

The first act of the New Year is for the *toshi-otoko* to proceed at dawn to the well or stream whence the household water is supplied. He throws into it a small offering of rice, and draws water in a new pail crowned with *shimenaha*. To drink this water, called *waka-midzu* or young water, brings luck and exemption from disease during the year.

On New Year's day *zoni*, a stew of various kinds of vegetables is eaten and a spiced sake called *toso* is drunk and offered to visitors. No work is done. Visits are exchanged between friends, and formal calls made on superiors. The phrase *Shinnen o medetô gozarimasu* (New Year's congratulations to you) is in everybody's mouth. The *ujigami* are visited and also the Shinto temples which lie in the direction (*ehô*) indicated by the cyclic name of the year. Thus the year of the Hare is associated with the East. The Gods who preside over this particular year are called the Toshi-toku-jin (year-virtue-Gods).

In some places a lamp, consisting of a coarse earthenware saucer with a wick, is lighted at the New Year In honour of the God of the Privy. Sick people at this time throw away their stockings or drawers on a frequented road, and if any one picks them up they expect to recover. Samurai boys receive presents of *hamayumi* (devil-quelling bows).

The seventh of the first month is called Nanakusa, or seven herbs, because in ancient times people went out into the country to gather wild pot-herbs which were made into a mess with rice and eaten on this day.

The New Year's celebrations end with the Sahe no Kami festival (now called *dondo* or *sagichô*) on the fourteenth or fifteenth of the first month, when the decorations above described are made the material for a bonfire.*

**Tatari-gami wo utsushi-tatematsuru norito** (service for the respectful removal of deities who send a curse).— This *norito* (No. 25) is long, but it contains nothing worthy of special notice. The mischievous deities are reminded of the divine right of the Mikado, and of the quelling by Futsunushi and Takemika-dzuchi of the evil beings who plagued Japan before the descent of Ninigi. Offerings of cloth, a mirror, jewels, bows and arrows, swords, a horse, sake, rice in ear and in grain, and various kinds of flesh and vegetables, are set before them, with the request that they should retire to enjoy these good things in some pure

* See above, p. 313.

spot among the hills and streams and remain there, rather than work curses and violence in the Palace.

It is to be distinguished from the Michiahe ritual, which was addressed to the Protective Road-deities in order to keep off pestilence. The present formula is a direct appeal to the evil deities themselves. It is not quite clear who they were. Perhaps all possibly harmful Gods were meant to be included.

**Ceremony when Envoys were despatched to Foreign Countries.**—On such occasions the Gods of Heaven and Earth, with the phallic Chiburi no Kami, or Road-Gods, were worshipped outside the city, the envoys taking part in the ceremony and reading a *norito*. The wood-Gods and mountain-Gods were worshipped before cutting the timber for building their ship.

The *Yengishiki* preserves a *norito* (No. 26) used on one of these occasions. It is addressed to the Sea-Gods of Sumiyoshi, and presents thank-offerings to them for providing a harbour there more convenient for the envoys to sail from than a more distant port in Harima.

**Ho·shidzume no Matsuri** (fire-calming-service).—This ceremony was performed on the last days of the sixth and twelfth months by the Urabe, or diviners, at the four outer corners of the Imperial Palace, in order to prevent its destruction by fire. The Urabe kindled a fire by means of the fire-drill and worshipped it. The following *norito* (No. 12) was read on the occasion :—

" *I humbly declare according to the celestial the great pronouncement (norito) delivered to the Sovran Grandchild by his Sovran, dear, divine ancestor and ancestress when they granted to him the Under-Heaven, commanding him to rule tranquilly as a peaceful realm the fair Rice-ear-land of the Rich-reed-plain, as follows : ' The two Gods Izanagi and Izanami, having become united as husband and wife, procreated the eighty countries and the eighty islands and gave birth to the eight hundred myriads of deities. When Izanami's last son, the God Homusubi (fire-growth), was born her pudenda were burnt and she became rock-concealed.* *She said, " For nights seven and for days seven look not on me, oh my husband." But before the seven days were fulfilled, Izanagi, wondering at her concealment, viewed her, and behold, her pudenda had been burnt in giving birth to the Fire.†  " Oh, my honoured husband" said Izanami, " thou hast insulted me by looking on me despite my having besought thee to refrain from doing so at such a time. Therefore thou must govern the upper world and I the lower world." So saying, she was rock-concealed. When she had reached the Even Pass of Yomi, she bethought herself : " I gave birth to, and left behind me in the upper world ruled by my honoured husband, an evil-hearted child." So she went back and gave birth to other children, namely, the God of Water, the Gourd, the River-weed, and the Clay-mountain-lady, four kinds in all. Moreover, she taught him, saying, " When the temper of this evil-hearted child becomes violent, do thou assuage it with the Water-God, the Gourd, the River-weed, and the Clay-mountain-lady."*

*" ' Therefore do I fulfil thy praises as follows : To the end that thou mayest deign to control thy transports against the Palace of the Sovran Grandchild, I offer thee bright cloth, shining cloth, smooth cloth, and rough cloth, of various colours. Of things which dwell in the blue sea-plain, I offer the broad of fin and the narrow of fin, even unto the weeds of the offing and the weeds of the shore. Of sake, I raise up the tops of the jars, and fill and range in order the bellies of the jars. Nor do I omit rice, cleaned and in the husk. Heaping up these things like a cross-range of hills, I fulfil thy praises according to the Celestial, the Great pronouncement' "*

It will be observed that the tone of this *norito* is not particularly reverent. It reads more like an offer to pay

---

* That is, died.
† What was the God of Fire in the previous sentence is here simply " Fire."

blackmail than a prayer. The phraseology implies that the Mikado is the God's superior. And surely there is a malicious humour in the reminder that the God was a bad boy, to provide the means for whose control and chastise-. ment his mother came back expressly from Hades.

**Kasuga no Matsuri.**—This service is comparatively modern, having been first used in 859. It is in honour of the Gods worshipped at Kasuga, near Nara, namely, Take-mika-dzuchi, Futsunushi, Koyane, and a Goddess who is supposed to be the wife of the last-named deity. It was celebrated twice annually by a priestess despatched from Kioto to Nara for the purpose. I take from Sir Ernest Satow's 'Ancient Japanese Rituals' in the *T. A. S. J.* the following account of the ceremonies used on this occasion. They may serve as an example of the elaborate ritual of Shinto at this period, and to illustrate the intimate associa tion of government with religion.

Before the celebration of the service, orders were given to the Divination Office to fix a day, hour, and locality for a purification (*harahi*) to be performed. On the day preceding the purification a sort of tent was erected near the river (*i.e.*, the Kamogaha at Kioto), and at the hour appointed the priestess who had been selected for the occasion proceeded to the place of purification in a bullock-car. The procession was magnificent, and was ordered with extreme precision. It consisted of nearly one hundred and forty persons, besides porters. First went two municipal men-at-arms, followed by two citizens and eight officials of rank. They were succeeded by the bailiff of the priestess's official residence with four attendants, after whom came ten corporals of the Guard of the Palace Gates, and a few men from the other four Imperial Guards. Next came the car of the priestess herself, with eight attendants in brown hempen mantles, two young boys in brown, and four running foot pages in white dresses with purple skirts. A silk umbrella and a huge long-handled fan were borne on either side of the car by four men in scarlet coats. Ten more servants completed her immediate retinue. Then came a chest full of sacrificial utensils, and two carriages containing a lady, who seems to have acted as a sort of duenna to the priestess, and the Mikado's messengers, surrounded by attendants in number suited to their rank. Close behind them were borne two chests full of food-offerings, and four containing gifts from the Mikado intended for those members of the Fujihara family who attended on the occasion. Seven carriages carried the female servants of the priestess, each of them being a lady of rank, and therefore accompanied by half-a-dozen followers of both sexes. Two high officials of the provincial government of Yamashiro awaited the procession at a convenient point, and conducted it to the spot chosen for the ceremony of purification. A member of the Nakatomi tribe presented the *nusa*, consisting of a white wand with hemp-fibre hanging from its upper end, the symbol of the primitive offerings of greater value, and a diviner read the purification ritual. After the ceremony was over, refreshments were served out, and the Mikado's gifts distributed. The priestess then returned to her official residence.

On her journey to the temple of Kasuga, the priestess was preceded by various priests, diviners, musicians, cooks, and other functionaries of inferior grade, who set out one day earlier in the charge of an officer of the Ministry of Religion. At the boundary of the province of Yamato she was received by officers of the Provincial Government, who accompanied her to the temporary building erected for her accommodation on the bank of the Saho-gaha. During the day the rite of purification was performed on the western side of the temple, and the offerings placed in readiness for the final ceremony. At dawn on the following day officials of the Ministry of Religion superintended the cleaning of the shrine by a young girl (*mono imi*) who had been carefully guarded for some time previous from contracting any ceremonial uncleanness, while other officials decorated the buildings and set out the sacred treasures close to the shrines and by the side of the arcade round the innermost enclosure. Everything being now in readiness, the high officers of State who had come down from the capital for the service entered by the gate assigned to them, and took their seats in the outer court, followed by members of the Fujihara family of the sixth rank and under. The priestess now arrived in a palanquin, with a numerous retinue of local functionaries, infantry and cavalry soldiers, and followed by porters carrying the offerings of the Mikado, his consort, the heir-apparent, and of the priestess herself. Next came race-horses sent by the Mikado's consort, by the heir-apparent, and from the Six Guards of the Palace, the rear of the procession being brought up by a crowd of lesser officials and men-at-arms. The palanquin of the priestess was surrounded by a large body of guards, torch-bearers, and running pages, umbrella and screen-bearers, and women and girls on horseback. After them came the chest of sacrificial vessels, a number of servants, three chests full of food-offerings, six chests of clothing for the Gods, with carriages containing some of the Mikado's female attendants, the priestess's duenna, and some young girls. On arriving at the north gate, on the west side of the temple enclosure, the men got off their horses and the women descended from their carriages. The priestess then alighted from her palanquin, and passing between curtains held by her attendants in such a way as to render her invisible to the crowd, entered the waiting-room prepared for her inside the courtyard, followed by the women of the Mikado's household. The Mikado's offerings were now brought forward by the Keeper of the Privy Purse and laid on a table outside the gate, while the women of the Household entered the inner enclosure, and took their places in readiness to inspect the offerings. In a few minutes they were joined by the priestess, who had changed her travelling dress for sacrificial robes. The

Keeper of the Privy Purse now brought the Mikado's presents in through the gate, and placing them on a table in front of the *midzu-gaki*, or inner fence, saluted the chapels by clapping his hands four times, alternately standing upright and bowing down to the ground. On his retiring, the same ceremony was performed by the persons charged with the offerings of the Mikado's consort and heir-apparent, after which the offerings of the Fujihara and other noble families were deposited on lower tables, with similar ceremonies. The *kandomo*, or subordinate officials of the Ministry of Religion, next carried up the Mikado's offerings and delivered them to the *mono-imi*, who carried them into the chapel. The *kandomo* then spread matting on the ground in front of each of the four chapels, and members of the Fujihara clan* who held a sufficiently high rank carried in and arranged the tables destined to receive the food-offerings. Two barrels of *sake* were then brought in and placed between the first and second and third and fourth chapels, in a line with the tables, a jar of *sake* brewed by the priests being also placed in front of each chapel. This over, every one quitted the enclosure, making way for the women of the Household, who uncovered the food-offerings and poured out two cups of *sake* for each deity. The liquor appears to have been of the turbid sort called *nigori-zake*. All the preparations being thus complete, the high officers of State and the messengers sent by the Court entered the enclosure and took their seats. Four saddle-horses intended as offerings to the Gods and eight race-horses were now led up in front of the temple, preceded by a major-general of the Guards and a Master of the Horse. A superior priest, with his brows bound with a fillet of paper mulberry fibre (*yufu-kadzura*) then advanced and read the ritual, bowed twice, clapped his hands four times, and retired. The congregation after-

---

* A branch of the Nakatomi, who claimed descent from Koyane, one of the four Gods worshipped,

wards withdrew to the refectory, where the food-offerings were consumed by the participants in the solemn act of worship, and the *sansai*, or thanksgiving service, was con ducted by the *kandomo* of the Ministry of Religion.

The sacred horses were then led eight times round the temple by the grooms of the Mikado's stables, who received a draught of consecrated *sake* as their reward. The general of the body-guard next directed some of his men to perform the dance called *Adzuma-mahi*, and when they had finished a meal of rice was served to them with much ceremony by the Mikado's cooks. At the command of the Vice-Minister of Religion, the harpists and flute-players were summoned to perform a piece of music, called *mi koto fuwe ahase* (the concert of harp and flute) ; the flutes played a short move ment alone, and were then joined by the harps, whereupon the singers struck in. An officer of the Ministry of Religion sang the first few bars, and the official singers finished the piece. This was followed by one of the dances called *Yamato-mahi*, performed in turn by the principal priests of the temple, by members of the Fujihara family and by the Vice-Minister of Religion himself. After the *sake*-cup had been passed round three times, the company clapped their hands once and separated. Then everybody adjourned to the race-course, and the day was wound up with gallop ing matches.

The *norito* (No. 2 of the *Yengishiki*) read on this occasion has been translated by Sir Ernest Satow. It is of minor interest.

**Hirose Oho-imi no Matsuri** (service in honour of the Food-Goddess of Hirose).—The *norito* of this ceremony (No. 3 of the *Yengishiki*) announces offerings to the Food-Goddess and makes promise of more if good harvests are granted by her. The Gods of the ravines which supply water for irrigating the Crown-farms are joined with her in this service. Sir E. Satow has translated this *norito*. It contains nothing of special interest.

M

**Tatsuta kaze no kami no Matsuri** (service of the Wind-Gods at Tatsuta).—The *norito* (No. 4 of the *Yengishiki*) of this service has been translated by Sir E. Satow. It contains a legend which professes to account for its first institution and for the founding of the shrine at which it was celebrated. For several years in succession violent storms had destroyed the crops. The diviners having in vain endeavoured to discover the cause of this calamity, the Wind-Gods revealed themselves to the Mikado in a dream and proposed to him a bargain, namely, that if he built them a shrine, and made them certain offerings, they would in future bless and ripen the grain and vegetables. The "golden thread-box," "golden shuttle," and "golden reel" enumerated in this *norito* as offerings to the Goddess were in reality of painted wood, one of the numerous cases of cheaper substitutes in Shinto ritual.

The *Nihongi* mentions very frequent embassies from the Mikado to this shrine in the seventh century. Princes were selected for the office of envoy.

In addition to the above, the *Yengishiki* has brief mention of ceremonies for "calming" the roaring of the kitchen-furnace, calming (or propitiating?) the God of Water, the August Abiding-place (of the Mikado), the Earth-Prince, the site of a new palace, in honour of the kitchen-furnace, of the august well (such as that from which water was taken for the Ohonihe ceremony), of the birth-well (from which water was drawn for washing a new-born prince), of the water of a privy, and a ceremony performed when the Mikado went out from the Palace. The same work contains schedules of offerings to various local deities, of whom we know little or nothing.

**More recent norito.**—In addition to the old *norito* of the *Yengishiki*, a good number have come down to us of more recent date, chiefly from the ninth century. We find among them for the first time *norito* addressed to deceased Mikados, a practice which was, no doubt, introduced from China. I give the substance of some selected examples.* They exhibit numerous traits of Chinese origin.

A.D. 733. The protection of the Sea-Gods of Suminoye was invoked for ships sailing to China.

805. The wrath of the God of Iso no kami was depre cated. He was supposed to have sent an illness upon the Mikado because his "divine treasures" had been removed for convenience to a place nearer the capital.

825. Envoys were sent to the tomb of a deceased Mikado to promise that it should be removed elsewhere the Urabe having discovered that he was dissatisfied with its site.

827. The Sun-Goddess was besought to stay a pestilence, and a member of the Imperial family promised her as priestess.

827. The diviners having attributed the Mikado's illness to the cutting down of the trees of the shrine of Inari, envoys were sent to recite a *norito* asking for pardon, and that he should be restored to health.

836. Degrees of rank were conferred on Futsunushi (lower third), Mikatsuchi (upper second), and Koyane (upper third), with the lower fourth rank for the Himegami (lady-deity). Prayer was made that the envoys should have a safe journey.

839. Trees on the Empress Jingo's tomb having been cut down, the Mikado feared that a drought might be the con sequence, and sent envoys to deprecate her wrath.

840. The Mikado being affected by an evil influence (*mono no ke*), the diviners attributed it to a curse from the Great Abstinence (*oho-imi*) deity of Deha.† At the same time envoys to China were cast away among southern savages. The savages were many and they were few, but by the help of some God, they had the victory over them. A report was received from Deha that on the same date a noise of

---

* From a modern collection entitled *Norito Bunrei*.
† In the north of Japan.

fighting was heard in the clouds of the Great God and a rain of missile stones fell. The Mikado in a *norito* expressed his gratitude and wonder at the far-reaching power of the God, and conferred on him the lower fourth rank with two households of peasants to serve him.

841. The Mikados Jimmu and Jingo were prayed to for rain, and apology made for previous neglect.

850. The Mikado Mondoku announced to his predecessor his accession to the throne in the following *norito*, which was read at his tomb by a high official commissioned for the purpose :—

"*I humbly make representation : ' He [the Mikado] with profound reverence declares—with respect be it spoken—to Your Sovran Majesty. In accordance with the commands bequeathed by Your Majesty the Court nobles repeatedly besought him to take over the celestial succession, but as the date [of his predecessor's death] was still fresh and his heart distracted by grief, he twice and three times humbly declared his inability to accede to this request. But when they strongly insisted, saying that it was the wish of Your Majesty, he felt that he ought not to indulge his own inclination. After considering the matter in all its bearings, he therefore purified the Great Abiding place, and reverently assumed the celestial succession, which he now with reverence announces to Your Majesty his intention to maintain'*

"*Furthermore he says, with profoundest reverence, ' That he hopes Your (with respect be it spoken) Sovran Majesty will deign to bestow on him your gracious loving favour, so that he may continue peacefully to maintain the government of the celestial succession as long as Heaven and Earth, the Sun and Moon endure.'*"

850. The Wind-Gods of Tatsuta were thanked for their protection, awarded the lower fifth rank, and begged to continue their guardianship.

850. The Mikado Jimmu was prayed to on behalf of the reigning Mikado, who was dangerously ill.

851. Floods having been caused by pollution, prayer was made for fine weather to the Gods of Ise, Kamo, Matsu no wo, and Otokuni.

857. The Mikado Mondoku despatched envoys to all the famous shrines to announce the change of the year-name (*nengo*) to Tenan (celestial tranquillity) which had been made in consequence of the good omens of trees whose branches had grown together and of the appearance of a white deer.  He sent offerings with prayers for abundance and immunity from storms and floods.  He further peti tioned the Gods to guard him by day and by night and to grant him a long reign.

864. Envoys were sent to Yahata (Hachiman) Daibo-satsu* in Buzen to give thanks for preservation from calamity.  But as a boiling of the Lake of Aso (a volcano in Kiushiu) was held by the diviners to portend war and pestilence, and numerous other portents occurred, a lucky day had been chosen and offerings (which would have been sent sooner only for pollution) made.

866. Envoys were sent to all the Gods of Nankaido asking their protection against rebellion, for a good harvest &c., and apologizing for a delay caused by pollution.

866. An envoy was sent to Ihashimidzu with an offering of shields, spears, and saddles to the God Hachiman Bosatsu. It is explained that of three saddles two only have been sent ; the third is to be despatched by a later opportunity. He is asked to guard the Mikado by day and by night and to watch over the affairs of the Empire.

866. A fire having destroyed one of the gates of the Palace, the diviners said that it portended sickness to the Imperial person with disasters by conflagration and battle. After some delay, caused by various pollutions, the Mikado sent an envoy to the shrine of the Sun-Goddess at Ise with prayer to avert these calamities, and more especially to

* A Buddhist title.

send down a sweet rain on the land which was then suf-
fering from drought.

868. Envoys were sent to Hirota and Ikuta praying the
Gods of these places that earthquake shocks attributed to
them should cease. A patent of rank was sent to them,
and they were besought to bless the Mikado and the
country. Thanks were also given for a good harvest.

874. Inari was raised in rank and prayed to for many
blessings, of which some do not apparently belong to the
province of a Rice-God.

For an account of Shinto festivals at the present day,
Mr. B. H. Chamberlain's 'Things Japanese' or Capt.
Brinkley's 'Japan and China' may be consulted. Their
nearest counterpart is the carnival of Southern Europe.
The Chinjiu Matsuri, or annual festival of the local patron
deity, is everywhere a great event, with processions, dramatic
performances, wrestling, fireworks, races, new clothes for
the children, &c.

# CHAPTER XIII.

## MAGIC, DIVINATION, INSPIRATION.

THE reader will find few traces of normal religious development in the practices to be described in this chapter. The pathological element is decidedly predominant.

**Magic.**—The older view of magic is that of Prof. Zimmern, who defines it as "the attempt on man's part to influence, persuade, or compel spiritual beings to comply with certain requests or demands." With this the view of the modern Japanese lexicographer Yamada, who calls magic (in Japanese *majinahi*) "the keeping off of calamity by the aid of the supernatural power of Kami and Buddhas," is in substantial agreement. Prof. Zimmern's definition is open to several objections. It is too wide, as it would include prayer and sacrifice ; it assumes that all the sentient beings appealed to are spiritual, and it excludes the numerous cases of magic in which Gods and spirits are in no wise concerned. It is, however, impossible to leave out of consideration the last-mentioned class of magic, though it might be convenient to distinguish it by a different name, as "charms." Sir Alfred Lyall and Mr. J. G. Frazer have shown that magic of this kind has preceded religion, and that it is in principle the same as science, although based on wrong premises.

**Magic and Medicine.**—Magic is the bastard brother of medicine. The two arts are associated in many countries. Hirata says that in China medicine had its origin in magic. In Japan, in Kotoku's reign (645-654), we find State departments of medicine and of magic organized on a similar footing. A *Nihongi* myth states that mankind owes both arts to the teaching of the Gods Ohonamochi and Sukuna-bikona. Evidently the myth by which these institutions are referred to a divine origin is of later growth than the institutions themselves. The same is plainly the case with the deification of the phallic emblems used to repel disease,[*] and with the various magical appliances described on p. 196. The object of the myth-maker in these cases was to lend a religious sanction to what was in its origin a non-religious magical procedure. The same principle might be copiously illustrated from non-Japanese sources. On the other hand, there are cases in which a practice based on religion has its original character obliterated, so that it might easily be mistaken for a charm of no religious import.

**Bakin on Magic.**—I have before me a collection of "vulgar magical practices" (*majinahi*) made early in the last century by the famous novelist Bakin.[†] It illustrates the confusion, even with highly educated men, between science and magic on the one hand, and between non-religious and religious magic on the other. A good many of Bakin's so-called *majinahi* turn out to be merely recipes, such as how to remove oil stains from books by an appli cation of lime ; to cure costiveness in fowls by doses of saltpetre ; to kill the parasites of gold-fish by means of a preparation of human excrement ; to keep away book worms by exposing the books in the sun : " If a pot-tree withers in the middle and seems likely to die, take it out, shake the earth from its roots, and expose it to the sun for one day. Then steep its roots in a drain for one night. When replanted it will thrive." The scrapings of a copper ladle mixed with fish will cure disease in cats. We approach true magic more nearly in the following : " When stung by a wasp, take up a pebble which is half sunk in the ground, turn it over, and replace it, when the pain will at once leave you." The cure of illness from eating poisonous fish by swallowing the ashes of an old almanac seems also to belong rather to magic than to medicine. There

---

[*] See above, p. 197.
[†] ' Yenzeki Zasshi,' v. 1.

are traces of a religious element in the following : " To cure toothache, apply to the tooth the ashes of a sardine which has been set up over the door on the last day of the year."* Another plan is : " Inscribe on a slip of wood certain incantations (given) in the ordinary Chinese cha racter, in the seal character, and in Sanskrit. Beside the inscription make two circles. If the toothache is in the upper jaw, knock a new nail with a purified hammer into the upper circle ; if in the lower jaw, into the lower circle. If the pain does not go away, continue knocking the nail with the hammer. The slip of wood should be afterwards thrown away into a stream."† Bakin tried this plan and found it effectual. He attributes his immunity from con flagration to his respect for fire. He always avoided stamping it out with his foot, and enjoins on his descend ants to follow his example. If the master of a house before going to bed goes round calling out, " Be careful of fire : fasten well the doors," the spirit (of his words) will fill the house, and it will be preserved against fire and robbery. On the last night of the year, and on other festival occasions, water should be drawn from the well at sunset, placed in a clean vessel, and offered without a drop being spilled to the God of the kitchen furnace. It should be returned to the well the next morning. This will pre vent danger of fire.

A Korean book of household recipes contains, along with instructions for making cakes, spiced wine, &c., such magical, but non-religious devices as the following : " To make a runaway slave come back of his own accord. Take a garment which he has worn and put it down the well, or hang some of his hair on a wheel and turn it round. He will then not know where to go and will come back to you."

---

* When demons and evil influences are expelled. See above, p. 308.
† After the manner of the Oho-harahi offerings.

**Imitative or Sympathetic Magic.**—These Korean ex
amples illustrate the principle of imitative or sympathetic
magic thus described by Mr. J. G. Frazer[*]:—

"Manifold as are the applications of this crude philosophy
—for a philosophy it is as well as an art—the fundamental
principles on which it is based would seem to be reducible
to two; first, that like produces like, or that an effect
resembles its cause; and second, that things which have
once been in contact, but have ceased to be so, continue to
act on each other as if the contact still persisted. From
the first of these principles the savage infers that he can
produce any desired effect merely by imitating it; from
the second he concludes that he can influence at pleasure
and at any distance any person of whom, or anything of
which, he possesses a particle. Magic of the latter sort,
resting as it does on the belief in a certain secret sympathy
which unites indissolubly things that have once been con
nected with each other, may appropriately be termed
sympathetic in the strict sense of the term. Magic of the
former kind, in which the supposed cause resembles or
simulates the supposed effect, may conveniently be described
as imitative or mimetic."

The sympathetic or imitative principle is not very con
spicuous in the instances of vulgar (that is, non-professional)
magic quoted by Bakin. It is, however, illustrated by other
Japanese customs. There is a round stone in a shrine in
Sagami which brings rain when water is poured over it.
The stone is supposed to be the *shintai* of an Aburi no Kami
(rain-fall-God), to whom the shrine is dedicated. Here we have
a combination of religion with magic.[†] Whistling in order
to raise the wind[‡] is a purely non-religious piece of imitative

* 'The Golden Bough,' second edition, p. 9.

† I cannot offer any explanation of the magic used by women and children
in order to bring fine weather. They hang upside down to the eaves or on
the branch of a tree human figures cut in paper, and called *Teri-teri-bōsu*
(shine-shine-priest).

‡ See above, p. 115.

magic, but in the *Nihongi* myth it is associated with religion by being represented as taught by a God. We should probably regard as a form of sympathetic magic the modern practice of devout visitors to the shrine of Tenjin, near Kiôto, who, in order to obtain relief from their ailments, rub the corresponding part of a bronze bull which stands before the shrine. A characteristic example of non-religious imitative magic is the custom of *kasedori*. When a marriage is unfruitful, the old women of the neighbourhood come to the house and go through the form of delivering the wife of a child. The infant is represented by a doll. The date selected for this ceremony is not immaterial. It is that of the festival of Sahe no kami. This, no doubt, gives it a quasi-religious flavour. To this class we may also refer the New Year's practice of going to sleep with a picture of a boat under the pillow. If lucky dreams follow an anchor is painted to it, if unlucky dreams a sail.

The *Nihongi** records a case in which a woman took earth from Mount Kako in Yamato, which she wrapped in her neckerchief and prayed, saying : " ' This earth represents the country of Yamato.' Then she turned it upside down." The common witchcraft of ill-treating a figure of the intended victim in order to make him suffer in a corresponding manner is well known in Japan. The *Nihongi* (A.D. 587) speaks of a rebellious Minister preparing figures of the Heir to the Throne and loathing them. Dr. Griffis† gives the following description of a magical ceremony performed by a woman in revenge for her lover's desertion of her :—

" At two o'clock in the morning she proceeds to the shrine of her patron-God, usually the *Ujigami.* Sometimes she wears a crown, made of an iron tripod reversed, on which burn three candles. In her left hand she carries a straw effigy of her victim; in her right she grasps a hammer. On her bosom is suspended a mirror. Reaching the sacred

* I. 157.
† 'The Mikado's Empire,' p. 474.

tree before the shrine, she impales the effigy upon it with nails, adjuring the Gods to save their tree, impute the guilt of desecration to the traitor, and visit him with their deadly vengeance. The visit is repeated nightly until the object of her sorcery sickens and dies. At Sabae, before a shrine of Kompira, stood a pine tree about a foot thick, plentifully studded with such nails."*

The possession by the operator of the hair or nails of his victim adds greatly to the potency of his devices. Hence they are carefully kept by the proper owners and thrown away together in the twelfth month.

Another form of witchcraft is represented by the later custom of Inu-gami (dog-deity) thus described by Motoöri: " A hungry dog is tied up in sight of food which he is not allowed to eat. When his desire is keenest, his head is cut off and at once flies to seize the food. This head is put into a vessel and worshipped. A serpent or a weasel will do as well." It constitutes a mighty charm, which evidently owes its power to the keenness of the animal's sufferings.† The Fuzoku Gwaho tells a story which was probably invented in order to account for this custom. " An old woman buried her pet dog, leaving only the head above ground. Then she cut him about with a bamboo saw, saying, ' If thou hast a soul, kill such a one, and I will make thee a God.' The man really did die afterwards in strange fashion. From that time the dog-deity dwelt in the old woman's house and wrought many wonderful curses." In Tosa each village has several Inugami-mochi (dog-deity-owners). They are shunned by their neighbours. A match maker's very first inquiry is whether there is such a person in the family. Leprosy is the next subject of his questions,

---

* See also Ch. K. 263.

† According to Van Helmont, the reason why bull's fat is so powerful in a vulnerary ointment is that the bull at the time of slaughter is full of secret reluctancy and vindictive murmurs, and therefore dies with a higher flame of revenge about him than any other animal.

sudden death (supposed to be hereditary), riches or poverty, wisdom or foolishness, are of subsidiary importance.

The same idea of a materialized emotion is illustrated by a practice common near Yamaguchi. In order to drive away certain destructive insects from the rice-fields a straw figure, made to resemble a cavalry soldier, is led round in stately procession, and finally flung into the sea. This figure represents the leader of some fugitives from a battle who hid in these fields, but were pursued and slain there. The noxious insects are their materialized resentment at this fate.

The principles of sympathetic and imitative magic, so copiously illustrated in ' The Golden Bough,' are not applic able to all magical procedures. Many defy specific explana tion, and are possibly the result of some chance association of ideas no longer traceable, or of a mistaken empiricism. *Post hoc, ergo propter hoc* is responsible for much that is called magic.

The description of magic in Hastings's ' Dictionary of the Bible ' as a " means of binding superhuman powers, either to restrain them from injuring oneself, or to con strain them to injure others and put them under a spell, or to reveal what to mortal man was unknown," scarcely applies at all to Japanese magic. I have not met with any mention in the older literature of pacts with demons or the coercion of spirits.

**The Symbol in Magic.**—In Japan, as in other countries, magic makes great use of the Symbol, the Talisman, and the Formula, spoken or written, This seems to depend on the more general notion that things which are associated in thought must have also a direct physical influence on each other, of which a familiar example among ourselves is the objection to receive a knife as a present, because it might cut the friendship between the giver and receiver. Possibly this association of the subjective with the objective (in Dr. Tylor's words " mistaking an ideal for a real con-

nexion ")* was in Hirata's mind when he used the somewhat
cryptic phrase, " Magic (*majinahi*, or magic, means etymologically mixture) is so called because it mixes the spirit
(*tama*) of that which is here with the body of that which
is there." We have seen† that the phallus, as a symbol of
robust animal life, was used to exorcise evil things, whether
demons or diseases. Roof-tiles impressed with a symbol
(bubbles) which is indicative of water, are used at the
present day as a charm to protect houses from fire. The
deification of the gourd, the clay and the water-plant, no
doubt, points to a previous magical use as preventives
of conflagration. Rice, perhaps as a representative of the
kteis, is used for several magical purposes. In one of the
*Fudoki*, unhulled rice is scattered broadcast by Tsuchi-
gumo,‡ to disperse a strange darkness which turned day
into night.

**The Talisman.**—When the meaning of the symbol is
altogether obliterated or unknown, we have the Talisman.
It is not clear what was meant by the "tide-ebbing " and
"tide-flowing " jewels given by the Sea-God to Hohodemi,§
or even that they had any meaning at all. A sort of scarf
(*hire*) was much used as a talisman. In the *Kojiki* we
are told of a scarf, which, when waved thrice, quieted
snakes. Another kind gave protection against wasps and
centipedes.‖ The *Nihongi* has the following account of
magical practices, suggested apparently by some acquaint
ance with the art of acupuncture :—

* See ' Primitive Culture,' i. 116, where numerous examples of symbolic
magic are given.
† See above, p. 187.
‡ The *Tsuchigumo* (earth-hiders) were men of a low class, who lived in
dwellings sunk in the earth, and gave much trouble to the Japanese Govern
ment in ancient times. Dr. Tylor, in his ' Primitive Culture,' i. 113, has
noted the tendency to attribute magical powers to pariahs and foreigners.
Sukunabikona, the teacher of magic to Japan, came from abroad.
§ See above, p. 115.
‖ See above, p 106.

" *Summer, 4th month, 1st day. The Koryo student-priests said that their fellow-student Kura-tsukuri no Tokushi had made friends with a tiger, and had learnt from him his arts, such as to make a barren mountain change into a green mountain, or to cause yellow earth to become clear water, and all manner of wonderful arts too many to enumerate. More over, the tiger bestowed on him his needle, saying : ' Be watchful ! be watchful, and let no one know ! Treated with this, there is no disease which may not be cured.' Truly, as the tiger had said, there was no disease which was not cured when treated by it. Tokushi always kept the needle concealed in a pillar. Afterwards the tiger broke the pillar and ran away, taking the needle with him*"

Shaking or jingling talismans or other objects is sup posed to have a magical virtue. Izanagi shakes the jewels which he takes from his neck to bestow on the Sun-Goddess. The Sun-Goddess and Susa no wo shook the jewels from which their children were produced. Shaking a number of talismans was part of the ceremony of *Mitama furishiki*, above described.[*]

Part of the outfit of a district wise-woman or sorceress in recent times was a small bow, called *adzusa-yumi*, by twanging which she could call from the vasty deep the spirits of the dead, or even summon deities to her behests. Another small bow, called *ha-ma-yumi* (break-demon-bow) is given to boys at the New Year. I conjecture that both of these had something to do with the bows used in the ceremony of *tsuina* described above.

Another magical appliance for the restraint of demoniac or evil influences is the *shime-naha*, or close-rope. It is made of rice-straw plucked up by the roots, the ends being allowed to dangle down at regular intervals. A rope of this kind was used to prevent the Sun-Goddess from returning into the Rock-cave of Heaven. At the present

* See p. 292.

day it is hung in front of shrines, and at the New Year before ordinary dwellings. Sacred trees are girt with it, or it may be suspended across a road to prevent the passage of evil spirits. Some people wear *shime-naha* on their person. The twin rocks at Ise, between which there is a view of Fuji and the rising sun, are connected by an immense *shime-naha*, with which a legend is associated to the effect that Susa no wo, in return for hospitality, taught his host how to keep out the God of Pestilence by stretch ing such a rope across the door. The *shime-naha* is sometimes called *Hi no mi tsuna* (sun-august-rope). The *shime-naha* is the counterpart of the consecrated rope which in Siam is fastened on the last day of the year round the city walls to prevent the banished demons from returning.

'Garlic has the same power over evil spirits in Japan that it has in Europe.

**The Formula in Magic.**—The magic power of set forms of speech, quite distinct from any meaning which they may possess, is well illustrated by the use of the numerals from one to ten as a magic formula for the cure of disease. But in the instructions of the Sea-God to Hohodemi to return the lost fish-hook to his brother with the words, "A hook of poverty, a hook of ruin, a hook of downfall," the proper meaning of the words is retained, though they are evidently supposed to be accompanied by some mysterious potency, independent of it. Beyond the circumstance that they were taught by Gods, these incantations do not seem to have had any religious character. Nor, when a judge* is about to execute some criminals by casting them into the fire, and uses the charm, "Not by my hands are they cast," is there apparently any God invoked. The words themselves avert any evil result. There is no hint of a religious origin in the passage of the *Nihongi* which states that the first

* *Nihongi*, ii. 82.

Mikado, Jimmu, invented magical formulæ for the dissl
pation of evil influences. Of course, there are many
formulæ of this kind which stand on a different footing.
When, at the present day, a Japanese calls out *Kuhabara /
Kuhabara!* (mulberry-grove) during a thunderstorm, it is
no doubt with the idea of suggesting to the Thunder-God
that the place is a mulberry grove, which, it is believed, is
never struck by lightning. Charms often consist of a
ticket with the name of the God (usually the *ubusuna*) and
a statement that the bearer is under his protection.

**Magic and Shinto.**—The treatment of magic by Shinto
is not uniform. We have seen that it lends its sanction to
some practices of this kind by affirming that they were
taught or practised by Gods, or by deifying the objects
used in them. But there are others which it condemns,
including them in the offences against the Gods enumerated
in the Oho-harahi.[*] It is, however, for their malicious pur
pose that they are reprobated. There is no trace in the
old records of any scepticism as to their efficacy. A scientific
knowledge sufficient to arouse doubts of the power of magic
did not then exist, and would have been equally fatal to
much in Shinto itself. Even in modern times such highly
educated men as Bakin and Hirata had an implicit belief
in the efficacy of this art. The latter complains that there
is a tendency among physicians of the Chinese school to
neglect it. Some diseases, he says, are caused by evil
spirits and some by minute insects (microbes?). Magic
and medicine should therefore, in his opinion, be combined.

The decay of magic in modern Japan is not owing to
religious but to scientific progress. It is due to China,
whose philosophy, imperfect as it is, taught far truer views
of the limitations of man's powers than anything Japan
was able to discover for herself.

**Divination.**—Divination (in Japanese *uranahi*) is magic
which has a special object, namely, the revelation of the

---

[*] See above, p. 294.

unknown. This is implied by the Japanese word, which is derived from *ura*, the rear, heart, lining, obverse, and hence that which is concealed. Ordinary experience, and, at a later stage of progress, science, enable us to reason with more or less certainty from the known to the unknown ; but mankind, not satisfied with legitimate methods, have supplemented them by divination, which comprises various irregular and ineffective processes specially directed to discovering the will of the Gods, ascertaining what will be lucky or unlucky, and predicting future events.

**Objects of Divination.**—In Japan we find divination practised to ascertain whether an expedition would be successful or unsuccessful, the reason of the disturbed state of the country and its remedy, the best site for a temple, tomb, or dwelling-house, whether the Mikado should make a progress to a certain place and perform sacrifices there, what crops it is best to sow, what days will be lucky or unlucky, when to expect a lover, the name of a future husband, &c. The priestess of Ise was selected by divina tion, and the provinces from which the rice for the Ohonihe ceremony should be taken. Ominous occurrences were interpreted by the help of this art. The purity of persons about to take part in a religious ceremony was tested in this manner. Or divination might be applied to the baser use of recovering lost property or discovering thieves. There was a special divination on the 10th day of the 12th month to ascertain what ill luck threatened the Mikado during the ensuing six months, so that the Gods whose curse was feared might be propitiated in advance.

**Religious and Non-religious Divination.**—Divination, like magic, does not necessarily involve the intervention of superhuman sentient beings, as we may see by our own palmistry, fortune-telling by cards, and Shakespeare crypto grams. That the art passed through a non-religious phase is highly probable. In Japan, however, the cases met with in the oldest records are commonly associated, explicitly or implicitly, with an appeal for divine guidance. Hirata defines divination as "respectfully inquiring the heart (*ura*) of the Gods." Motoori takes the same view, though both writers admit that in modern times divination which has no religious sanction is sometimes resorted to, playfully, or in unimportant matters.

**The Greater Divination.**—The greater, or official, divi-. nation consists in drawing conclusions according to certain conventional rules from the cracks which appear in a deer's shoulder-blade when exposed to fire. This practice is known not only to the Chinese, Kalmucks, Cherkeses, and other races of North-Eastern Asia, but to the ancient Germans and Greeks. Nearer home we have the "reading the speal" (*épaule*), a sort of divination by examining the marks on a shoulder-blade of mutton, practised not very long ago in the Highlands of Scotland. The *Nihongi* tells us that the Gods themselves made use of the Greater Divination in order to learn the reason of Izanagi and Izanami's abortive children the Hiruko and the Island of Ahaji. The God Koyane, ancestor of the Nakatomi, was specially charged with this form of divination. In the numerous passages of the *Nihongi* where divination is mentioned without further description, it is no doubt the Greater Divination which is intended. Chinese methods of divination were introduced into Japan from Korea at an early date. In 553 it seems to have been an established practice that Koreans learned in medicine, in divination, and in calendar-making should take turns of service at the Court of Japan. It was no doubt owing to their influence that the tortoise-shell was substituted for the deer's shoulder-blade in this divination. A reference to the "divine Tortoise" in the *Nihongi* under the legendary date B.C. 92 is merely an anachronism. But the tortoise was really in use for this purpose in the eighth century. The *Yengishiki* recognizes no other, though in the country districts the shoulder-blades of deer were long retained.

In an old book purporting to describe *he practice of the Tsushima college of diviners at a much later period than the *Yengishiki*, we are told that the diviner, after practising religious abstinence for seven days, took his place in the divination plot (*uraba* or *uraniha*), from which all other persons were rigorously excluded. He was provided with the tortoise-shell, some *hahaka* wood, and other requisites. Having prayed to the God of the divination plot,* who is besought to grant a true divination, the diviner recites the *Kami-oroshi* (formula which brings down the God), and kindles in a blazing fire a stick of *hahaka* about four or five inches long, and of the thickness of a chopstick. When it has taken fire, he blows it out, and with it pricks the tortoise-shell from the back. Divination is then made from the lines thus produced. When the divination is over, the *Kami-agari* (ascent of the God) is recited, and the ceremony is at an end.

The *Shinto Miōmoku Ruijiu* gives the following description of a form of tortoise-shell divination practised at Kashima to select young girls for the service of the God (*mono-imi*). Two candidates who have not reached puberty perform rites to the God for 100 days. On the final day a caldron is set up before the shrine and two tortoise-shells are placed in it, each of which bears the name of one of the girls. These are roasted from early morning till dusk. The tortoise-shell with the name of the successful candidate is then found to be wholly uninjured by the fire whilst the other is reduced to ashes. It is said that the girl selected attains a great age and that she never menstruates.

**Tsuji-ura** (cross-roads divination).†—This form of divination was much practised in ancient Japan, especially by

---

* Koyane. Hirata speaks with scorn of the Chinese methods of divining current in Japan in later times, in which no invocation of the Gods was used. Sometimes other Gods, and even Buddhas, were invoked.

† "The King of Babylon stood at the parting of the way, at the head of the two ways, to perform divination."—Ezekiel xxi. 21.

women and lovers. It consisted in going out to the road at dusk, planting a stick in the ground to represent Kunado, the phallic God of roads, and interpreting the fragmentary talk of passers-by as an answer to the question.* Another account says that to perform *tsuji-ura* you take a box-wood comb in your hand, go to cross-roads and sound it three times by drawing your finger along it (*tsuge*, " box-wood," also means "inform me"). Then, with devotion to the Sahe no Kami, repeat this verse three times : " Oh, thou God of the cross-roads-divination, grant me a true response." Good or bad luck is to be inferred from the words of the next (or the third) person who makes his appearance. Some times a boundary line was marked out and rice sprinkled to keep away evil influences. The words of the passer-by who first entered the charmed limit constituted the response.

**Hashi-ura** (bridge-divination). Little is known of this kind of divination. The procedure was the same as in *tsuji-ura*, and the Gods concerned were probably the Sahe no Kami. The end-post of a bridge was, and still is, a *wo-bashira*, that is, male pillar or phallus.

**Ishi-ura**, or stone-divination, is mentioned in the *Man-yoshiu* along with *tsuji-ura*. The "stone" is probably the stone emblem of Kunado or Sahe no Kami. It consisted in judging of future fortune by the apparent weight of the stone when lifted. Such stones were called *Ishi-gami* (stone-deities) and were no doubt phallic.

**Mikayu-ura** (divination by gruel). This kind of divina tion is also associated with the Sahe no Kami. It was practised in various forms at Hirawoka in Kahachi, Suha in Shinano, and other places, on the 15th day of the 1st month† in order to ascertain what crops it would be best to sow that year. A pot was set up before the God in

---

* Pausanias says that in ancient Greece the inquirer, after asking his ques tion of the God and making his offering, took as the divine answer the first words he might hear on quitting the sanctuary.

† The date of the festival of the Sahe no Kami.

which adzuki beans* were boiled.   Then tubes of reed, five or six inches long, marked with the names of all manner of crops were plunged into the gruel.   The *negi* (priests) stood by, and taking out the tubes with chopsticks divined from the manner in which the grains of rice (mixed with the gruel) entered them whether the crop in question would be good or bad.   At Haruna the priests published the results to the peasants in a printed form.

Hirata mentions another form of divination in which beans are set in a row round the hearth and fire brought close to them.  Some are roasted black while others remain white, and from this the weather and luck of the ensuing year are divined.

**Koto-ura** (harp-divination) was formerly (11th century) practised at Ise with the object of ascertaining whether the priests who were to take part in the three great religious services of the year and the utensils employed were pure or not.   Prayer having been made to the Sun-Goddess, the officiating priest struck a harp three times,† uttering with each note a loud Hush!  He then recited the following *Kami-oroshi* (bringing-down the Gods) :—

> "*Ah! we protest that we are in earnest,*
> *To your pure seat deign to descend*
> *All ye Gods of Heaven and Earth,*
>
> *Ah! we protest that we are in earnest,*
> *To thy pure seat deign to descend*
> *Thou Thunder-God also.*
>
> *Ah! we protest that we are in earnest,*
> *To your pure seat deign to descend*
> *Oh thou upper great brother and thou lower*
> *great brother* "‡

The names of the priests were then called over and the question asked in the case of each, " Is he clean or unclean?"

---

* See above, p. 193.

† The *Kami-yori-ita* (God-resort-board), struck in later times to bring down the Gods, is believed to be a substitute for this harp.

‡ It is not known who these Gods were.

The officiating priest then struck the harp and tried to whistle by drawing in his breath. If the whistle was audible it was a sign of purity, and *vice versâ*. The same procedure was observed with regard to the persons who had prepared the offerings, the offerings themselves, and the utensils required in the service.

**Caldron-Divination.**—At the shrine of Kibitsu no miya in Bittchu there is a mode of divining good and ill-luck from the sound made by a caldron in boiling. The priests, on the application of a worshipper, recite *norito* and kindle a fire of brushwood under a caldron. If the sound produced resembles the bellowing of a bull, the prognostic is good, if otherwise, it is bad.

**Divination by Lots.**—Sticks with numbers inscribed on them, or slips of paper, were much used for divination. The succession to the Imperial throne has been decided in this way. Prayer to the Kami often preceded their use. The following is a form of divination by lot which is used by sailors when they have lost their reckoning. The names of the points of the compass are written on slips of paper, placed in a measure of rice, and the whole mixed up. A *harahi-bako* of the Great Deity of Ise is put on the top. Prayer is offered and the lot which is found to adhere to the *harahi-bako* is looked upon as the answer of the Deity. Another form of divination by lots is thus described : " You place three sticks, numbered one, two, three, in a bamboo tube and inquire of the God as to good or ill luck, saying reverently, ' If the thing is lucky, let it be such a number, if unlucky, such another number.' " In what is called *harahi-kuji* " you write lucky or unlucky, or whatever your prayer may be, on papers which you fold up and roll into a ball. Then having offered reverent prayer to the God, rub the lots with *harahi ko-nusa* * when that which adheres to them is concluded to be the answer. This is common at all shrines."

* Smaller *gohei* used in the *harahi* ceremony.

Lots were, and still are, used for all manner of non-religious purposes. If a solitary passenger appears at a jinriksha stand, he is often cast lots for by means of a set of cords of various lengths knotted together at one end which is kept for the purpose. The 'Yih-King,' a Chinese book which sets forth a non-religious system of divination depending partly on drawing lots is much used in Japan.

**Divination by Means of the Stars** was first introduced in A.D. 675 by the Korean teachers of Chinese arts.

**Kitsune-tsukahi.**—"Amongst the ordinary diviners is one called *Kitsune-tsukahi*, *i.e.*, a fox-possessor. The divination is carried on by means of a small image of a fox, made in a very odd way. A fox is buried alive in a hole with its head left free. Food of the sort of which foxes are known to be most fond is placed just beyond the animal's reach. As days pass by the poor beast in its dying agony of hunger makes frantic efforts to reach the food ; but in vain. At the moment of death the spirit of the fox is supposed to pass into the food, which is then mixed with a quantity of clay, and shaped into the form of the animal. Armed with this extraordinary object, the *miko* is supposed to become an infallible guide to fore telling future events of every kind."*

Augury by various kinds of birds was known. The geomancy practised to some extent in Japan is of Chinese origin.

The *Nihongi* mentions a number of isolated cases of divination invented on the spur of the moment. The following is an example :—

" When the Emperor was about to attack the enemy, he made a station on the great moor of Kashihawo. On this moor there was a stone six feet in length, three feet in breadth, and one foot five inches in thickness. The Emperor prayed, saying : ' If we are to succeed in destroy-

---

* Weston, ' Mountaineering in the Japanese Alps,' p. 307. See also Index, *Inugami ;* and Mr. Chamberlain's ' Things Japanese,' third edition, p. 110.

ing the Tsuchi-gumo, when we kick this stone, may we make it mount up like a *kashiha* leaf.' Accordingly he kicked it, upon which, like a *kashiha* leaf, it arose to the Great Void. Therefore that stone was called Homishi. The Gods whom he prayed to at this time were the God of Shiga, the God of the Mononobe of Nawori, and the God of the Nakatomi of Nawori—these three Gods."[*]

**Omens** are frequently mentioned. A leg-rest breaking without apparent cause was a bad omen. The migration of rats from the capital, the movements of a swarm of flies, comets, a dog bringing in a dead man's hand and depositing it in a shrine, prolonged darkness, to meet a blind or a lame person are examples of evil omens. Earthquakes, floods and storms were supposed to portend war. A wren's entering a parturition-house is described as a favourable omen. White animals of all kinds were good omens, and also three-legged crows or even sparrows, no doubt because the Sun-crow had three legs.

**Dreams.**—At all stages of human progress, the rational, normal, and usual attitude of mankind towards dreams is a disbelief in their reality. The ivory gate is recognized to be their ordinary, every-day thoroughfare. There are good reasons for this. Most dreams are so palpably absurd that the common sense even of the primitive man, enlightened by daily experience, rejects them as something not to be depended on. A man dreams that he has partaken of a hearty meal and wakes up hungry. The cogent logic of an empty belly leaves him no choice but to reject unhesitatingly the proposition that his dream was a reality. He dreams that he has broken his leg. Will he, therefore, lie up for a month to give it time to heal? In his dreams he can fly. Nature exacts a stern penalty if he is idiotic enough to act on the belief that he can do so in reality. The practical necessities of life prohibit a

---

[*] Compare the story of Gideon's fleece in Judges vi. 37. See also *Nihongi*, i. 237, and Ch. K. 194.

man who has to earn a living and support a family from indulging in any such foolish imaginations. The analogy of his own day-dreams, which he must know to be unreal, is too obvious to be disregarded.

It is true that we do not find much evidence of this attitude of mind in books of travel or history. Nobody thinks it worth while to commit to paper instances of so very evident a fact. Most men are comparatively un interested in the normal and familiar. Travellers, and some times even men of science, are prone to neglect the universal and commonplace for the strange and unusual. Like Desdemona, they seriously incline to hear of

> "The Anthropophagi, and men whose heads
> Do grow beneath their shoulders."

Herbert Spencer[*] thinks that the primitive man accepts the events dreamed as events that have actually occurred, and adduces evidence which no doubt shows that there really is a current of thought to that effect among savages and others. For the reasons above stated I prefer to regard such cases as abnormal and exceptional. The *Kojiki* and *Nihongi* have many instances of Gods appearing to men in dreams and giving them instructions. These are doubtless inventions of some scribe, but they indicate a belief in the possibility of such occurrences. Hirata thought it possible by witchcraft to cause people to have dreams.

A more frequent view of dreams is that, although not in themselves realities, it is possible by suitable interpretation to deduce truth from them—usually in the form of pre dictions of the future. There are cases of this kind in the old Japanese records. A deer, for example, dreams that a white mist has come down and covered him. This portends that he will be killed by hunters and his body covered with white salt.

There is evidence that some men occasionally attain in

[*] 'Sociology,' i. 154.

dreams to a deeper spiritual insight and a keener emotional sensibility to divine influences than in their waking moments. Those who have had such experiences do not speak lightly of them. At the present time science is not in a position to deal adequately with this matter. Shinto helps us nothing.

**Ordeal** is a species of divination. Under the date A.D. 277 the *Nihongi* has the following :—

" *The Emperor forthwith questioned Takechi no Sukune along with Umashi no Sukune, upon which these two men were each obstinate, and wrangled with one another, so that it was impossible to ascertain the right and the wrong. The Emperor then gave orders to ask of the Gods of Heaven and Earth the ordeal by boiling water. Hereupon Takechi no Sukune and Umashi no Sukune went out together to the bank of the Shiki river, and underwent the ordeal of boiling water. Takechi no Sukune was victorious. Taking his cross-sword, he threw down Umashi no Sukune, and was at length about to slay him, when the Emperor ordered him to let him go. So he gave him to the ancestor of the Atahe of Kii.*"

The same authority informs us that in A.D. 415 the Mikado, in consequence of the great confusion caused by the assumption of false names and titles, commanded the people of the various houses and surnames to wash themselves and practise abstinence.

" *Then let them, each calling upon the Gods to witness, plunge their hands in boiling water. Hereupon every one put on straps of tree-fibre, and coming to the caldrons, plunged their hands in the boiling water, when those who were true remained naturally uninjured, and all those who were false were harmed. Therefore those who had falsified [their titles] were afraid, and, slipping away beforehand, did not come forward. From this time forward the Houses and surnames were spontaneously ordered, and there was no longer any one who falsified them*"

A note adds :—

*" This is called Kugadachi. Sometimes mud was put into a caldron and made to boil up. Then the arms were bared and the boiling mud stirred with them. Sometimes an axe was heated red-hot and placed on the palm of the hand."*

In a case which occurred in A.D. 530, it is stated that a judge, in order to save himself trouble, was too ready to resort to the boiling-water ordeal and that many persons were scalded to death in consequence.

At the present day plunging the hand into boiling water, walking barefoot over a bed of live coals and climbing a ladder formed of sword-blades set edge upwards are practised, not by way of ordeal, but to excite the awe and stimulate the piety of the ignorant spectators.[*]

**Inspiration.**—Such knowledge as we possess of the divine will and nature comes in the first place to the nobler individuals of our race, men in whom high intellectual powers are harmoniously allied to keen and healthy emotional susceptibilities and ripened by long years of experience and reflection. They it is—the seers, inspired prophets, men of genius, or by whatever name we may call them—who furnish the material out of which religion is developed, not the vulgar, with their superstitions which are only a product of its decay.

Inspiration is not an isolated phenomenon. Like all our thoughts and doings, it is the resultant of three component factors—namely, our own *ego* and that of our fellow-men, and the all-pervading influence of that divine environment in which we live, and move, and have our being. Each of these may predominate according to circumstances. In what we call inspiration, the two former are, as far as may be, in abeyance, and the mind is left free to be acted on by such higher influences as it is capable of receiving.

In the case of Shinto, we have, unfortunately, no record

[*] See Mr. P. Lowell's ' Occult Japan,' p. 36.

of the conditions under which such truths as it contains became revealed. The deification of the Sun and the recognition of the fact that there is love for mankind in the warmth and light which proceed from him was a truly magnificent idea in a world destitute of religion. The Izanagi myth, by which so many of the Gods were assigned a common parentage, was a brilliant conception, paving the way towards monotheism. Musubi, the God of Growth, marks a further stage of progress in this direction. To these may be added such few and vague glimpses as were caught of the truth that offences against our neighbour are also displeasing to the Gods. But we have no knowledge of the circumstances attending these discoveries or of the persons who made them. The only true seer of whom the old records tell us anything was an unfortunate man who in A.D. 644 taught his countrymen to worship—albeit in the form of a caterpillar—the God of the Everlasting World, the God of Gods, and suffered death in consequence.

The seer is not equally clear sighted at all times. He has temporary enhancements of lucidity due to conditions which are very imperfectly understood. Some are of a physical nature. The moderate use of certain drugs and stimulants is an acknowledged help towards producing such exalted states of mind. Music, quiet, sympathy, voluntary concentration of mind (lapsing sometimes into the hypnotic trance, or something resembling it), general abstemiousness, and occasional fasting, are all aids of recognized value which are not neglected by the individual, compact of common clay, who vainly aspires to fill the high office of interpreter between Gods and men.

The Japanese word for inspiration is *Kangakari*, which means God-attachment, and is nearly equivalent to our "possession." It is indicative of the passive attitude claimed by the seer in all countries, with an earnestness which, however genuine, notoriously does not exclude the possibility of error. The most transparent bodies deflect or modify the light which passes through them. Other words for inspiration are *takusen* and *shintaku.* They are of Chinese origin, and involve the idea of a divine message or commission.

In the notices of inspired communications recorded in the Shinto books we seldom or never recognize the true prophet. Instead of revelations of divine truth, we are given the fruits of hypnotism, imposture, and a credulous interpretation of meaningless things. The reader will discern few traces of genuine inspiration in the following examples, of which the earlier are taken from the *Nihongi.*

The Goddess Uzume gave forth an "inspired utterance" as part of her performance before the Rock-cave of Heaven into which the Sun Goddess had retired. It consisted of the numerals from one to ten.

B.C. 5. The Sun-Goddess instructed the Princess-priestess Yamato-hime that a shrine should be erected to her in the province of Ise.

B.C. 38. A young child pronounced an unintelligible speech which sounded like the names of deities, and was thought to be inspired. Worship was offered in consequence.

B.C. 91. A God inspired Yamato totohi momoso hime (a Princess) to say as follows : " Why is the Emperor grieved at the disordered state of the country ? If he duly did us reverence it would assuredly become pacified of itself."

A.D. 193. The Empress Jingo was inspired by a certain God to urge her husband the Mikado to invade Korea.

"*200. 3rd month, 1st day. The same Empress, having selected a lucky day, entered the Palace of worship, and discharged in person the office of priest.* * *She commanded Takechi no Sukune to play on the lute, and the Nakatomi, Igatsu no Omi, was designated as Saniha.†* *Then placing one thousand pieces of cloth, high pieces of cloth, on the top*

---

* *Kanrushi.*

† *Saniha* (pure court) is explained as the official who examines the utterances prompted by the Deity.

*and bottom of the lute, she prayed, saying : ' Who is the God who on a former day instructed the Emperor ?  I pray that I may know his name.'  After seven days and seven nights there came an answer, saying: ' I am the Deity who dwells in the Shrine of Ise.' "*

*" 487. A certain man, inspired by the Moon-God, said, ' My forefather Taka-musubi had the merit of creating Heaven and Earth.  Let him be honoured by dedicating to him people and land.  I am the Moon-God and I shall rejoice if this my desire is complied with.' "*

555. Mention is made of a divine inspiration by which the *Hafuri*, a century before, had advised humble prayer to the " Founder of the Land " before going to the assistance of a Korean king.

*" 672. Kome, Takechi no Agata-nushi, Governor of the district of Takechi, suddenly had his mouth closed so that he could not speak.  After three days, a divine inspiration came upon him, and he said: ' I am the God who dwells in the Shrine of Takechi, and my name is Koto-shiro-nushi no Kami.'  Again, ' I am the God who dwells in the Shrine of Musa, and my name is Iku-ikadzuchi no Kami.'  This was their revelation : ' Let offerings of horses and weapons of all kinds be made at the misasagi (tomb) of the Emperor Kamu-yamato-ihare-biko.'  Further they said : ' We stood in front and rear of the Imperial descendant and escorted him to Fuha, whence we returned.  We have now again taken our stand in the midst of the Imperial army for its protection.'  Further they said : ' An army is about to arrive by the Western road.  Be on your guard.'  When he had done speaking, he awoke [from his trance].  For this reason, therefore, Kome was sent to worship at the Imperial misasagi and to make offerings of horses and weapons.  He also made offerings of cloth and worshipped the Gods of the Shrines of Takechi and Musa.*

*" After this Karakuni, Iki no Fubito, arrived from Ohosaka.  Therefore the people of that day said : ' The*

*words of the instructions of the Gods of the two Shrines are in accordance with the fact.'*

"*Moreover the Goddess of Muraya said by the mouth of a priest: 'An army is now about to arrive by the middle road of my shrine. Therefore let the middle road of my shrine be blocked.' Accordingly, not many days after, the army of Kujira, Ihoriwi no Miyakko, arrived by the middle road. The men of that day said: 'So the words of the teaching of the God were right.' When the war was over, the Generals reported the monitions of these three Gods to the Emperor, who straightway commanded that the three Gods should be raised in rank and worshipped accordingly*"

812. A decree was passed denouncing punishment on peasants who, without reason, predicted good or bad fortune. The authorities were at the same time enjoined to report any genuine predictions.

1031. While a service to the Sun-Goddess was being performed at Ise, a storm of thunder and lightning came on. The Saiwo (virgin priestess of Imperial blood) was inspired and said : "I am the Ara-matsuri no miya, the first of the separate shrines of the Great Shrine, and I now speak by command of the Great God. The Sato [an official designation] Sodzu and his wife have for years past made absurd pretensions, such as that the two great Deities have flown to and attached themselves to them, the Ara-matsuri and the Takamiya to their children and the [deities of] the five separate shrines to their domestic. Such extraordinary assertions evince a want of loyalty both to the Gods and to the Mikado. Their disregard of the ceremonial regulations and the fewness of the offerings are not (in themselves) deserving of severe blame, but they show a want of respect to the Gods. Iga no Kami reaped the rice officially set apart for the service of the shrine and slew the peasants of the Deity. Yet, by the remissness of the Government officials, it was the third year before he was banished..,....Let Sodzu be sent into exile at once."

After delivering this message the Saiwo drank several cups of the sacred sake. Nowadays, with ourselves, recourse is had, under like circumstances, to a letter to the *Times* or a question in the House of Commons.

1225-27. Though not an inspiration, I may mention here an oracle which was delivered at Idzumo by wormholes in the wood of the old Temple which took the form of Chinese characters. It intimated that the God did not care for lofty buildings, but that the people should turn to virtue. Motoori strongly suspects its authenticity. No Shinto God, he thinks, would be likely to use Chinese for his oracles.

1348. A Buddhist priest of the province of Ise, having made prayer for 1,000 days at the Shrine of the Great Deity, saw on the thousandth day a bright object floating on the sea. This he found to be a sword two feet five or six inches in length. At this time a boy of twelve or thirteen, being divinely inspired, said : "This is one of the three regalia, the precious sword sunk in the sea."* The matter was reported to Kioto, where the authenticity of the sword was corroborated by dreams, but ultimately not officially recognized.

The *Wa Rongo*, a work published in 1669, contains a number of oracles (*Kangakari*) attributed to a great variety of Deities throughout Japan. Some account of this work will be given in the next chapter.

Numerous other cases of inspired utterances are recorded in Japanese history. They have generally relation to the worship of the God concerned, directing the erection of a new shrine, indicating religious observances which will do him pleasure, or complaining that he is neglected or insulted. The Buddhist priests, who converted Shinto to their own purposes, made frequent use of this means of sanctioning their encroachments, and it was also made to serve political purposes.

* At the battle of Dannoüra, in 1184.

Some of the above notices are purely legendary, and of the rest many are open to a suspicion of imposture. It is probable, however, that in most cases the writers who recorded or invented them had in view the hypnotic trance, a kind of condition which is well known in Japan at the present day. The following description of a hypnotic *séance* is abridged from Mr. Percival Lowell's interesting book, ' Occult Japan.'

A place having been chosen, either holy or else purified *ad hoc*, a *gohei* is set up with lighted candles beside it and flanking these, sprigs of *sakaki*, the sacred tree of Shinto. In front of the *gohei* is set out a feast for the God. Some five feet in front a porous earthenware bowl is placed on a stand, and in the bowl a pyre of incense sticks. The purification of the place consists in enclosing the spot with strings, from which depend at intervals small *gohei*, and from the space so shut off driving out all evil spirits by prayer, finger - charms,* sprinkling of salt, striking of sparks by flint and steel, and brandishing a *gohei.*

The persons of the officiators are purified by bathing and putting on fresh white garments.

In its full complement the company consists of eight persons, the *naka-za* (middle-seat) corresponding to the medium, the *mae-za* (front-seat), who is the director of the proceedings, and puts the necessary questions to the medium, and several others whose business it is to ward off evil influences, &c.

A purification service having been chanted under the leadership of the *mae-za*, and songs sung to the accom paniment of the *shaku-jo*,† a sort of staff with metal rings attached to it, the pyre is lighted, and as the flames ascend into the air prayers go up to Fudosama.‡

* *In-musubi*, a Chinese practice.
† A Buddhist religious implement.
‡ A Buddhist deity. The incense is also Buddhist.

The *gohei* having been removed and set up in the middle, the men take their seats for the descent of the God. Facing the *gohei*, they go through a further short incanta tion. Then one of the subordinates holds the *gohei* while the *naka-za* seats himself where it had been and closes his eyes. The *mae-za* takes the *gohei* and places it between the hands of the *naka-za*. Then all the others join in chant, and watch for the advent of the God.

For a few minutes, the time varying with the particular *naka-za*, the man remains perfectly motionless. Then suddenly the *gohei* begins to quiver. The quiver gains till all at once the man is seized with a convulsive throe. In some trances the eyes then open, the eyeballs being rolled up half out of sight. In others the eyes remain half shut. Then the throe subsides again to a permanent quiver, the eyes, if open, fixed in the trance look. The man has now become the God.

The *mae-za*, bowed down, then reverently asks the name of the God, and the God answers, after which the *mae-za* prefers his petitions, to which the God makes reply. When he has finished, the *naka-za* falls forward on his face. The *mae-za* concludes with a prayer, then, striking the *naka-za* on the back, wakes him up. One of the others gives him water from a cup, and when he has been able to swallow it the rest set to and rub his arms and body out of their cataleptic contraction.

The *Sankairi*, a work published in 1853, mentions a kind of inspired medium known as *yori-dai* :—

" *There are numbers of these in Ôsaka who practise Kami-oroshi (bringing down the God). An altar to Sho-ichi-i Inari Miôjin (first of first rank illustrious God Inari) is consecrated within their dwelling-house, before which the medium takes his seat. Some of these bringers-down of the God are men, others women. They take a gohei in each hand and repeat the Rokkon shojo no harahi [a bastard Buddhist form of harahi], muttering at the same time something or*

*another so that one might think they were veritable official
bringers-down of the God.*

*"At Tenōji there is a Miko-machi, or street of mediums
who pretend that it was established by Shotoku Taishi.
When the cries of these mediums reach the street, people look
in at the windows. They differ, however, from the Inari-
oroshi. Some there are who use the formula, ' Is it a living
mouth or a dead mouth ?' so that they probably belong to the
Shinano mediums, who talk of [the God] being drawn by the
adzusa bow. There is also a kind of witchcraft called Inu-
gami* But the Miōjin-oroshi [or yoridai] we speak of
repeats over and over again the phrase ' Be pleased to cleanse,
be pleased to purify,' so long as he retains his senses. Then
his complexion changes and he becomes pale, while the gohei
in his hands shake themselves erect. He will then answer,
one after another, by manifest inspiration, any questions which
the applicant may put to him."*

Tne *Sankairi* is a Buddhist book, and goes on to tell a
story of a *Kami* being brought down by *nembutsu* (Buddhist
prayers) and the medium repeating a Buddhist hymn.†

It need hardly be said that, as in the case of our own
spiritualistic *séances*, the net value of the information
obtained by this process is *nil*. It is hardly fair to Shinto
to call this sort of thing " esoteric Shinto," as Mr. Lowell
does. Spiritualism is not esoteric Christianity, but a
diseased excrescence on it. The higher Shinto func
tionaries do not condescend to such practices, and, indeed,
they are commonly performed by laymen, or even by
Buddhist priests. The official Shinto mode of ascertaining
the will of the Gods was by the " Greater Divination," that
is, by the deer's shoulder-blade or the tortoise-shell. *Kangakari*, or inspiration, was, however, known at all periods of
Japanese history ; and although no detailed accounts have

* See above, p. 332.

† An excellent account of a Japanese hypnotic *séance* is given in Mr. Weston's
' Mountaineering in the Japanese Alps,' p. 282.

reached us of the methods used to produce it, there are indications that they were of a similar character to those described by Mr. Lowell. The *kannushi* of the ceremony of the Empress Jingo's inspiration* seems to be the same as Mr. Lowell's *naka-za*, and the *saniha* corresponds to his *mae-za*. We may presume that his office sometimes resembled that of the functionary at Delphi, whose business it was to clarify the obscurities of the Pythian priestess's utterances. The *miko* of the shrine of Ise gave inspired utterances. The sprinkling of boiling water is said to have been part of the process by which they were induced.

True inspiration, such as that which touched Isaiah's hallowed lips with fire, belongs chiefly to the male sex. The *kangakari*, or hypnotic trance, on the other hand, has in Japan, as elsewhere, a decided preference for women or boys.†

'Occult Japan' deals only with the hypnotic trance as a condition in which communications are received from the Gods. But there are also mediums, called *miko* or *ichiko*, who when hypnotized deliver messages from deceased relatives and others.‡ Hirata speaks of the *miko* and *hafuri* providing *yori-bito* (mediums), by whom they brought near (*yoru*) by prayer the spirits of Gods or men and questioned them. *Ichiko* is defined in the dictionary, *Kotoba no Idzumi*, as a woman who, as the representative of a God or living soul, or dead man's soul, delivers their thoughts from her own mouth.

Possession by foxes, badgers, and other animals is a well-known phenomenon in Japan, but as it has no special connexion with Shinto I shall only refer the reader to Mr. B. H. Chamberlain's 'Things Japanese,' which contains a

* See above, p. 350.

† "Antiquity regarded the soul of woman as more accessible to every sort of inspiration, which also, according to ancient opinion, is a πάσχιον."— Müller, 'Sc. Myth.,' p. 217.

‡ See above, p. 206.

scientific account of this form of disease from the pen of Dr. Baelz.

There are in Japan families who are believed to own foxes, by whom they are assisted and protected, and who watch over their fields and prevent outsiders from doing damage. Such families are avoided, and none but members of similar fox-owning families will intermarry with them.*

* See above, p. 344.

# CHAPTER XIV.

## DECAY OF SHINTO.—ITS MODERN SECTS.

**Rise of Buddhism.**—The later history of Shinto is one of neglect and decay. Such vitality as it retained was owing mainly to the Buddhist ideas which were engrafted upon it. The influence of Chinese systems of ethics and philosophy was also very perceptible, especially in more recent times. The Buddhism of Japan is not simply the doctrine of the founder, described by some as atheistic. It is a real religion, and besides the worship of other Buddhas, comprises that of an Infinite Being—the Buddha Amida—having certain attributes which we should term divine, and of his assessors, with doctrines far more abstruse and profound than those which were taught by Sakyamuni himself. In the main a form of the northern branch of Buddhism, it found its way originally to Japan *via* Tibet, Western China, and Korea.[*]

In A.D. 552 the King of Pekché, in Korea, sent an embassy to Japan with a present to the Mikado of an image of Shaka (Sakyamuni) and several volumes of Sutras. They were gladly received, and were entrusted to the charge of a Minister with instructions to practise the new faith. But the jealousy of the adherents of the older religion was aroused. When a pestilence broke out soon after, they attributed it to the wrath of the native deities, and found means to have the Buddhist temple burnt and the holy image thrown into a canal. Other attempts to propagate Buddhism were little more successful, and it was not until the time of the Regent Shotoku Taishi that it made any

[*] For an account of Japanese Buddhism consult Murray's 'Japan,' or the more comprehensive description in Grifns's 'Religions of Japan.'

substantial progress. At his death in 621 there were in Japan 46 temples or monasteries and 1385 monastics, male and female. In 686 it was decreed that every household should have its domestic Buddhist shrine.

When Buddhism, after Christianity the great religion of the world, had once gained a foothold in Japan, its ultimate victory was certain. There was nothing in Shinto which could rival in attraction the sculpture, architecture, painting, costumes, and ritual of the foreign faith. Its organization was more complete and effective. It presented ideals of humanity, charity, self-abnegation, and purity, far higher than any previously known to the Japanese nation. Its doctrines of sin and repentance, of fate, of future bliss and woe, its profound metaphysics, and, perhaps more than aught else, the satisfaction which it offered to the yearnings of many a wounded spirit for a holy contemplative life, detached from the toil and worry, the sorrow and the disturbing passions of the world, were well calculated to find a welcome in their hearts.

At first the two religions held aloof from one another. But while Buddhism flourished more and more, Shinto was gradually weakened by the diversion into another channel of material resources and religious thought which might otherwise have been bestowed upon itself.

Ryobu Shinto.—The two religions came into more direct contact in the eighth century, when there began a process of pacific penetration of the weaker by the stronger cult, which yielded some curious and important results. Buddhism is not a militant religion in the sense that Islam was. It owes little or nothing to the aid of the secular arm, and avoids rather than seeks open conflicts with other faiths. What the Japanese call *hoben* (pious device) and to which we should often apply the harsher terms "pious fraud" or "priestcraft," are more congenial to it. A notable application of the *hoben* method occurred in the time of the Mikado Shomu, who reigned at Nara from 724 to 756.

Wishing to celebrate his reign by the erection of a great Buddhist temple and image, he took advice of Gyogi, a priest renowned to this day for many services to civilization, and despatched him to Ise with a present for the Sun-Goddess of a relic of Buddha. Gyogi spent seven days and seven nights in prayer under a tree close to the gate of the shrine, and was then vouchsafed an oracle in the form of some couplets of Chinese verse couched in purely Buddhistic phraseology. It spoke of the Sun of truth enlightening the long night of life and death and of the Moon of eternal reality dispersing the clouds of sin and ignorance. This was interpreted to mean that the Sun-Goddess identified herself with Vairochana, called by the Japanese Birushana or Dainichi (great Sun), a person of a Buddhist trinity and described as the personification of essential *boahi* (enlighten ment) and absolute purity. The Sun-Goddess subsequently appeared to the Mikado in a dream and confirmed this view of her character. The temple (Todaiji) founded by Shomu —though not the original building—is still in existence. It contains the famous colossal statue of Birushana, which is at this day one of the wonders of Japan.

The principle of recognizing the Kami as avatars or incarnations of Buddhist deities, of which the case of the Sun-Goddess and Vairochana was the first in Japan—it had been already applied in China to Laotze and Confucius —was subsequently much extended, and, with a spice of Chinese philosophy added, formed the basis of a new sect called Ryobu Shinto. Its Buddhist character is indicated by its name, which means "two parts," the two parts being the two mystic worlds of Buddhism, namely, the Kongokai and the Taizokai. The principal founder of Ryobu was the famous (and fabulous) Kobo Daishi (died 835), to whom the invention of the Hiragana syllabary and quite a mira culous number of sculptures, writings, and paintings are ascribed. The sect of Buddhism engrafted by him on Shinto is that known as Shingon (true word). It is not one of its highest forms, and deals much in magic finger-twistings, endless repetitions of mystic formulæ unintelligible to the worshipper, and other superstitious practices.

Despite its professions of eclecticism, the soul of Ryōbu is essentially Buddhist. It borrows little more from Shinto than the names of a few deities, notably Kuni-toko-tachi, to whom it gives an importance by no means justified by anything in the older Shinto writings.* Ryōbu owed much of its success to forgeries and other means, which were con sidered less objectionable in those days than they would be at present. Great indulgence has always been shown in Japan towards means of edification (*hoben*) that would hardly recommend themselves to our more scrupulous minds. Yet there was something more than priestcraft in the attempt to weld Buddhism, Confucianism, and Shinto into one consistent whole. It is surely a true instinct which leads mankind to recognize an essential unity in all religions, and to reconcile, as far as possible, the outwardly conflicting forms in which it is clothed. The religious history of Japan is full of such endeavours.† But Shinto, Buddhism of various sects, Confucianism, and Sung philosophy consti tuted a very refractory mass of material, and the results obtained, while they testify to much industry and ingenuity, are more curious than valuable.

**Yui-itsu.**—The Yui-itsu Shinto was a branch of Ryobu. It was invented about the end of the fifteenth century. Yui-itsu is short for Ten-jin-yui-itsu (Heaven-man-only-one), a doctrine borrowed, according to Hirata, by the Chinese philosophers from Buddhism. Of course in this connexion Ten does not mean the visible sky. It is rather a conception which fluctuates between Nature and God.

---

* See above, p. 175.

† The novelist Bakin, who cannot be charged with priestcraft, says : "Shinto reverences the way of the Sun : the Chinese philosophers honour Heaven ; the teaching of Shaka fails not to make the Sun a deity. Among differences of doctrine the fundamental principle is the same."

It will be seen that the fundamental problem which has so much occupied the minds of Western theologians and philosophers—namely, that of the relation which exists between the human and the divine—has not escaped the attention of Far Eastern thinkers. Motoori treats the doctrine of the identity of Ten and man with much contempt. " How can there be anything in common," he asks, " between Ten, the country where the Gods live, and man ? "

To the people, a Ryōbu shrine was one where Buddhist priests officiated, a Yui-itsu shrine one where none but Shinto functionaries were seen.

Other sects, or rather schools, of Shinto were those of Deguchi and Suwiga, both of which arose in the seventeenth century. The former explains the phenomena of the Divine Age on principles derived from the Yin-King, an ancient Chinese book of divination ; the latter is a combination of Yui-itsu Shinto with Sung philosophy.

All these sects were much given to strained analogies and fanciful comparisons in support of their views. The conversion of Saruta-hiko into a great moral teacher by the Deguchi Shinto is an example. Saruta-hiko is worshipped at road sides. He therefore came to be considered the God of roads and the guide and protector of travellers. But the road or way may be used metaphorically for the path of duty or virtue. Hence we have the astonishing result by which a phallic deity figures as the chief Shinto apostle of morality.

Other instances are the symbolic meanings ascribed to the regalia and the notion that the cross timbers of the roof of the typical Shinto shrine represent the (Chinese) virtues of benevolence, justice, courtesy, and wisdom.

These and many more of a similar character are argute scholastic speculations in which the people take little concern.

The Ryobu, which retained its predominance until the

eighteenth century, was by far the most important of these so-called Shinto sects.

It is impossible to trace here their somewhat complicated history. I may, however, note a few facts which will illustrate the character and extent of the encroachment of Buddhist and Chinese ideas on the native faith and cult.

As early as the eighth century a Mikado began the custom, subsequently continued during many centuries, of abdicating the throne after a few years' reign and assuming the Buddhist tonsure. The mode of imperial burial was modified in accordance with Buddhist ideas of the worthlessness of these mortal frames of ours. Some Mikados were cremated. One described himself as a slave of Buddha, and another in an official ordinance spoke of the Kami as obeying the laws of Buddha. After such an example was set by the high priests of Shinto, it could not be expected that their Court should be more faithful to the older cult. In the Heian period the nobles could not be induced to trouble themselves about the Shinto ceremonies, which were either deputed to subordinates or omitted altogether. The regular embassies to the shrines were neglected, except on some great emergency, such as famine, plague, or earthquake. Even the greatest Shinto rite of all—the Ohonihe, or coronation ceremony—was in abeyance for eight reigns, viz., from 1465 to 1687. What would have seemed even more shocking to an old Shintoist was the circumstance that Buddhist priests were allowed to take part in it.

Buddhist priests had the custody of nearly all the shrines read Sutras, and performed Buddhist ceremonies there, such as baptism and *goma* sprinkling. Relics of Buddha were deposited in them. Buddhist temples had Shinto shrines of a Chinjiu, or protecting Kami, built in their court yards. Buddhist architecture and ornaments were used for the Miya and *ni-wô* (the two kings, guardians of the gate) or *shishi* (lions) set up before them. The latter are an Indian conceit. They were originally set up at cemeteries in order to frighten wild beasts and prevent them from tearing up the dead. We are told that in the reign of Horikawa (1099) nearly all the shrines were in ruin.

The Onyôshi, or official college of professors of the Yin and Yang natural philosophy of China, who were equally prepared to compute an almanac or to exorcise a demon, were for many centuries entrusted with the performance of the *harahi* (purification ceremonies), and other Shinto functions.

The accompanying illustration shows another form of the admixture of Buddhism with Shinto which prevailed until quite recently. Of the three shrines here represented, the central only is dedicated to a Shinto Deity, viz., Atago, or the Fire-God, who, moreover, has the Buddhist epithet Daigongen affixed to his name. The other two are dedicated to the Buddhist deities Benzaiten and Bishamon.

The myths of the *Kojiki* and *Nihongi* did not escape from admixture with Indian cosmology and Chinese philosophy, a process which yielded the strangest results. Thus a fourteenth-century writer described the Yin and Yang as evolving by their mutual interaction Izanagi and Izanami, the earlier generations of the *Nihongi* story being omitted. Their child, the Sun Goddess, proves to be a manifestation of Buddha, one of whose services to humanity was at some far remote period to subdue the " Evil Kings of the Six Heavens " of Indian myth, and compel them to withdraw their opposition to the spread of the true doctrine (that is, Buddhism) in Japan.

Still there were a few exceptions to the general decay. At the two great shrines of Ise and Idzumo, the old cult was maintained in tolerable purity, and doubtless many local shrines were preserved by their insignificance from Buddhist encroachment. It should not be forgotten, moreover, that, although the history of Shinto under foreign influence was one of neglect and decay, in so far as its original elements were concerned, it borrowed from

野々宮

Buddhism and Confucianism germs of a higher thought, which under more favourable circumstances might have borne precious fruit. I have before me a book entitled, 'Wa Rongo; or, Japanese (Confucian) Analects,' which shows the later Shinto in a more favourable light. It was published in 1669. The preface states that the original work belongs to the reign of Gotoba no In (1184-1198), and gives a list of successive editors or compilers from 1219 to 1628. It is a collection of oracles of Shinto gods and wise utterances of mikados, princes, and others, of a tolerably heterogeneous kind. Most of them, however, bear the stamp of the Ryobu Shinto. They are Buddhism, Confucianism, or Sung philosophy in a Shinto dress. The first volume contains 108 (the number of beads in a Buddhist rosary) oracles attributed to the Gods of various Shinto shrines throughout Japan.

These oracles are by no means consistent with one another. Some are frankly Buddhist in character, others inculcate the doctrine of the identity of Kami and Buddhas, while others, again, denounce the practice of alien religions. In some Heaven-and-Earth is recognized as a sort of pantheistic deity, distinct from the physical universe. Here we have Chinese inspiration. Purity of heart, charity to the poor, and the avoidance of vain repeti tions are much insisted on. No moral code is anywhere set forth. When virtue is spoken of, it is the Confucian morality, or the observance of the Buddhist command ments, that must be understood.

In the following examples the reader will find himself in a wholly different and far higher moral and religious atmosphere from that of the unadulterated older Shinto described in the preceding chapters.

**Shinto Oracles.**—The Sun-Goddess enjoins uprightness and truth, on pain of being sent to Ne no kuni.* Men

---

* In the old Shinto, Ne no kuni, or Hades, is not a place of punishment for the wicked. Here it stands for the Jigoku, or Hell, of the Buddhists.

should make their hearts like unto Heaven-and-Earth.*
Wearisome ceremonies and repetitions (of some Buddhist
sects) should be abandoned, and reverence shown to the
Gods of the ancestral shrines.†

The Mikado Gotoba no In received the following
inspiration in a dream from the two shrines of Ise :—

*In the last days the world will be disturbed and all men
troubled. The sovereign house will show respect for the
military house, and local governors will make friends with
wearisome fellows (Buddhist monks). Buddhist priests will
take to them wives, eat flesh, and propagate base doctrines.
The land of Ashihara of the fair rice-ears is the rightful
property of my descendants.*

An oracle of Hachiman :—

*I refuse the offerings of the impure of heart. Some Gods
are great, some small, some good and others bad. My name
is Dai jizai wo bosatsu.*‡

An inspired poem (A.D. 1204) :—

> *Loving-kindness is of the Buddhas :*
> *Uprightness of the Kami :*
> *Error of the sons of men.*
> *Thus of the same heart there is a triple division.*

The Gods of Kamo promise their divine help and the
fulfilment of their prayers to their worshippers, especially
those who regularly visit the shrine.

Oracle of the Gods of Kasuga :—

*.Even though men prepare for us a pure abode and offer
there the rare things of the land, though they hang up
offerings of the seven precious things, and with anxious
hearts pray to us for hundreds of days, yet will we refuse
to enter the house of the depraved and miserly. But we will*

---

* That is, Nature—a Chinese idea.
† This is Chinese.
‡ A Buddhist designation.

*surely visit the dwellings even of those in deep mourning\** *without an invitation, if loving-kindness is there always. The reason is that we make loving-kindness our shintai.*

*Hear all men! If you desire to obtain help from the Gods, put away pride. Even a hair of pride shuts you off from the Gods as it were by a great cloud.*

*Hear all men! The good Kami find their strength and their support in piety. Therefore they love not the offerings of those who practise tedious ceremonies.*

The Deity of Matsunowo says :—

*Any one who makes a single obeisance to one Kami will receive infinite help: much more so any one who makes pure his heart and enters the great way of single-minded up rightness.*

Oracle of *Temman tenjin*, the deified Minister Sugahara no Michizane† :—

*All ye who come before me hoping to attain the accomplish ment of your desires, pray with hearts pure from falsehood, clean within and without, reflecting the truth like a mirror. If those who are falsely accused of crime‡ come to me for help, within seven days their prayer will be granted, or else call me not a God.*

An oracle of Mume no miya promises that if an offering of sand is made help will be given to women in child-birth, and children to those who have none.

An oracle of Atago (the Fire-God) denounces his vengeance on those who pollute fire, and on the wealthy who do not assist their poorer neighbours.

*Leave the things of this world and come to me daily and monthly with pure bodies and pure hearts. You will then enjoy paradise in this world and have all your desires accomplished.*

* And therefore unclean.
† See above, p. 179.
‡ As Sugahara himself was.

Oracle of the God of Kashiṃa* :—

*I am the protector of Japan against foreign violence and break the spear-points of Heavenly demons and Earthly demons. All enjoy my divine power. I derive strength from the multiplication of devout men in the land. Then do the forces of demons melt away like snow in the sun. When devout men are few, my powers dwindle, my heart is dis tressed and the demon powers gain vigour while the divine power is weakened.*

Oracle of the God of Atsuta :—

*All ye men who dwell under Heaven. Receive the just commands of the Gods. Regard Heaven as your father, Earth as your mother, and all things as your brothers and sisters. You will then enjoy this divine country which excels all others, free from hate and sorrow. Obey the instructions of the Heaven-shining Deity and honour the Mikado. If any are rebellious, come before me and name their names. I will surely crush the foe and yield you satisfaction.*

An oracle of the God of Suhat promises to hear the prayers of all true worshippers, even though they may have eaten flesh. No outward purity avails a whit.

Oracle of Tatsuta (the Wind-God) :—

*All ye of high and low degree, rather than pray to Heaven-and-Earth, rather than pray to all the Kami, dutifully serve your parents. For your parents are the Gods of without and within.‡ If that which is within is not bright it is useless to pray only for that which is without.*

An oracle of Inari, near Kioto, speaks of this polluted world (a Buddhist phrase), and recommends the reading of Sutras and Dharani.

---

* See above, p. 155.
† See above, p. 177.
‡ Alluding to the inner and outer shrines of Ise.

The following sentiments are ascribed to the God of Fujiyama :—

*Ye men of mine. Shun desire. If you shun desire you will ascend to a level with the Gods. Every little yielding to anxiety is a step away from the natural heart of man. If one leaves the natural heart of man, he becomes a beast. That men should be made so, is to me intolerable pain and unending sorrow.*

A son of a Mikado received the following inspiration in a dream :—

*It is the upright heart of all men which is identical with the highest of the high, and therefore the God of Gods. There is no room in Heaven-and-Earth for the false and crooked person.*

The following poem was revealed in a dream to the Mikado Seiwa :—

*If we keep unperverted the human heart, which is like unto Heaven and received from Earth, that is God. The Gods have their abode in the heart. Amongst the various ordinances none is more excellent than that of religious meditation.*

The God of a Tajima shrine says :—

*When the sky is clear, and the wind hums in the fir-trees, 'tis the heart of a God who thus reveals himself.*

An oracle of Hachiman (the War-God) enjoins on his worshippers to be full of pity and mercy for beggars and lepers, and even for ants and crickets. Those whose pity and charity are wide will have their precious cord (of life) extended immeasurably ; their posterity will be spread abroad like the wings of a crane. They will become the upright heart of the Gods of Heaven.

Another oracle of Hachiman :—

*All men's love of children and love of self are heinous crimes. Nothing is more admirable than to sever, were it only for a time, all earthly relations.*

*If men will have upright hearts they must be neither foolish nor clever, they must indulge neither in grief nor in hate, but be as the flowers which unfold under the genial warmth of a vernal sun.*

*If there be any who, having studied the books of China or practised the teachings of India, despise the instructions of the Gods of our own Japan, I will go to their houses and either slay their infant children or visit them with sore disease, or turn away from them their followers, or by the God of Fire destroy their dwellings. This is not because I hate the doctrines of China or India, but because it is rejecting the root for the branches.*

Oracle of Itsukushima in Aki :—

*Of old the people of my country knew not my name. Therefore I was born into the visible world and endured a base existence. In highest Heaven I am the Deity of the Sun, in the mid-sky I show my doings. I hide in the great Earth and produce all things : in the midst of the Ocean I am the eight Dragon-kings, and my power pervades the four seas. If the poorest of mankind come here once for worship, show me their faces and declare their wishes, within seven days, fourteen days, twenty-one days, or it may be three years or seven years, according to the person and the importance of his prayer, I will surely grant their heart's desire. But the wicked of heart must not apply to me. Those who do not abandon mercy will not be abandoned by me.*

**Revival of Pure Shinto.**—The seventeenth century witnessed a great revival of Chinese learning in Japan. It embraced not only the renewed study of the ancient classics of Confucius and Mencius, but the philosophical writings of Chu-hi and other sceptical writers of the Sung Dynasty (960-1278). The Samurai, or governing caste of the nation, devoted themselves to these studies with amazing zeal and enthusiasm, to the great neglect of Buddhism, which from this time forward was left mainly to the common people.

This movement reached a climax in the eighteenth century, when a reaction set in. Kada, Mabuchi, and other patriotic scholars, resenting the undue preponderance allowed to Chinese thought, did their utmost, by commentaries and exegetical treatises, to recall attention to the monuments of the ancient national literature, such as the *Kojiki*, *Nihongi*, and *Manyoshiu*, which had been so long neglected that they were in great part unintelligible even to educated men. Under their pupil and successor Motoori (1730-1801), this movement assumed a religious character. His patriotic prejudices were offended by the foreign elements which he found in the Ryobu and other prevailing forms of Shinto, while the Sung doctrine of a "Great Absolute" was not only odious to him on account of its alien origin, but failed to satisfy his soul-hunger for a more personal object of worship. He therefore turned back to the older form of Shinto. To its propagation by lectures and books he devoted many years of his life, and not without success. He had numerous followers among the more educated classes.

Motoori's principal work is the *Kojiki den*, a commentary on the *Kojiki*, in which he loses no opportunity of attacking everything Chinese and of exalting the old Japanese customs, language, and religion in a spirit of ardent and undiscriminating patriotism. He seems to have been wholly blind to the fact that the exotic faiths and philosophies, whose intrusion into Shinto he so bitterly resented, contain elements far otherwise valuable to mankind than the ritual of the *Yengishiki* and the old-world myths of the *Kojiki*

His pupil Hirata (1776-1843) was less of a literary man and more of a theologian than his master. In a long life he wrote numbers of books, amounting to hundreds of volumes, and delivered innumerable lectures urging the claims of the old Shinto. His teaching was so successful that it at last drew upon him the attention of the Shogun's Government, who, finding that their own authority was being undermined by the prominence given to the *de jure* sovereign rights of the Sun-Goddess's descendants, forbade his lectures and banished him to his native province of Dewa. Hirata's anti-foreign prejudices did not prevent him from believing in the immortality of the soul—a doctrine of Buddhist origin—or from borrowing from China a worship of ancestors quite different from anything in the old Shinto. He adopts the Chinese duty of " filial piety," and makes strenuous but unavailing efforts to find coun tenance for it in the *Kojiki* and *Nihongi*. Though he says that the Kami detest Buddhism because it teaches us to abandon lord and parent, wife and child, and is therefore destructive of morality, and because its adherents are filthy beggars, who boast of wearing cast-off rags and eating food given in charity, in another place he goes so far as to admit Buddha to his Shinto Pantheon, on condition that he shall be content with an inferior position. He tacitly accepts the moral code of China, while protesting that such things are unnecessary, as we are endowed by nature with an intuitive knowledge of right and wrong.

The agitation for the revival of Pure Shinto was a retro grade movement, which could only end in failure. It con tributed substantially, however, to the success of the political revolution which in 1868 brought about the resto ration of the Mikado to the sovereign position which was the logical outcome of Motoori's and Hirata's teachings. The Shinto reformation of the same date, when the Buddhist priests were removed from the Ryobu shrines, and a certain purification of ritual and ornaments was effected, was also due to their influence.*

Shingaku.—A school of preachers who called their doctrine *shingaku* or " heart-learning," and professed to combine Shinto with Buddhism and Confucianism, had

* For a full account of the Revival of Pure Shinto, see Sir E. Satow's papers contributed to the *T. A. S. J.* in 1875. Our knowledge of Shinto dates from this time.

some vogue in the first half of the nineteenth century. These men were in reality rationalists, who took the maxims of Confucius and Mencius as the basis of their doctrines. Any Shinto element which they may contain is quite inappreciable. Their sermons, of which a good number have been printed, are in the colloquial dialect. They are very entertaining and, despite an occasional bit of indecency, not unedifying.

Tenrikyô,* or the "teaching of the Heavenly Reason," is a modern sect. The founder was a woman named Omiki, who was born in the province of Yamato in 1798, and died in 1887. Her religion owes much to the Shingaku and Ryobu doctrines. While professing to worship Kunitokotachi, Izanagi, Izanami, and seven other Shinto deities, practically Izanagi and Izanami are her only Gods. The former (identified with the sun) is taken to represent the male, and the latter the female principle, corresponding in nature to Heaven and Earth, and in human society to husband and wife. These Gods are spiritual beings, chiefly revealed in the heart of man, and are endowed with personal attributes. Tenrikyô has high moral aims, and has made rapid progress. In 1894 there were claimed for it 10,000 priests and preachers, and 1,400,000 adherents.

Remmonkyo.†—The name of this sect implies that, like the spotless lotus-flower, which has its roots in the mud, it attains to purity in the midst of a wicked world. It is stated to have originated with a certain Yanagita Ichibeimon, but its real founder was his disciple, a woman named Shimamura Mitsuko, who was still alive and preaching in 1901.

The Remmonkyô professes to be a reformed Shinto, but in reality it owes little to this source beyond the names of the Gods Ame no minaka nushi, Taka-musubi, and

---

* An interesting account of this sect is given in a paper by Dr. Greene in the *T. A. S. J.*, December, 1895.

† See papers by Dr. Greene and Rev. A. Lloyd in the *T. A. S. J.*, 1901.

Kami-musubi, who are termed the three Creator Deities. They are considered, however, to be only manifestations of the Ji no Myôhô, or "Wonderful Law of Things," and the real God of the sect is the personified Myôhô (wonder ful law) a conception borrowed from the Buddhist Nichiren sect. The followers of Shimamura call her an *ikigami* (live God), and regard her as identical with the Myôhô. How often in Japanese religious history do we meet with this idea of the incarnation of the God in his priest or prophet !

The *shintai*, or material representative of the Myôhô, is a slip of paper bearing the words "Ji no Myôhô," written by the founder herself. It is sold as a charm against disease and danger. Faith-healing is a practice of this sect, as it is of the Tenrikyô. Their moral code is of the ordinary Confucian type.

The last-named two sects are not likely to play an important part in religious history. The founders of both were ignorant women, and their doctrines are a mere jumble of conflicting ideas borrowed from various sources, and inspired by no great central thought. We may, perhaps, compare their position in Japan to that of the Salvation Army or the Plymouth Brethren in this country.

**Official Shinto.**—The official cult of the present day is substantially the "Pure Shinto" of Motoori and Hirata. But it has little vitality. A rudimentary religion of this kind is quite inadequate for the spiritual sustenance of a nation which in these latter days has raised itself to so high a pitch of enlightenment and civilization. No doubt some religious enthusiasm is excited by the great festivals of Ise, Idzumo, and a few other shrines, and by the annual pilgrimages—which, however, have other *raisons d'être.* The reverence paid to the Mikado is not devoid of a religious quality which has its source in Shinto. But the main stream of Japanese piety has cut out for itself new channels. It has turned to Buddhism, which, at the time of the Restoration in a languishing state, is now showing signs of renewed life and activity. Another and still more formidable rival has appeared, to whose progress, daily increasing in momentum, what limit shall be prescribed?

As a national religion, Shinto is almost extinct. But it will long continue to survive in folk-lore and custom, and in that lively sensibility to the divine in its simpler and more material aspects which characterizes the people of Japan.

THE END.

# INDEX.

*N.B.—Where there are several references the most important is placed first.*

# I

# J

# K

PRINTED BY JOHN EDWARD FRANCIS, BREAM'S BUILDINGS, CHANCERY LANE, E.C.

Printed in Great Britain
by Amazon

PRINTED BY JOHN EDWARD FRANCIS, BREAM'S BUILDINGS, CHANCERY LANE, E.C.

Printed in Great Britain
by Amazon